An
Buddhadharma

By

Master Sheng-yen Lu

Translated by

Janny Chow

Purple Lotus Society

San Bruno CA

An Overview of the Buddhadharma

First Edition

Library of Congress Cataloging-in-Publication Data

Lu, Sheng-yen, 1945-
[Fo hsüeh tsung shuo. English]
An overview of the Buddhadharma / by Master Sheng-yen Lu; translated by Janny Chow. -- 1st ed.
p. cm.
ISBN 1-881493-06-7 (pbk.)
1. Buddhism--Doctrines.
I. Chow, Janny, 1952- . II. Title.
BQ4165.L83613 1997
294.3'4--dc21 97-11942
CIP

Printed in the United States of America. 1997

About the Author

◆Master Sheng-yen Lu is a prominent religious figure throughout Southeast Asia. As of 1997, over 4 million people have taken refuge in his True Buddha School. With over 300 chapters worldwide, the True Buddha School is recognized as a major component in Buddhism today.

◆Master Sheng-yen Lu was born in 1945 in Taiwan. In 1982, he settled in the United States to promote Buddhist teachings in the West. He has since built a major Buddhist temple, the Ling Shen Ching Tze Temple, in Redmond, Washington, and a large retreat center in the Cascade Mountains.

◆Originally a Christian, Master Lu was twenty six years old when a profound mystical experience led him to study Taoism, Sutrayana and Tantric Buddhism. After intense training and practice over a period of fourteen years, he became a Master of exceptional accomplishment in these disciplines and achieved Perfect Enlightenment.

◆Master Lu is revered as a Living Buddha by his students. By practicing the True Buddha Tantric Dharma, as taught by the Living Buddha, one can realize Awakening and Liberation in this present life.

◆Master Sheng-yen Lu is also a prolific writer, having published over 120 books in Chinese on such varied topics as Tantric Buddhism, Geomancy, Zen Buddhism, and Taoism. Many of these books are now being translated into English.

Acknowledgments

The Purple Lotus Society would like to thank the following persons for making this translation possible:

Grand Master Sheng-yen Lu for His blessing and guidance; Master Lian-hsiang for her encouragement; Master Samantha Chou for her encouragement and support; Janny Chow for translation; K.C. Ng for checking the accuracy of the translation; Pamela Ziv Johnson for editing; Kevin Henderson for desktop publishing; Ellen Hsu for the cover design; and the many students involved in transcribing the Chinese text on which this translation is based.

Table of Contents

Anyone who desires to practice the True Buddha Tantric Dharma should first take refuge in Grand Master Sheng-yen Lu to obtain the power of lineage transmission.

First Day:
May 3, 1993

Masters, fellow cultivators, good afternoon. This is the second Dharma teaching held at the Rainbow Villa and the topic is An Overview of the Buddhadharma. On one hand, this may seem to be a very easy subject because its scope is so broad that, no matter what one discusses, the subject would be covered. On the other hand, this is a very difficult topic, because one must be able to extract all the essences from the vast Buddhadharma and present them in a very systematic and orderly manner. Therefore it is both easy and difficult. Anyway, difficult or not, I am going to attempt it. [laughter] I am going to talk about it. [laughter] Although I have studied the Buddhadharma for many years, taken refuge in many teachers, and penetrated deep into the treasury of the sutras, it still requires careful thinking, intense inner focus, and eloquent communication skills to present, in a very short period of time, a complete presentation of the Buddhadharma. This is a subject as vast as the ocean itself! I hope that everyone will be able to understand the teachings contained in this Dharma discourse, and that they will derive benefits from what they have learned. By putting these teachings into future practice, one may attain Realization. This will bring a great significance to this Dharma teaching.

Great Vehicle — Small Vehicle — Diamond Vehicle

This is the first day and I shall begin today by talking about the different "vehicles" in Buddhism. In Buddhism, there are the so-called Great Vehicle [Mahayana], Small Vehicle [Hinayana], and Diamond Vehicle [Vajrayana], which is the same as Tantrayana. Actually when Buddha Shakyamuni was alive, he did not mention anything about the Great Vehicle, Small Vehicle, or Diamond Vehicle; these differentiations were created by people after the Buddha's parinirvana. The Buddha himself did not make any reference to "vehicles." As he was the True Buddha, therefore only the True Buddha can be considered as the True Vehicle. Apart from that, there is no other vehicle. The practice of differentiating the three vehicles came into existence after the Buddha had passed on.

However, in our discussion today, we will be making references to different "vehicles." Why? This is because the three vehicles are traditions which have been passed down to us by our predecessors in the practice of Buddhism. In reality, the true Buddhadharma has only One Vehicle, which encompasses the Great Vehicle, Small Vehicle, and the Diamond Vehicle. It would not be correct to talk solely about one particular vehicle. This would be like describing a person by considering only the head. The head alone does not represent a person! Similarly, concentrating on the trunk alone would produce only a partial representation of a person. Likewise, it is not correct to consider only the limbs when one is discussing a person. One must describe the head, the trunk, and all four limbs in order to give a complete description of a person. One must also consider all aspects in a description of the true Buddhadharma. Therefore, the true Buddhadharma contains all of the Great Vehicle, Small Vehicle, and Diamond Vehicle. In reality, there is only One Vehicle.

In the context of the Buddhadharma, what does the Great Vehicle teach? It teaches one to seek Enlightenment for the sake of the welfare of all beings. When one generates the bodhicitta, which is a desire to help all sentient beings to reach Liberation, one is generating the Heart of the Great Vehicle.

What is the Small Vehicle? The Small Vehicle seeks the Liberation of oneself. One mainly engages in practices that concentrate on one's own Liberation.

How about the Diamond Vehicle? This is the esoteric pathway which uses esoteric methods of cultivation to enable one to quickly achieve Realization. After self-realization, one then proceeds to help other sentient beings as in the Great Vehicle. The practice of the Diamond Vehicle is known as the practice of attaining Buddhahood in the Present Life, because one engages in actual practices of inner realization which enables one's body, speech, and mind to enter into a union with the body, speech, and mind of the Buddha. These methods of inner realization are methods of the Diamond Vehicle.

Although the Buddhadharma encompasses tenets from all three Vehicles, discord exists among followers of the three Vehicles. Small Vehicle practitioners like to criticize Great Vehicle practitioners for being impractical and for wanting to help other sentient beings without first engaging in actual practice. They also like to point out that the Buddha himself never preached on the Great Vehicle. On the other hand, Great Vehicle practitioners criticize Small Vehicle followers for indulging in their own salvation, while ignoring other sentient beings and failing to generate the bodhicitta. They contend that the highest achievement of the Small Vehicle practice only equals the level of the Arhat and, therefore, falls far short of that of Buddhahood. Such arguments have occurred throughout the history of Buddhism. What about the Diamond Vehicle or Vajrayana? This Vehicle is subdivided into Tibetan Vajrayana, Japanese Vajrayana, and Tien-tai Vajrayana. Many differing views exist among these Vajrayana schools. For example, just the Highest Tantra section alone of the Tibetan Vajrayana has received much slander from other Vehicles. The Japanese Vajrayana has been criticized as consisting of only the lower three parts of esoteric teachings and lacking an authentic Highest Tantra practice. The Tien-tai Vajrayana has been accused of placing too much emphasis on rituals while being deficient in inner realization practices. Therefore, it will take a long period of time before there can be a true integration of the Vajrayana with all the other scriptural schools. The fact is that the three traditional divisions of the Buddhadharma — the Great Vehicle, Small Vehicle, and Diamond Vehicle — have so far proven unable to be integrated.

Faith

What motivates one to start the practice of the Buddhadharma? There are always certain events at the beginning that give one the impetus to embark on the path.

All of you here have been motivated by different forces to practice the Buddhadharma. As for myself, I started the practice because I experienced an extraordinary event. You all know that in this direct experience, I was transported from the samsaric world to the Maha Twin Lotus Ponds. When I reached that spiritual realm, I saw my previous existence, the Light Radiating Pai Lian Hua Tung Tsu (White Padmakumara). I saw with my own eyes the White Padmakumara who radiated a great light, and I heard a voice telling me the name of the White Padmakumara. These were real experiences, by which I mean I actually travelled to that realm, where I truly saw and heard these things. This incident was the first event that led me to start on the path of the Buddhadharma.

Now all of you here have, of course, read the description of this experience in my books. A faith was inspired in you. Therefore, you are also treading the same path on which I have walked. In truth, the source of this Padmakumara [Lotus Bodhisattva] is the Female Buddha with Buddha Eyes whose own source is the Great Sun Tathagata. At the Twin Lotus Ponds of the Female Buddha with Buddha Eyes, Padmakumara manifested. Padmakumara, the Bliss Body of the Buddha, is also currently teaching the Dharma at the Maha Twin Lotus Ponds. I, teaching the Dharma here today, am the Emanation Body of the Buddha. Teaching at the Maha Twin Lotus Ponds is the Bliss Body of the Buddha. Teaching at the Great Sun Tathagata is the Dharma Body of the Buddha. The Great Sun Tathagata is the Dharma Body, the Padmakumara is the Bliss Body, the present incarnation is the Emanation Body.

Last night one of the students here was taken to the Realms of Heavens in his sleep. He came to a place called Hsi Chien Ch'eng [City of Happy Sights] and heard many heavenly beings talking about going to attend a teaching. Out of curiosity, he asked them, "Who is giving the teaching?" They replied that they were going to hear the Padmakumara teach. He was surprised, "Isn't the Padmakumara Sheng-yen Lu? Isn't Sheng-yen Lu going to give a Dharma teaching tomorrow at the Rainbow Villa? When has he come to this City of Happy Sights to teach the Dharma?" The reply was that the Padmakumara at the City of Happy Sights had been teaching at their city for almost two months. This student exclaimed, "That can't be right! Our Grand Master, Sheng-yen Lu, will give his first day's teaching tomorrow, so how could he have been teaching at the City of Happy Sights for two months now?" He went along to hear the teaching and, when he arrived at the podium, he looked up and saw that the Padmakumara was indeed the Grand Master. He asked himself, "The Grand Master is clearly still in the Seattle area, how could he be teaching at the City of Happy Sights in front of so many heavenly beings, and have been teaching for almost two months?" This morning the student came to tell me about his experience. He mentioned that the theme being discussed by the Padmakumara at the City of Happy Sights was "Penetrating Into Madhyamaka [the teaching of the Middle Way]."

This morning the student asked me how could there be two Sheng-yen Lu's? Why is there a Sheng-yen Lu in the City of Happy Sights and another one here in Seattle? This is what I told him, "Sheng-yen Lu is present everywhere, not just in Seattle. At this time, there are many Padmakumaras teaching simultaneously in many Heavenly Kingdoms and Pure Lands." This is the phenomenon of manifestation of multiple bodies which may number in the billions and assume any kind of form or shape. This is extremely difficult to perceive. It cannot be expressed in words. We know that the Dharma Body of the Buddha is pervasively present throughout the whole universe. The Bliss Bodies of the Buddha can manifest in any of the myriad Buddha Lands. The Emanation Bodies of the Buddha are equivalent to the Buddhas emanating from each of the skin pores of the Bliss Bodies. Here lies the greatness of the Buddhadharma. The three bodies of the Buddha — the Dharma Body, the Bliss Body, and the Emanation Body — are limitless and extend into Infinity. That is why there are Padmakumaras presently teaching the Dharma in the Heavenly Realms while a Padmakumara is teaching here in the samsaric world. Therefore, one should not harbor any doubts when one listens to the Buddhadharma. The Buddhadharma is unimaginably difficult to conceive. There are exceedingly great numbers of worlds and phenomena that one cannot see and hear with one's physical faculties. The penetration into the Buddhadharma begins with "faith" and not with "doubt." Therefore there is this quotation found in the Buddhist scriptures: Only faith can penetrate the vast ocean of the Buddhadharma. Only through faith can one enter this doorway.

For example, *A Complete and Detailed Exposition on the True Buddha Tantric Dharma* is a teaching which has taken me years of painstaking labor to develop and which I have shared openly with you. You are able to obtain this teaching for a very small price. With the installation of the video cameras here, you may now purchase video tapes of these precious teachings. I understand that the price of the whole set of video tapes ranges between NT 1,500 — 2,000 (approximately US $60 — $80). You might decide to purchase the NT 1,500 set because you think the NT 2,000 set is too expensive. The difference is only a few hundred Taiwan dollars. Do you realize that this painstaking labor of my whole life is worth only two thousand Taiwan dollars? [audience laughter] My teaching is always open to videotaping and one is free to buy whichever tapes one chooses. One is, of course, happy to find the cheapest and best produced work! But this is not what I want to bring to your attention; the purpose of my teaching here today is not to endorse the more expensive and inferior set. You are free to buy whichever set you like[1]. What I mean is that *A Complete and Detailed Exposition on the True Buddha Tantric Dharma* is a labor of love that has taken me more than twenty years of painstaking effort to produce. When I first went to my guru to ask him to teach me, I had to go through innumerable hardships and the offerings I made to him were the monthly wage pouches I received from my military service. You are able to tape all these teachings in one week's time. I have spent a long time studying them and distilling their essence, so they could be delivered in a week's teaching.

[1] Two local chapters had taped and produced two different sets of video tapes on *A Complete and Detailed Exposition on the True Buddha Tantric Dharma*. Grand Master's comments here on the price and quality of the tapes were in response to issures raised by some students regarding the tapes.

Actually, the teaching is priceless. If, after viewing the tape, one has faith in what I said, the teaching is, priceless. If one finds those details, which I explain in the teaching, make great sense and if one agrees with them and truly uses one's consciousness to practice them, then the teaching become invaluable. It is beyond any price. When one generates this kind of faith, one will receive the priceless treasure. Such being the case, if one tells me, after viewing the tapes or listening to the actual teaching that was given here, that one does not like the True Buddha Dharma and wants to leave the True Buddha School, will I grieve or not? I have laid bare my heart and my blood is on the ground for the sentient beings to tread upon.

In any case, I have already offered you my heart and my blood. When you practice the teaching thoroughly, you can attain Buddhahood. If a student comes to me and says, "I don't like the True Buddha School, I want to leave," he is stepping upon my heart and breaking it into pieces! Shouldn't I be crying my heart out? I have given you the best thing in the world and I have completely disembowelled myself to offer you my heart and all that is inside me. That is why a cultivator once said that, before Enlightenment he lived a miserable life; after Enlightenment he still lived a miserable life. The first misery was due to the fact that he has not attained the Truth of the Universe. The second misery was that, when he realized the Truth and offered this Jewel to others, others did not want it. It was a double blow of misery.

Therefore, in the future, if a student wants to leave the True Buddha School, he can come to tell me directly and I shall prostrate to him. Why should I pay homage to him? The prostration is to signify my respect for him, as well as to indicate that I have forsaken everything that I have. As the True Buddha School does not forsake any individual, if a student decides to leave, then I must prostrate to him for the two above mentioned reasons. Do you understand the meaning of this or not?

Only faith and confidence can penetrate the Buddhadharma. Why do I have such strong faith and confidence? Whether one has left the True Buddha School, or is still with the True

Buddha School, one should understand the importance of faith. Even if one has left the True Buddha School, as long as one still believes in Buddhism, one is still within the True Buddha School. One is no longer within the True Buddha School only if one has decided not to practice Buddhism. This is because our True Buddha Dharma is the authentic Buddhadharma! In this teaching one may practice the very insightful Buddhadharma, attain the very profound skill of Zen meditation and Supreme Wisdom. Wherever one goes, one is still within the Supreme Wisdom! So, can one really become disengaged from the True Buddha School?

In the days when Buddha Shakyamuni was teaching, he did not teach us so many things! When someone joined the group, the Buddha would teach the newcomer to generate the bodhicitta and to abide by the disciplines. When meal time approached, they all went outside to accept food offerings from others. When they came back, they practiced meditation to cultivate stillness. This was what the Buddha taught: how to carry out the normal daily activities which included eating (accepting food offerings), dressing (the donning of cassocks), practicing (entering into meditative stillness), and participating in the spiritual community (the monks went places as a group). The Buddha also taught the use of disciplines and the bodhicitta to govern conduct. What is the goal for doing all these things? The aim is to arrive at a state of stillness! One must develop the meditative stabilization! What does one need stabilization for? In stabilization the power of confidence is generated. In practicing meditation today, if one is able to enter into stabilization, one will definitely grow in confidence and no longer be confused. When one says that one wants to leave the True Buddha School, this indicates that one has not yet acquired stabilization! That is why, in the beginning, the most important thing the Buddha wanted us to learn was stabilization. The whole teaching of the Buddhadharma may be summed up in this one word — stabilization. Stabilization is important because it gives rise to confidence. The series of events that lead one to sprout an initial faith in the Buddhadharma is not sufficient to sustain one. Spiritual evolvement is a process that takes ongoing tempering and polishing.

We know there are many kinds of faith. "Superstition" is a kind of faith, but it is a blind faith that one has before obtaining the Right View. The practice of the True Buddhadharma always starts with a faith which precludes superstition and is characterized by the possession of Right Faith and Wisdom Faith. Right Faith is Right Knowledge. One has already contemplated and stripped the Buddhadharma to its core and decided that it is a correct teaching based on correct views. This kind of faith is Right Faith. What is Wisdom Faith? In the Wisdom Faith, one works and trains one's wisdom until it opens up and reaches the Supreme Wisdom. This kind of faith is called Right Faith and Wisdom Faith. It is not superstition.

Today you are here, listening to my teaching of the Buddhadharma. There are outsiders who would ask you not to be so superstitious, who would ask you not to believe in transcendental powers and things that are intangible. These people say they will believe it when they see and hear it. How many people are there who have this kind of faith?

There are not that many people who truly possess the Right Faith in their belief of the Buddhadharma. The number of people in possession of the Wisdom Faith is also few.

Take a look at your own faith and examine its components. How much of it is superstition? How much Right Faith is there? How much Wisdom Faith is there? Examine it slowly and make a judgment. Are you seeking blessings from the Buddhas and Bodhisattvas? Are you seeking a longer life? Children? Marriage? Do you wish the Buddhas and Bodhisattvas to bestow some fortune on you? Are you seeking Enlightenment from the Buddhas? Or are you seeking self enlightenment through self cultivation? In this last case, you are not seeking anything, but at least you are working on yourself.

Why are you practicing the Buddhadharma? The most important goal is to liberate yourself from all kinds of emotional afflictions and from the cycle of life and death. Are you seeking "elimination of emotional afflictions and liberation from the bondage of life and death"? How many of you are truly seeking this goal? If you are not seeking this goal, not training yourself and walking on the path towards the goal of "elimination of emotional afflictions and liberation from the bondage of life and death," then don't you really belong to the group of people whose faith is superstitious and blind? Therefore give this question some thought and ask yourself if you are walking on the right path or the wrong path.

The purpose of the Buddhadharma and its practice is to attain Liberation from the bondage of life and death, to attain Enlightenment, and the elimination of emotional afflictions. If you have deviated from these goals, then there is a possibility that your faith is just a superstition, a blind faith, and you are doing something wrong.

For example, there was this one person who wanted to practice and take refuge in the Buddhadharma. Perhaps he was so excited at the thought of taking refuge, he bounded down the stairs too fast, slipped, and sprained his foot. He uttered, "This is a bad omen. I am not taking refuge!"

There are also many students who, besides studying the Buddhadharma, also do practices to ask riches from the Dragon King and money from the Yellow Jambhala's mongoose. The Ganapati statue over here has gotten the most requests, as one can tell from the number of colorful ribbons people have put around his neck. Many people have gone all out to beseech money from the Ganapati because he had once manifested to me and said that any request from me would be fulfilled. These students don't realize that this promise was made to me alone. After I related this incident, many students tried desperately to beseech riches from Ganapati and have given him all these extra adornments. [audience laughter] You have not listened carefully, those words were spoken to me and not to you. Therefore, requests from me will always be fulfilled, while those made by you may not always materialize. But I do think Ganapati should have a bit of sympathy for you and answer some of your requests. After all, you have put in such a great effort. There was one student who, after receiving no response for his request, sent back his refuge certificate to us. I don't really know what to say to that. When we practice the Buddhadharma, we have a very high and lofty ideal, an ideal that is rarely found in ordinary life, which is to liberate oneself from worries and troubles in life, transcend the bondage of life and death, and realize Enlightenment. This kind of faith is the Right Faith.

Now I always pray that all of your businesses will thrive and that none will close down. I am afraid that, if you go bankrupt, the Buddhas and Bodhisattvas will get blamed. In reality, according to my knowledge, the amount of fortune a person will have is already determined. How much food and drink, even including snacks, that one can consume is determined and related to how many blessings one has accumulated. How much money one can earn is also fixed. It is true that doing the practice can improve the situation, but one cannot expect an instant turnaround. I don't mean to rule out all such possibility, as sometimes the result can be quite swift. [audience laughter] If I tell you blessings do not come so quickly, you will stop your practice. [audience laughter] So I tell you that sometimes, under the right conditions, the supplication will be quickly answered.

Therefore it is important to have the Right Faith. Although fate is inevitable and Buddhism does not discuss readings of fate, it does offer the viewpoint that one can use the Buddhadharma to rupture fate's hold on one. It is precisely because karma exists that there exists ways to release one from its bondage. This is a type of conceptualization, a kind of wisdom. A Wisdom Faith recognizes karma as well as the shattering of karma. I will give a simple illustration. I have said in the past there was nothing that I would not eat with the exception of two things: gold and diamonds. Gold is too hard to swallow and diamonds are too expensive. Since how much one can consume is predetermined, I now find that, after approaching fifty, there are certain things I have to refrain from eating. I have gone from being able to eat anything to being able to eat nothing! [audience laughter] Simply put, this is inevitable. One cannot eat too much sugar, because of diabetes. One cannot consume too much salt, because of hypertension. One cannot eat too much fat, because it will cause blockages in the arteries as well as other health problems. My mother says that squids have a high amount of cholesterol in them and a high blood cholesterol level can lead to narrowing of the blood vessels. So one cannot eat too many high cholesterol foods. Some people will tell you that a certain food can cause cancer and that other foods can cause hormonal imbalances. Therefore, every spoonful of food or drink a man takes is predetermined by fate. This kind of faith is based on wisdom and is called Wisdom Faith.

Your practice of the Buddhadharma has to be qualified by Wisdom and Right Faith. Only by possession of Wisdom and Right Faith will you be able to achieve illumination and accomplishment on the path to Buddhahood. Otherwise, you are no different from ordinary people. Like them, you are just worshiping gods, wishing for fortune, longevity, children, marriage, fame, and profit. When your wishes are not met, you stop worshiping. This is the behavior of ordinary people. Therefore, practicing the Buddhadharma differs from ordinary worship, which seeks fortune, leans towards superstition, and is still within the boundary of conventionalism.

Your practice of the Buddhadharma today is a walk on the path towards Wisdom, the Supreme Wisdom. The goal is to transcend the bondage of life and death, to understand the meaning of life, to reach Enlightenment, and to eradicate all your neurosis and problems. Today you have come to listen to this discourse on An Overview of the Buddhadharma. Now you have to understand what is Right Faith and Wisdom Faith, and walk on their corresponding paths; then you will not go wrong. If today your faith is blind, or if you only seek to enhance your fortune, longevity, children, marriage, fame, or profit, then your faith is just a kind of superstition within the conventional world.

What I would like to emphasize today is that faith marks the beginning of the practice of the Buddhadharma. One sprouts an initial faith because one wants to understand the Truth in life, to achieve Liberation and the Supreme Wisdom. With this initial faith, one enters the door of the Buddhadharma.

Impermanence

After the "initial faith," the next concept to be discussed should be "impermanence." This world is impermanent. In fact, not just this world, everything in our lives is impermanent. In Buddhism, "impermanence" is the most frequently discussed idea. Padmasambhava asked us to give the idea of impermanence some sympathetic consideration. You have to know that the span of a human life is very short. Our assembly here today was brought on by some very subtle causes and conditions and will only last a very short while. Very quickly people are brought together and very quickly people are dispersed. Buddha Shakyamuni has very clearly explained the condition of "impermanence." Birth is definitely followed by death. If one is living, one is inevitably walking towards death. A good health will eventually deteriorate. When the Buddha was in his old age, his health was poor. A perfectly healthy body can also become unhealthy. Death follows birth, withering follows flourishing, and dispersion follows assembling. We have gathered together for this extraordinary occasion but, in a few days, we will go our separate ways. In the future, such assemblies at the Rainbow Villa will probably take place only once or twice a year and the teachings will probably focus on internal practices, with the enrollment of students numbering forty, fifty or, at most, one hundred. This time our talk is open to more students, but the next time, there will only be fewer. Therefore, one can say that this is the second and last time for an open seminar here at the Rainbow Villa. In the future, a student will need to submit a dissertation before being admitted to the classes. This assemblage will only last a moment, as all assemblies will inevitably be followed by dispersals. This is "impermanence."

I have given an example earlier of how I used to be able to eat almost any kind of food. I used to have a tremendous sweet tooth. I loved to eat all kinds of sweet cakes, including the Japanese style and Taiwanese style cakes. I loved cakes stuffed with sweet bean paste, and my favorite was the kind of big, round wedding cakes popular in the Tainan area. In the past, whenever Mrs. Lu happened to see me eating the cakes, she would always be alarmed by how fast I could gulp down a big chunk of those cakes. She would say, "You shouldn't eat anymore." As soon as she said that, I would immediately consume two more pieces in a row. [audience laughter] I had this personality trait of self-determination and would not listen easily to others. If someone asked me not to eat anymore, I would deliberately eat a little bit more. When we were invited out for dinners, we were served desserts at the end which would include pastries, fruits, or a sweetened soup. In the past, whenever this sweet soup was served, I would always help myself to a second bowl when I finished the first bowl. [audience laughter] When Mrs. Lu, who was sitting next to me, noticed that, she would say, "How could you eat two bowls?" Then I would eat a third bowl. [audience laughter] But you should know that, when you exceed your limit of sugar consumption, "impermanence" makes its call. When "impermanence" beckons you, you cannot eat anymore because your blood sugar level is too high! Then you have to refrain from sugars. So I tell everyone, don't be stubborn. When you exceed your amount of food consumption, "impermanence" will signal you to stop. Then you have to obey quietly. Well, when I realized what was happening to me, I decided to defend myself against these chemical imbalances by practicing some chi exercises. Fortunately, the Buddhas and Bodhisattvas care very much for me and they told me that practicing certain chi exercises would be enough to help me.

Generally speaking, many people have illnesses. I also have illnesses! You can tell others about this, it doesn't matter. I am not afraid of others talking about me. Many spiritual cultivators feel that they cannot be ill, as if illness signifies a loss of spiritual power. [audience laughter] Actually I have had many illnesses, such as diabetes, heart problems, hypertension, dermatitis, and also cancer [laughter], bone cancer! Very severe illnesses! And there was also, I remember in the past, athlete's foot! These were ailments I have had in the past! [audience laughter] I remember when I was small I even had polio for a while. I still remember that, for a while, I was limping on my way to grade school. I also suffered from a skin illness where both of my legs looked like red bean popsicles with red beans-like bumps all over them. I also have had rheumatoid arthritis, back pain, and imbalance of kidney and bladder functions. You know when your bladder muscle is weak, you become incontinent [audience laughter]. There were also bony spurs, stomach pains, and many other problems related to the stomach. I also have suffered from respiratory problems and bronchitis. It's not *that* type of bronchitis, though. [The term "bronchitis" in Mandarin sounds like the term for being "henpecked."] It is the real kind of bronchitis. And there was allergic rhinitis and red eye. [audience laughter] My red eye disease was healed by the Kuan Yin Bodhisattva and this I remember very well. My ears were often congested and I had to clean out the wax every three months. [audience laughter] This is true. That was why I liked to visit Taiwan because one can obtain the service of having one's ears cleaned out. I visited Taiwan every three months in order to have my ears cleaned out. This side of my temple hurts and my cerebellum isn't that highly developed [audience laughter] I will probably get the Alzheimer's disease in the future. With Alzheimer's disease, the brain shrinks somewhat. Sometimes, the corners of my mouth would crack and become inflamed, and my tongue would be scraped, making eating quite a chore. There were also nose bleeds. When I first arrived in the United States I had a very serious nose bleed problem, as well as allergic dermatitis.

Where is Master Chang Jen? You notice that he looks as if he has gained quite a bit of weight recently. Why? This is because he has been poisoned! [audience laughter] After coming down with a flu and ingesting a mixture of several different kinds of cold medicines, his skin became red all the way from the soles of his feet to the top of his head! The redness has now disappeared, but his face and body are still very much swollen. This is a toxic reaction.

Why am I now so obese? I used to be very skinny, so what has caused me to gain all this weight? My younger sister was a saleswoman for a product called "Eagle Brand Three Ocean Nutrient Formula" and after I started taking that nutritional supplement, my appetite was greatly increased. That supplement induces great changes in one's body chemistry, which is tantamount to poisoning one's body. Therefore obesity can be attributed to many factors. One factor is the accumulation of excessive water in the body, another is the body has been poisoned or chemically changed, still another is that one's consumption of calories exceeds its expenditure, as in the case of Master Richard Yan. I think he belongs to neither the first nor second condition. His case belongs to the last condition of over-consumption of calories. [audience laughter]

Do I have any tumors inside my body? I do. When I cure someone of a big tumor, a small tumor will grow inside me. This is due to "supercedence"! The number of small tumors correlates exactly to the number of tumors I have helped to get rid of in others, but I will maneuver my internal chi to eliminate these small tumors. When I cure someone of cancer, I will get the cancer myself. Therefore I have many kinds of cancer in my body. I have had bone cancer and several of my intimate disciples were aware of this. But then I gradually eliminated the cancer. When I cured someone of a bony spur, I found myself come down with a bony spur and it was very painful. I had to do practice to grind it off. I also have had stomach cancer, and all kinds of cancer except uterine cancer! (audience laughter) When I conducted the Healing Fire Ceremony in Hong Kong, for three consecutive days I experienced hundreds of different kinds of illnesses. Wouldn't you say that this was a miracle? During those three days and nights I was in a stupor and did not eat any solid food at all. Many people witnessed this and were puzzled at the time. Why was Grand Master starving himself and refusing to eat his favorite foods? Was he demonstrating his transcendental powers? No, I was not. I was really unable to swallow anything except water. For three days and nights I was doing the task of "supercedence." Because of this supercedence, I was able to make the child with polio and muscular dystrophy stand up from his wheelchair, the man with the crooked spine stand up straight, and the tumor disappear from the baby! To effect such healing, I had to take over their illnesses during those three days and nights.

The human body is a transitory phenomenon. In fact, impermanence is the fundamental essence of existence. Can things remain unchanged forever? Is there a norm that stays unvaried forever? Why do high officials start practicing Buddhism? Why do generals start practicing Buddhism? I have said before, generals are often arrogant fellows but, in their old age, they start to see the shadows of ghosts. The people they have killed come back to haunt them. They have no choice but to practice Buddhism.

Has anyone been to the Buddha Light Temple at the Kuan Yin Mount in Pu Li in Taiwan? That was the residence of Dharma Master Reverend Lo Kuo who was one of my teachers in the scriptural schools. He had given me the refuge name of Tao Yen and Mrs. Lu the name of Tao Hua which sounds like "sweetpea flower" in Taiwanese. [audience laughter] When I visited the temple, I learned that many of the monks there were retired generals who had nonetheless held on to some of their old habits. Why did these high officials and generals turn, in their retired years, to Buddhism and live as monks? This is impermanence! No matter how high a position one occupies, one must eventually descend from it. Even the president, who is the highest ranking official, has to someday come down from his position, let alone more minor officials. Likewise, rich men could become impoverished while poor men could become prosperous. This is impermanence! The generals who had assembled there at the temple to do their practice were still quite set in their old ways. When the kitchen failed to buy any hot chili peppers, the monks started hitting the tables and causing a racket. The old soldiers wanted hot chili peppers for every meal and they just did not feel good without them. Considering the fact that they had been generals, it was amazing that they did not have the dining tables overturned. The feng-shui at the Buddha Light Temple is not very ideal, the monks there always fight with each other and once a nun was beaten to death by the monks. Reverend Lo Kuo himself did not know much about feng-shui. When I went to take a look at the geomancy, I found that the temple was standing on land that is known as Fire Star Dragon in geomancy terms, which is associated with very hot and dry air. That is why people living in the temple cannot help but have hot and irritable tempers.

It is impermanence when retiring high officials and generals turn to Buddhism, when rich people turn to Buddhism in their old age, and when healthy people turn to Buddhism when their time comes. Many married couples have taken renunciation vows together to do Buddhist practices. Do you think the affinity between two people can stay forever unchanged? That is not always possible! There is of course much love and affection in newlyweds, but some love relationships last a very short time. Just a week into their marriages, some couples are already fighting. They might call each other "darling" in the morning but in the evening they are heading towards divorce. This is the phenomenon of impermanence.

That is why Padmasambhava has asked us to consider and experience impermanence. If one often contemplates "impermanence," one will sprout a strong faith and grow confident in the Buddhadharma. Why is it that I am able to extricate myself from all the worldly troubles? Because I am mindful of impermanence. In this life of mine, I have encountered many twists and turns, multitudes of obstacles, and heaps of outside criticism and slander. Why am I able to rise above these things? Because I am mindful of impermanence! I am mindful that, although I have been healthy in the past, my health might deteriorate one day; although I have a good life now, there might be a day when I will become very miserable. Our True Buddha School is growing and flourishing now, but there might be a day when ... The Tathagata himself had said that Buddhism would only flourish in India for five hundred years. This is impermanence. Why would the excellent Buddhadharma only thrive for five hundred years in India? This is due to impermanence.

The transience of health and sickness, prosperity and poverty, prestige and anonymity, and within human relationships enables us to experience the impermanence inherent in all worldly phenomena. It is due to this constant awareness of impermanence that I am able to sprout and maintain my faith. After profoundly experiencing impermanence, one will find that the whole phenomenon of the Universe is a state of Emptiness. Due to the penetration into this Emptiness, one may rest in peace and tranquility. The fundamental nature of all phenomena is impermanence! So how can one be perturbed and upset by any problems? When one day the originally wealthy you suddenly become poor, it will of course trouble you! But, as long as you are mindful of impermanence, you will rise above the trouble. When the previously healthy you suddenly become stricken with a grave illness, you have to be aware of impermanence, then you can rise above the trouble. You have been the executive of a company, but suddenly your job is taken away from you; if you can understand and penetrate impermanence, you will not grieve. You must know that all phenomena of the world are inherently transient. When you penetrate deeply into this impermanence to experience it, you will not feel that you have gained or lost anything. One has to understand this truth before one can transcend worries and troubles.

Because of the impermanence in the worldly phenomena, we have to search for the Supreme Wisdom. That is what gives meaning to our lives. Why do you think we are practicing the Buddhadharma? It is because of impermanence. Because of impermanence, we want to seek the meaning of life. The most meaningful thing in life is to practice the Buddhadharma and do spiritual cultivation. Apart from this, each of us is in a state of transitory change, so why compare oneself to others? What is there to be proud of? Why be so arrogant? Everything is constantly changing. There is a Taiwanese saying, "A family's prosperity does not last three generations." In fact, sometimes prosperity does not even last one or two generations. Do you think you have really made a lot of money? Do you think you have really built yourself a big mansion? Didn't I give an example of this the other day? A man is building a mansion for himself and his family. While the mansion is still being built, the "demolition man" has already arrived. The owner is so happy when the mansion is finished! Subsequently, inside that mansion his wife gives birth to a child who turns out to be the demolition man. The child has come with the intention to dismantle the whole building. This is impermanence! So, do not be too overjoyed when you build a big mansion; neither should you grieve when the mansion is demolished.

Do not feel elated because the Buddhist religion founded by the Buddha is thriving, or sad because it is crumbling and disintegrating. In the future, when tens of millions, or hundreds of millions, of students come to take refuge in this True Buddha School, you need not be happy. Neither should you be sad when all students run away and not even one stays behind. At the beginning of this talk I described my grief a little overzealously. Actually there is no need to have any grief. I was trying to convey the state of my mind when this most precious practice, which is a labor of my love, is offered to others and others turn it down. In fact, to a truly Enlightened Being, there is no such thing as gain or loss. He is in a completely sovereign and satisfied condition.

The Buddhadharma emphasizes understanding and experiencing "impermanence" because it is the portal to liberation from neurosis and worries. If one cannot penetrate "impermanence," one will not be able to generate a spiritual faith and confidence in the Buddhadharma, and thus rise above neurosis and worries. Therefore Padmasambhava asked me and all of the Tantrayana students to carefully and intimately experience "impermanence" and to grow a staunch faith. Only by contemplating "impermanence" is one able to generate faith and confidence. Only through experiencing "impermanence" can one rise above the concepts of gain and loss. If today many people were to slander you, insult you, and take advantage of you, would you be able to stay mindful of "impermanence"? This is a world fundamentally devoid of a "norm"! A "norm" does not inherently exist! When you remain calm and unperturbed, you reach realization and are able to truly transcend troubles and worries. Otherwise, without penetration into "impermanence," how can you transcend worries and troubles? You will always be troubled and bound by emotional aflictions and your suffering will never end.

For example, I feel that my ability to attain self-mastery and become sovereign, my contentment with the world, and my decision to return life after life to this samsara, are a direct extension of this realization of impermanence. If one realizes impermanence, one will have no fear. If one has not realized impermanence, one will always have problems. This is why practicing the Buddhadharma can lead us to liberation from neurosis. We can take a look at the Great Zen Master Lotus Pond who has written the word "Death" above his headboard. "Death" is to die, all must die. I am not cursing everyone to die, but there is a principle which is absolutely inviolate — that all of us, including you and I, will eventually die. A hundred years from now, we will all have passed away! Can one live as long as the turtle? Can one live as long as the pine trees here at the Rainbow Villa and remain standing tall for several thousand years? Just any piece of rock or any one of the trees will outlive us! Understand "impermanence" from this. The Zen Master Lotus Pond wrote the word "Death" as a daily reminder that he would die the next day and that he had to maintain faith and confidence and to vigorously keep practicing the Buddhadharma here and now. This is why one has to be mindful of impermanence. How does one enter into the doorway of the Buddhadharma? Through "faith and confidence." How does one sprout this faith and confidence? By being mindful of impermanence!

The phenomena of birth, aging, sickness, death, and suffering are all transient. Do not be solely concerned with making money, one also has to give some consideration to Truth.

Let me tell you, many people have deviated from the path of cultivation when they gave in to the temptation of money! Money and fame have caused many to deviate from the path. The Tathagata has taught us to not become too enamored with fame or profit and he has compared money to poisonous snakes. In his time, the Buddha used to instruct us to "not look at ladies with our eyes or touch money with our hands." But nowadays people are not just touching money, they are embracing money! It is miserable to become entangled and trapped by money. I have said before that there are two great powers in this world. The first is the power of the Tao, the Buddha, the Tathagata, or the Buddha Nature — the greatest and most expansive power — which penetrates and encompasses the whole Universe. The second is the power of money! And you must not place the importance of money above that of the Tao, the Buddha, or the Buddha Nature; otherwise you will be trapped and cannot become liberated. To attain liberation, you must place the importance of the Tathagata first. Modern men would fare much better to have a more indifferent and reasonable approach towards money. One should never take money from others by force or trickery. Understanding impermanence will enable one to understand about money. After all, being wealthy is not always a blessing! Sometimes it can be a nuisance. Additionally, misuse of money can create evils and turn into one's own karmic hindrances. The more money one has, the more karmic hindrances one can create.

In the past the Buddha stated that money, like poisonous snakes, can bring about similar disasters. If you don't have money, no one will scheme to take it away from you! Today your wealth can increase the risks to your life. This money that you own is the poisonous snake at your side! Think this over, the Buddha's words do make sense, don't they? Because you have money, others will think about how to take it away from you! If you were penniless today, would anyone be scheming about you? They couldn't wait to run away from you. [audience laughter] Let me tell you, even the ghosts are afraid of the poor. [audience laughter]

Although the practice of the Buddhadharma requires one to enter deeply into the treasury of Buddhist scriptures, it is quite impossible to ask one to read all the twelve sections contained in the Three Buddhist Canons. Everyone of us lives in the world for a limited time only, so only those who are totally dedicated to the path can go and read all of the Buddhist works. Besides, even if one finished reading them all, one might not necessarily understand them or be able to penetrate their meanings. Even if one is able to read through the classics, one might not be able to gain anything useful out of them. Therefore, in today's discourse of An Overview of the Buddhadharma, I will concentrate on the main points: Faith and Impermanence. After one generates this faith and confidence, the next step is Comprehension.

Comprehension

What comes after one generates faith and confidence? One next has to achieve "comprehension." Comprehension involves contemplation, analytical thinking and understanding.

Generally the monks advise one to go and read the sutras. They say, "Go and study the sutras! Go and turn the sutras around!" Does the studying of sutras offer any benefits? Of course they offer some benefits. Many people are able to eventually experience this: when they open the scriptures, they can see Buddha Shakyamuni and Kuan Yin Bodhisattva emerging from the sutras. This happens when one deeply penetrates the sutras and enters into the realm wherein the Buddha manifests to directly expound the sutras to one. Many people, however, read the sutras perfunctorily! They just casually read over them. They will read and chant the *Diamond Sutra*, the *Amitabha Sutra*, the Article of Universal Gateway from the *Lotus Sutra*, the *Ksitigarbha Original Vow Sutra* and any other kind of sutra! But when you ask them if they know what the essences of the sutras are, they say, "I don't know! I am only chanting!" [laughter] That is like playing a record! [laughter] Why? The record just spins around. In such chanting, one has not used one's heart or mind to comprehend the sutras.

"Comprehension" means understanding the scriptures and this understanding is known as the "Enlightened Wisdom." We study the sutras today so we can understand their meanings, which entails a deep penetration and not just a superficial reading. What does "turning the sutras around" mean? Does it mean holding the sutra in hand and turning it around? Or does it mean the turning of the prayer wheel in the style of the Tibetans who spin the prayer wheel with each recitation? It means neither. It means that one has become a living proof of the teachings of the sutras. One has turned one's normal activities and the sutra into one inseparable state of being. This is what "turning the sutra around" means. A skillful adept can truly enter into the state of being of the sutras. If it snows outside, he can sit upon the snow and start floating and gliding with the snowflakes. When he thirsts, he can hide himself under the stamens and pistils of flowers to drink from their water. When the flowers sway with the wind, the adept can hide himself inside the flower to sip from its nectar. He can also sit upon the snowflake and float along with the other snowflakes. In reading the sutras, the adept has reached the state of merging his body and mind with the wind and can thus sail up and down just as the wind does. This state of being is a kind of free and liberating state. Only when one is able to read the sutras and enter into a state of union, to open up a more expansive consciousness, and to become as free as the world of Nature, can it be considered as "penetration into the treasury of the sutras" or "comprehension."

As Buddhist believers, what exactly is it that we believe in? We believe in the teachings of Buddha Shakyamuni. In penetrating into the treasury of the sutras taught by the Buddha, we obtain his teachings. Then the next step is to practice his teachings, to become one with the Buddha, and to attain sovereignty and transcendental powers just like the Buddha. Isn't one also the Buddha? This is a kind of "comprehension" in practicing Buddhism. That is why we go to listen to Dharma teachings. You have come to hear me talk about the Dharma, you have come to be close to the disseminator of true knowledge and to obtain the true Buddhadharma. When you acquire a tacit understanding of the teachings, the teachings will become yours — this is why we go to listen to Dharma teachings. After viewing *A Complete and Detailed Exposition on the True Buddha Tantric Dharma*, the knowledge becomes yours. You only spend US $60 — $80 to obtain the knowledge, and you can verify this when you practice the liturgy accordingly.

To "comprehend" is to penetrate deeply into the Buddhadharma. Therefore one has to listen to the Dharma teachings, to read the scriptures and to contemplate their meanings. The three steps in the learning of the Buddhadharma are: Hearing (exposure), Contemplation, and Practice. To hear, to contemplate, and finally to practice and verify one's learning. When one is able to contemplate and understand the meaning in the sutras, one attains the wisdom of the sutras. Simply put, this is "comprehension."

In this first talk of An Overview of the Buddhadharma, I have talked about "Faith," "Impermanence," and "Comprehension." Regarding "Comprehension," it is very important to attend more talks given by Dharma masters and sages. One must study scriptures and read the sutras. To penetrate into the treasury of the sutras, one has to ponder and deeply contemplate their meanings. "Comprehension" is when one is able to tacitly understand the meanings. Implicit in the term "Comprehension" is Hearing (exposure) and Contemplation.

In these several days, I shall be teaching to you a synopsis of the Buddhadharma. These are important teachings that I have gleaned from my Buddhist knowledge. They are also what I have contemplated on and understood. Take time to slowly understand and experience these Dharma teachings, and you will be able to achieve a yogic response. After achieving a yogic response, continue to follow your faith and to practice it, you will then receive great empowerments and blessings from many Buddhas and Bodhisattvas. Your consciousness will expand and you will achieve great accomplishments. These are the simple teachings on my first day of discourse.

Om Mani Padme Hum.

Second Day:
May 4, 1993

Masters, fellow cultivators, good afternoon. Today is the second day of my discourse on An Overview of the Buddhadharma and I would like to begin with a brief review of what I discussed yesterday.

Yesterday I covered the issues of "Faith," "Impermanence," and "Comprehension." Regarding the issue of "Faith," some people are correctly of the opinion that a "right faith" is superior to a "superstitious faith," and that the latter is preferable to not having any faith at all. People who do not believe in anything face the greatest obstacles in entering the door of Buddhism. After all, a faith that is "superstitious" is still a beginning faith. When one enters the door of the Buddhadharma and gains "comprehension," one's "superstitious faith" can gradually transform into the "right faith." Therefore, regarding the issue of Faith, right faith is superior to superstition while superstition is preferable to total disbelief or indifference. Some people claim that they do not believe in anything but, when you confront them with the fact that there must be at least one thing that they believe in (which is "money"), they will definitely concur with you. Money is still something everyone believes in. After all, truth is invisible but money is visible. People are enamored with the physical, materialistic aspects of the world, and are unaware of the invisible, transcendental aspects of mind and consciousness. Therefore, in practicing the Buddhadharma, the most important key is to have the right faith, the Wisdom Faith.

Regarding "Comprehension," one must gain access to virtuous and knowledgeable teachers and then listen to their teachings. One has to penetrate deeply into the treasury of sutras. One also must do contemplation. To comprehend is to hear and to contemplate. It is of utmost importance that one arrives at the right kind of comprehension, as any misunderstanding of the Buddhadharma will not lead to any fruition. The Buddhadharma that we are practicing is the holy teachings of the Tathagata [one of the epithets of the Buddha] and it will bring us great benefits when we are able to understand it correctly.

It can be quite troublesome if one misunderstands the Buddhadharma. Many people have only a smattering of knowledge of the Buddhadharma. You have come to hear my discourse because you want to obtain the right Buddhadharma which is the holy teachings of the Tathagata. When you understand this discourse, you will have obtained a very correct view of the Buddhadharma.

Although our school is being attacked by many people on the outside, the fact is they have only been able to attack my clothes, [audience laughter] my car, and my house. They cannot find anything in the True Buddha Dharma to attack. Isn't this true? There has never been anyone who has found fault with the True Buddha Dharma. No one has dared to claim that there is anything wrong with the True Buddha Dharma. Why? Because the True Buddha Dharma is the Right View! It is the authentic stuff! It only urges one to do practice. It does not ask one to wear this dress, to buy that car, or to do anything else! Outsiders can only aim their targets at the surface. They cannot say anything about the real contents of the True Buddha Dharma because the True Buddha Dharma is the holy teachings of the Tathagata, which has been passed to us from previous lineage holders. When you practice according to the True Buddha Tantric Dharma, you will attain the Right Fruition. So why should you be bothered by what kind of car your guru is driving, what clothing he is wearing, or what kind of rice — short grain rice from Japan or long grain rice from Thailand — he is eating? Why be bothered by what he eats? Those things do not really concern you! After all, you will be well fed when you attain the Dharma Taste! You will attain the Right Fruition! Therefore, when you have the Wisdom Faith, the Rational Faith, the Right Faith, and the Right Comprehension, it will be very easy for you to attain a tacit understanding and know what the Dharma Taste is.

Some people stop practicing because they cannot get along well with other people. This has much to do with human relationships but nothing to do with the Buddhadharma! There are always disagreements among people! How many people are there who could truly live in harmony with everybody? One should ignore such affairs and not let them interfere with one's practice of the Buddhadharma. In the past, my guru, the Reverend Liao Ming, told me this, "In one stroke, myriad worlds are shattered." What does this mean? It means that all the things that have happened in your past, including all the things people have said and done to you, and all your disputes, have to be completely swept away in one stroke. Go, take a nap. When you wake up, let bygones be bygones and start afresh. Renew everything on a fresh basis. A cultivator has to have this kind of boldness of vision. My guru, the Reverend Liao Ming, has sometimes reprimanded me. It made me very uneasy and I would get upset and declare that I would not make any more offering to him. [audience laughter] A few days later, I would mull over his words, "In one stroke, myriad worlds are shattered" and be reminded of his teachings to let bygones be bygones. We remained good friends and continued to have a guru/disciple relationship. He continued to teach me and I continued to learn from him. To forget everything in the past — a cultivator has to have this breadth of spirit! This way one will obtain the wonderful Dharma Taste! Can you forget yesterday? Not just yesterday, but all of the past? Let go of everything and you are instantly the Buddha, the Free and Sovereign Buddha. If you cannot forget, you will be forever bound.

Start right now to understand and believe and give some thought to Impermanence, which I discussed yesterday. Every phenomenon is fundamentally impermanent. My mother is sitting over here. In the past I found her to be very young. [audience laughter] I don't know if she still sees me as a child. [audience laughter] But now my mother is looking like this, actually she is still quite beautiful. [audience laughter] I heard that she still purchases clothing designed for people in their twenties. [audience laughter] This is impermanence! The flight of time is very terrifying. One passes from infancy to childhood, through one's teens, youth, middle and old age, and then finally one lies down and is gone. This is the procession of life's changes.

The holy teachings of the Tathagata says: Life is short and one must quickly contemplate impermanence and transcend the world. This is what the Buddha told us in the past. Contemplate on Impermanence and Transcendence and one will very soon be released from bondage and have in hand that which is most valuable. Of course one can go and study for one's doctorate, but two decades will be wasted in its pursuit [laughter], and then one will want to get married and have children! Much of one's life is spent pursuing a career, marriage, and raising children. How much time is left for spiritual cultivation? Therefore, the Tathagata teaches us to be mindful of Impermanence and to rise above the world. This is the significance of yesterday's teachings.

Practice

Today I will discuss Practice and Realization, which are the two steps which follow the generation of Faith and the attaining of Comprehension.

A Right Faith and Right Comprehension, together with a penetration into the treasury of sutras, concern the theoretical aspects of the Buddhadharma. A meal is served and it looks absolutely delicious but, if you don't eat it, you won't be fed. Although you know where to buy the ingredients, how to prepare the dishes, and how much salt, sugar, soy sauce, or flavor enhancers to use, not doing the practice is tantamount to not eating the delicious foods prepared. Therefore, today I will discuss the very important issue of Practice.

The Practice of the Buddhadharma can be divided into two major aspects. The study of the Buddhadharma is also known as the Inner Study. The Inner Study is simply the study of one's mind and consciousness. In the past, when the Buddhadharma was introduced into China, the Chinese referred to it as the Inner Study. We know that the famous Ouyang Chingju Licheng was the abbot of the Chinese Institute of Inner Study. Well, the so-called Inner Study refers to that portion of the study of the Buddhadharma which is a study of consciousness.

Actually, the Buddhadharma also contains an Outer Study. What is the Outer Study? The Outer Study pertains to "precepts and disciplines." In the practice of Buddhism, besides observing the precepts and disciplines (the outer aspect of Practice), one also has to be mindful of one's consciousness (the inner aspect of Practice). Although mastering one's inner world is generally more difficult than observing the percepts, the latter is also not easy to carry out.

The Five Precepts

As Buddhists, we know that the first Five Precepts we must observe are: refrain from killing; refrain from stealing; refrain from sexual misconduct; refrain from untruthful speech; and refrain from liquors or intoxicants.

Whenever I talk about the Five Precepts, you probably chuckle to yourself, as I was a drinker myself. [laughter] Let me tell everyone: I have quit drinking! [audience laughter] This is for real. Many people, including Mrs. Lu, were surprised at what a clean break I made with liquor. In the past I said, "In all these years of my practice of the Buddhadharma, I have not had any indulgences. If I have to quit drinking, what is there worth living for?" I used to savor a little liquor everyday. Oh! It was so nice to have a nightcap at bedtime; it produced a good night's sleep! [audience laughter] But strangely, I could quit just like that! When I said I would quit, I quit! This is possible when one is centered and has a strong will power. It has been a long time since I had my last sip. The last time was when I was in Los Angeles for a Dharma Ceremony. Since then I have not had a drop of liquor! Well, how come there is no applause? [audience laughter and applause] This is quite a feat! [audience laughter] It is very difficult to have an alcoholic quit cold turkey! [audience laughter] Really, I have become a teetotaler! So, in the future, you only need to make wine offerings to the Yellow Jambhala and Red Jambhala, you don't have to offer me any more wine! [audience laughter] No more XO, no more herbal liquors!

Regarding "refraining from untruthful speech" — what a difficult precept that is! I know that this is not an easy precept to abide by. Honestly, it is so easy to make an untruthful speech if one is not careful; even I am afraid of it! [audience laughter] But people who are practicing the Buddhadharma must not speak untruthfully. I remember once reading the personal column of a newspaper or magazine wherein someone had written a particular article. I am afraid many people will be hurt if I say it aloud. The headline began with "Born Liars" in large print. (I am scared to go on.) [laughter] This refers to the opposite of men. [audience laughter] Now, I have not really made any statement! [audience laughter] So, remember, do not speak untruthfully, even though this is not easy to carry out. Men as well as women can speak untruthfully, especially those who are in businesses. A merchant will claim that his goods are very fresh even though they are almost rotten. If he said they were rotten, would anyone buy from him? Therefore, he lies. Even if it is obvious that his goods are heftily marked up in price, a businessman still claims that they are a bargain. It is so easy for someone in business to break this precept. Business people talk only about their strong points, remaining silent about their shortcomings. A real estate agent will not disclose the flaws of a house but will rave about the merits of a property. Isn't this so? Take Master Chao for example. He is in the real estate business. [laughter] I have never heard him say anything bad about his properties! He only talks about the good points. That is why, when I ran into him, I had to buy from him. [audience laughter] Don't misunderstand me, I have not purchased any real estate property for myself! [audience laughter] I was referring to the Bodhi Lei Tsang Temple in Vancouver and the land on which the building to house the True Buddha News will be built. Master Chao only says good things about his properties, as no one would buy from him if he pointed out their shortcomings.

To refrain from lust or sexual misconduct is also one of the five precepts. We know that, as Confucius said, "food" and "sex" are the two basic human drives. Many people can't help falling into this trap. As for myself, I have walked on the edge of this trap, but I have not fallen into it! Although one of my feet was in descent, [audience laughter] I was able to withdraw it quickly and nothing happened! There once was a student of mine who told me the following. When she returned from her visit to Mainland China, she told me that she had done many good deeds. I asked her what kind of good deeds had she done? She said she had performed many acts of charity and much almsgiving. How were these performed? She proceeded to tell me that she had gone to bed with many men, including a certain Mr. Ho, a certain Mr. Wu, her brother-in-law, and someone whom she could not name or even describe. Well, I asked her why she was doing that. She retorted, "Didn't you ask me to do more charity?" [laughter] I asked her why she considered it charity. She replied, "Don't the Four Immeasurable Vows say that one must give happiness to the sentient beings? [audience laughter] Doesn't the first vow of Benevolence ask us to bring happiness to sentient beings?" For a moment I was speechless! I opened my mouth and, for a moment, could not say anything! She claimed that her activities were really acts of charity that brought others happiness!

Fortunately I practice the Buddhadharma and, to be able to give a discourse on An Overview of the Buddhadharma, I have to understand the tenets of the Buddhadharma. I told her, "That was wrong!" The Buddha has said that there are certain things one should refrain from giving to others. They include things that can increase others' desires, harm others, or ruin others' pursuit of Enlightenment. By engaging in such sexual activities, she was fanning others' desires. There are certain things one should not give to others as presents: things that enhance others' desire, poisons, or weapons such as knives and guns. Therefore, I reminded her of the words spoken by the Buddha. Whether she truly heard them or not, I do not know. Such activities are a transgression of the precept. As monogamy is what is legally accepted nowadays, householders have to observe monogamy. People who have taken the ordination vows must transform their sexual desire. There are practices which one can do to transmute such desire and lust.

That woman student was very good at distorting the truth. She could twist ideas in a way that was hard to take. My earlier statement about withdrawing my foot after a close call was a reference to this student. I did not go to her bedroom, but I clearly recall that it was she who came (in her nightgown and unannounced) to my bedroom. Well, the amazing thing was that I was completely in control of my elements and did not fall into her trap. I listened to her stories and, when she finished, I saw her out the door. That was all that happened. My clothes were tidily in order without a single button undone. [audience laughter] One comes across such things in life. This is why, when Buddha Shakyamuni was alive, defamatory stories were in wide circulation. There were incidents where various women made false accusations against the Buddha. Why? They found monks and spiritual cultivators to be easy targets. This is also why "refraining from sexual misconduct" is included in the Five Precepts.

Another precept is "to refrain from stealing." I feel that Western educational systems are somewhat deficient in emphasizing the importance of integrity in the building of moral character. In the Orient there is more attention given to the moral education of children. Especially in Japan, there is a very strict sanction against stealing. Children are taught from an early age that, "Things that don't belong to one are not one's. One is not qualified to be a human being when one steals from others." Stealing is a very serious transgression in the Buddhist precepts.

Next is the precept "to refrain from killing." Buddhists do not kill. The True Buddha School advocates not killing, as well as animal release. Whether one has to be a vegetarian or not is a different matter. The most important point is that one does not kill. These are the Five Precepts that govern exterior behavior and conduct.

In our True Buddha School, the True Buddha Tantric Dharma that we practice falls under the domain of Inner Study, whose goal is to purify the mind and consciousness. In this study, we practice the Great Homage, Mandala Offering, Armor Protection, and Vajrasattva Practice; we chant mantras and sutras, including the Fourfold Refuge Mantra; we hold mudras and enter into Samadhi. All these train one's mind to become pure. The purification of the mind is extremely important. The Buddha teaches, "One is practicing Buddhism when one refrains from all evil actions, enacts all benevolent deeds, and enters into a state of pure mind." The first two qualifications pertain to exterior behavior, while the last phrase refers to Inner Study and actual practice. Where else can one find a practice that offers the same elements as does the True Buddha Tantric Dharma? Today one can read the published liturgy for group practice of the Scriptural schools and will note that they revolve around "chanting, walking around the Buddha statues, bowing, and sitting in meditation." These are the same four steps practiced even in the Zen schools. The True Buddha Tantric Dharma is a practice that enables one to penetrate more deeply into the expansive and more subtle levels of consciousness where there is a stronger experience of "Dharma Taste." Where else can one find a system of practice with all these elements? Most Dharma masters now are teachers who espouse "Faith" and "Comprehension"; there are very few who teach others how to do "Practice" and achieve "Realization." Therefore, the True Buddha School is extraordinary in that it teaches everyone how to do "Practice."

In the beginning when Buddha Shakyamuni taught us, the Arhats, there were only a few precepts. The additional precepts came as a result of increasing numbers of followers breaking the precepts and making transgressions. At the very beginning, the Buddha only gave us four rules. Listen carefully to these four rules. If one could carry out all of them, one would be quite amazing. The first one is: Make no contact with the worldly people, but remain cloistered alone in an enclosed area such as in the mountains. For example, if one is staying at the Rainbow Villa, one should remain cloistered within the enclosing wall and not go outside. This is living a "mountain life." That was the way it was with the Dharma Master Hui

Yuen, the founder of the Pure Land Sect. He did not travel beyond a certain nearby brook. If a visitor came to see him, he would see the visitor off as far as the brook. Many spiritual cultivators lived such cloistered lives in remote areas, remaining thirty, forty, or fifty years. Such a life affords tranquillity. That is why the Buddha asked us to live in the mountains as an assembly of monks and to travel in a group, accepting alms from others. Everyone filed along, straight as a troop of soldiers, and was forbidden to gaze around, as such activity caused too much distraction. Therefore, by living a "mountain life," one's mind is able to remain in the mountain.

The second rule was, "No seeing," in the same sense as Confucius' ethical code of, "Not seeing anything that transgresses propriety." One was asked not to look at the opposite sex. That was why Buddha Shakyamuni had, at the beginning, not allowed women to join the order of renunciants. Among the disciples, Ananda was more partial to women and asked the Buddha to change the rule. Three other disciples, Mahakashyapa, Shariputra, and Maudgalyayana, strongly opposed Ananda's proposal, but to no avail. As a result of women joining the group, Buddhism only flourished in India for five hundred years instead of one thousand years, as the Buddha had originally proclaimed.

The third rule was, "Do not touch money." The Buddha taught us spiritual cultivators to refrain from touching money because money could tarnish the reputation. Nowadays many ascetics also claim that they do not touch money, but they use chopsticks to pick up money tossed to them by almsgivers. [audience laughter] Actually, this is still not acceptable. Even though one does not touch money directly when using the chopsticks, it shows that one still has greed. As long as meals were offered, renunciants did not need any other material things, for they dressed very simply and their living conditions were also very simple. At that time, Mahakashyapa lived under trees and slept between grave sites in the cemetery. He did not live in a beautiful house. This was a teaching of the Buddha himself.

The fourth rule was "No alcohol." This is because alcohol can unleash inhibitions and alter one's personality. Sometimes, an ordinarily timid person can become quite audacious after consuming alcohol, and will start verbally abusing anyone from the Jade Emperor in Heaven to all his past ancestors. Therefore it is very easy for drunkards to commit many transgressions. As for myself, I never became unruly during my drinking years. In my case, drinking only made me more subdued. [audience laugher] The more I drank, the more silent I would become. In my whole life, there were only three occasions when I actually got drunk. The first time was when I was still studying land surveying. I climbed outside the school wall to go on a binge of Kaoliang [a liquor made of sorghum]. The next morning during roll calls, the whole troop reeked of alcohol. The second time was when I got drunk at Luo Yu Ch'in's house. The third time was during a finger-guessing game between two other people, and I offered to drink for them, no matter what the outcome. [audience laughter] Of course I would get drunk that way. Those are the only three times in my whole life that I have gotten drunk. Ever since then I have kept very calm in my drinking. Anyway, I have now, of course, quit drinking altogether.

In India, there is this legend. A spiritual cultivator lived by himself deep in the mountains. All the nearby villagers knew of him and, since they liked very much to make offerings to cultivators, they would take the initiative and bring food to him. This spiritual cultivator was someone who led a "mountain life," and he did not want the villagers to get too close to him, so he drew a boundary line about fifty feet away from him. He told the villagers to place their food offerings outside the boundary line. There was one woman who went often to make offerings of cow's milk or goat's milk. Over time, the cultivator became aware of this woman, who brought him very fresh and delicious milk each time she came. One day, the woman spoke to the cultivator of how much she hoped to have a closer view of him. She had only seen him from a distance. Indeed, she had been making offerings to him for a very long time — almost a year now. The cultivator's sympathy for her was aroused and he gave her permission to move to a distance ten feet away to have a look at him. Oh, the woman was very beautiful. When she came closer, the cultivator glanced at her and, without saying anything else, he kept on with his practice, entering into a deep meditation. From then on, while everyone else continued to place their offerings fifty feet away, this woman would bring her offerings of milk to only ten feet away. This way, the two would look at each other. From ten feet away, this woman spoke again. She told the cultivator that she had heard that, when yogis focused their energy, they could generate a heat in their palms and that a vapor could emerge from the palms. She wanted to seek a confirmation of this from the yogi. So she asked, "Do you know if a yogi's palms get very hot? Can I have a look at your palms?" This cultivator decided that, since he had already made the allowance for her to get as close as ten feet away, what difference did it make if he showed her his palms? So he extended his palms to show her. To have a better look though, she had to get even closer. Then she started to feel his palm to see if it was hot! Well, as soon as they touched, they both became electrified. [laughter and audience laughter] First they looked at each other, then their hands touched. What happened next? Next the yogi became a herdsman and a shepherd [laughter and audience laughter] while the shepherdess carried and nursed their children.

That was why the Buddha originally taught that a renunciant should refrain from looking at the opposite sex. While gazing into each other's eyes can create an invisible electricity, touching hands creates an opportunity for the electricity to be translated into physical contact. As soon as the female and male energies touch each other, it can cause trouble for the cultivator! Unless one is very stabilized, one will be overwhelmed with the desire to give up one's renunciation and return to a householder's life. That's why one has to abide strictly by the Five Precepts of "No killing, no stealing, no sexual misconduct, no false speech, and no alcohol."

The Buddha taught us to live a "cloistered mountain life," to "not look at the opposite sex," to "not touch money," and to "abstain from alcohol." Of course, these four rules which I talk about today were rules in the past. Perhaps modern men are able to stay more centered and able to better resist distraction, so we do not practice precepts the way cultivators did in the past. Nonetheless, we still must abide by the Five Precepts that govern our exterior actions.

Actual Practice of Mind

Therefore, to engage in the practice of the Mind, or Inner Study, is to practice the True Buddha Tantric Dharma. In my discourse of *A Complete and Detailed Exposition on the True Buddha Tantric Dharma*, I have explained that, after one succeeds and achieves realization in the external practice, one moves on to do the internal practice, the esoteric practice, and the inner-esoteric practice. The four corresponding levels of empowerments are: Personal Deity Yoga Empowerment, Internal [Energy] Yoga Empowerment, Highest Tantra Empowerment, and the Great Perfection Empowerment. These four levels of empowerments are very important. When one follows this graduated pathway of Tantric practice, one is practicing the Inner Study.

What methods employed by the Scriptural schools are related to Inner Study? I am cognizant of their methods. In the case of chanting, a momentary purity of the mind is generated during the time one chants Namo Amitabha. In the event known as Ch'an Ch'i [a seven days event of sitting meditation], one seeks to enter into an empty state of mind or a realm of purity. All these are within the domain of "practice of mind."

In Tantrayana, we first practice "the Four Preliminaries," "Guru Yoga," and "Personal Deity Yoga" — after receiving their corresponding empowerments which are known as first level empowerments. After receiving the second level empowerments, one then practices "Treasure Vase Breathing," "opening of the middle channel," and the "opening of the Five

Chakras." With the third level empowerment, one can practice the "Highest Tantra" to realize the "Samadhi of Bliss and Emptiness." With the fourth level empowerment, one can practice the "Great Perfection" and enter completely into the Void or Emptiness. It is a system of Actual Practices. Our school today completely utilizes concrete methods of actual practices to show progression on the path. The methods employed by the Scriptural schools are relatively simple: one pure thought with the chanting of one epithet, meditating on emptiness, and entering into Emptiness. These are also the methods of the Zen school.

Regarding the rumors circulating about me, you are of course aware that my reputation on the outside, is not very good. Many students have written me to show their concern regarding the negative criticism. When I see the term "feng p'ing" [rumors] which literally means "review from the winds," I really feel that these are just a lot of hot air! I really do not concern myself with these rumors but, since the students have shown their concern, I will spend some time on it. Some people claim that the Grand Master does not follow the precepts. People have criticized me because they feel that I do not abide by the precepts. Actually I do abide by the precepts. The discipline that I observe is even stricter than that followed by the ordained monks. You know that in the past the Tibetan Lamas have been labeled derogatorily as "True Scriptures False Monks." What does this mean? True Scriptures refer to the Buddhist scriptures that were introduced into Tibet from India. The scriptures were translated first from Sanskrit into Pali, then from Pali into Tibetan. Since these are closely related languages, the Tibetan scriptures are considered true and are efficacious when one chants them. What does False Monks mean? This refers to the fact that the lamas consume meat, drink alcohol, and engage in the Consort Practice. Therefore the Tibetan lamas were considered to be false monks. This was the kind of criticism which was prevalent in Buddhist circles in the past. Then what about the monks in Mainland China and Taiwan? They were known as the "False Scriptures True

Monks." Why? When the Buddhist scriptures were translated from Pali into Chinese, many ideas indigenous to the Chinese were integrated into the translation. The idea of vegetarianism and certain codified behaviors were integrated into the sutras. Such adulterated sutras are no longer effective when one chants them and are called false sutras. What does True Monks mean? The Chinese monks are vegetarians, non-drinkers, they follow the Five Precepts, and observe celibacy. Since many Tibetan lamas are married, they are considered False Monks. The monks in our True Buddha School are true monks. [laughter]

The outside rumors claim that I do not follow the precepts; actually I am a very good observer of the precepts! How unruly can one be in Seattle? Some people criticize me for going dancing. Actually I have not been dancing for a long time. [laughter and audience laughter] You claim that I sing Karaoki. Actually this is forced upon me. [audience laughter] When I am home, do I go and sing by myself? It is only when I am out and am complying with the wishes of the students that I sing. Isn't it true? It is with reluctance that I sing. I have heard that singing can generate a grassroot intimacy and power; therefore I sing for everyone. When have I ever sung or danced at home? That was why I became a monk. [audience applause] Why are you applauding this? [laughter and audience laughter] I am telling the truth; this is absolutely the truth. I abide by the Five Precepts. I have never killed, I don't steal, and I don't indulge in sexual misconduct. I follow the precepts!

Regarding "false speeches," you can see that I only tell the truth! I talk about everything and, in my books, I write about everything. This is true speech. I have quit drinking, so am I not abiding by the Five Precepts? I do abide by the precepts, so as to set an example for you! [laughter and audience applause] You have to follow and abide by the Five Precepts. There are terrible outside rumors, accusing me of swindling people out of money by fixing prices on Initiation Empowerment, by charging people for registering for certain ceremonies, and by demanding monthly offerings from each student! There is no such thing. I have made it very clear from the beginning that all offerings are voluntary. Have I ever stipulated how much a student has to offer to me? Come and tell me, and I will pay you back a hundred times! My guru told me this, "In the future, when you leave the mountain to go into the world, you must let others pay you on a voluntary basis." I follow this precept of my guru's. Every Buddhist service is always paid for by the students on a voluntary basis. This precludes business transactions. In a business deal, there is a certain asking price for a certain commodity. But in temple services, such as registering for Bardo Deliverance, Purification and Blessing Ceremonies, Offerings, Taking Refuge, Installment of a plaque for ancestors or a lamp at the lamp pagoda, there is no set fee; the amount of the offering is voluntary. People have tried to swindle me instead of the other way around. You have to remember that I am the almsgiver, I am the one who is giving away the money. What you have given me are as droplets while what I am returning to you is a downpour. So, where is the swindling of money? We know that all those rumors which are circulated are all lies.

Next there is the rumor of sexual harassment. You know that swindlers usually swindle people out of money and sex. These are the two things a swindler is always after. What else can there be! Talking about sexual harassment, let me think if it ever took place. [audience laughter] It happened once, [audience laughter] but it was her trying to take advantage of me and not the other way around! [audience laughter] Someone tried to make a pass at me but she failed! How can it be otherwise? Isn't it true? You know the aesthetic standard of yogis is pretty high? [audience laughter] It is embarrassing to talk like this! [laughter and audience laughter] Anyway, if one gives this matter some thought, one will come to the right conclusion!

To become an adept, a cultivator must practice "chi." When a yogi who engages in the Internal Practice of "chi, channels, and light drops" [Energy Yoga] attains a true internal realization, a certain power will be generated. He does not have to coerce others into a sexual relationship with him. In fact others will try to pursue a sexual liaison with him! Therefore this rumor that I took sexual advantage of others is absolutely untrue; in fact, it was the other way around. [audience applause] Mrs. Lu made the remark, "Grand Master, if one day you were to announce that you wanted some girl friends, there would immediately be a long line formed, like the line outside a lady's powder room." [audience laughter] This was what Mrs. Lu said. I did not say that! [audience laughter] I would not dare to make such a bold statement! [audience laughter] Mrs. Lu said that if I publicly announced that I wanted a mate, people would flock to me! [laughter and audience laughter] This is because a realized yogi or yogini will radiate a certain invisible light and power, and many people, both male and female, find him or her irresistible and want to get close to him.

It is also inevitable that, out of a devotion for the guru, a feeling of adoration arises. Along the path of cultivation, when one attains certain realizations, such phenomena will occur. For example, when Buddha Shakyamuni was meditating under the pipal tree, women such as Sundari and Cinca-manavika found him attractive and were drawn to him. They made excuses to get close to him. The Buddha had not tried to take advantage of them, it was they who wanted to take advantage of the Buddha. That is why a cultivator must maintain stability and not succumb to the seductions of money and sex.

Through actual practice, one will generate a stability and emit a radiance. One will also obtain the Clear Light. In the Scriptural school, actual practice is chanting. A single chanting is associated with a single moment of pure consciousness. In the Tantric school, actual practice is entering into Samadhi through the unbroken integration of mantra, mudra, and visualization [the purification of speech, body, and mind].

Realization

Through actual practice, one will achieve "Realization." What is "Realization"? Realization is Enlightenment. By engaging in the process of actual practice, one will ultimately arrive at the realm of Enlightenment. Therefore, starting with "Faith," "Comprehension," and "Practice," one finally reaches "Realization."

Some people have practiced for a very long time (thirty or even fifty years) but have not attained Realization. When they give Dharma teachings, they just open the sutras and read what the Buddha has said. Sometimes they will add some of their own explanations. They urge people to have "Faith" and "Comprehension." Their definition of "Comprehension" is to read and explain the sutras. Do they engage in actual practice? No! This kind of Dharma master is numerous.

Oh! Today and the day before yesterday, I saw many clouds in the sky, covering up the sun. In the future I am going to call myself Master Wu Yun (Master Dark Clouds). [audience laughter] It is quite a good name! The Great Master Dark Clouds. These dark clouds are quite powerful. They have covered up the whole Seattle area and almost the entire state of Washington, and they are bringing much rain. From now on, just call me the Great Master Dark Clouds. [laughter and audience laughter] Or call me the Venerable Master Hsuan Nao (the Venerable Master Rowdy). Since sentient beings are so boisterous, I don't want to remain quiet all by myself. I also want to be rowdy. [laughter, and audience laughter and applause] After all, we are all mixed up in this together! I can think of an even better name. You know that among the Dragon Kings of the East, South, West, and North Oceans, the East Ocean Dragon King is the greatest. I should call myself the Supreme Master Tung Hai (the Supreme Master of the East Ocean), since Ching Hai is just a small inland lake! [audience laughter] From now on, when you write to me, just address your letters to Master Dark Clouds, the Venerable Master Rowdy, or the Supreme Master of the East Ocean. Those will be my aliases. [audience laughter and applause]

Dharma teachings given by people who have attained Realization are infused with the Dharma Taste. People who have not attained Realization do not really know how to give teachings with the Dharma Taste. These are two distinctly different kinds of Dharma teachings. An Enlightened master only needs to bring a little of his Realization into play and one will immediately recognize the Dharma Taste in his teachings. This Dharma Taste is the expression of Wisdom through spoken words. Wisdom arises when one gains an insight into Reality and when one resides permanently in the Condition of Ultimate Reality. This Wisdom can be expressed in the form of either verbal or written language.

Many Zen riddles are expressions of this Wisdom in the form of a spoken language. For example, the Fifth Patriarch Hung Jen met the Sixth Patriarch and asked, "Where are you from?" The Sixth Patriarch replied, "I am from Taiwan." The Fifth Patriarch then questioned, "How can someone from Taiwan attain Enlightenment? Do the Taiwanese have the qualifications to attain Enlightenment?" To this the Sixth Patriarch replied, "Although there are different kinds of people, all, whether they are Taiwanese, other Oriental, or Occidental, have the same Buddha Nature! Their Buddha Nature does not differ." As soon as the Fifth Patriarch heard this, he knew the Sixth Patriarch had understood the Equality Wisdom aspect of the Buddha Nature. Words spoken by a person who has attained Realization are infused with the Dharma Taste.

Similarly, even though the fellowship of our school in Los Angeles is not thriving as well as fellowships elsewhere, when the potential of the Los Angeles students to attain Enlightenment is being questioned, one can still answer, "Although people reside in different cities, such as Los Angeles, San Francisco, and Seattle, their Buddha Nature is the same." This answer demonstrates the same awareness as the Sixth Patriarch's and is also infused with the Dharma Taste. Zen riddles can be used to ascertain the level of one's Realization and, through their dialogue, the Fifth Patriarch was able to recognize the superior root qualities of the Sixth Patriarch. As the Sixth Patriarch had already obtained the View of Emptiness, the Wisdom of Equality (one of the Five Buddha Wisdoms) immediately shone through as soon as he spoke. This was, of course, perceived by the Fifth Patriarch.

When an iota of obscuration is removed, an iota of luminosity is revealed or "realized." This is what happens in our spiritual cultivation. Each time we do a practice, we enter into a period wherein obscuration is removed and where there is only pure consciousness [that transcends the ego]. When one is able to maintain these moments of pure consciousness and expand them into an unbroken continuity of pure consciousness, one realizes the Buddha Nature!

Wisdom has been classified into Wisdom generated from Insight into Reality or Wisdom generated from the Permanent Condition of Ultimate Reality. Wisdom has also been classified according to its mode of expression: through verbal or written language. The Zen School masters have traditionally abandoned the written words as a mode of transmission, preferring to speak directly to disciples in order to bring them to see their own original Buddha Nature and thus achieve Enlightenment. In Tantrayana, this transmission is effected through "the Empowerment of the Guru." Blessing and empowerment from a Realized Guru brings about transformation and quickens the process of Instantaneous Buddhahood or Enlightenment. This kind of Tantrayana transformation is effected through the secret power of mantra. Do you think your Grand Master is a Realized Guru? [Audience replies, "Yes!" and audience applauds] I am of course happy to hear this affirmation from you. How can I be sad with such an answer! [audience laughter]

There are several current events in my life which I would like to share with you. Although certain aspects of a Realized person are extraordinary, in some areas he lives an ordinary life like everyone else. Lately, many people have come to help with the correspondence at the True Buddha Tantric Quarter. As a result, the number of people staying for lunch and dinner has increased to more than twenty, sometimes even more than thirty. The two nuns, Bi Chen and Bi Yen, who are in charge of preparing the meals would call out to us, "We are running out of food!" Well, someone had to go and purchase more food. Since it is quite a chore for Mrs. Lu to do all the purchasing by herself, over the last several months I have been grocery shopping every night at the Uwajimaya, Safeway, QFC, Larry's Market, as well as a few other stores. [laughter and audience laughter] You might wonder why I have to go to so many different markets. Sometimes I even go to different Safeway supermarkets. This is because many little bodhisattvas, very small in size, were following me. They stayed on top of my head, above the ears, and also at other parts of my body. They were the happiest when I went grocery shopping. [laughter and audience laughter] Wherever I went, I just needed to clap my hands and announce, "Go and help yourself!" Then they would help themselves to a free meal! [laughter and audience laughter] After enjoying themselves and exhausting everything in one supermarket, we had to try a new one the next day! [laughter and audience laughter] That was why we shopped at the Safeway in Redmond one day and visited the Safeway in Bellevue the next day. I had to switch supermarkets everyday. The bodhisattvas came like a gust of wind or, rather, using a not very nice analogy, they suddenly descended like a dark cloud of locusts and in a few minutes all the corn was gone! [laughter and audience laughter] When I entered the supermarket, I knew when they were coming. The doors of the supermarket suddenly opened by themselves and, with a blast, closed again. Other people in the store were dumbfounded at the inexplicable automatic opening and closing of the doors! [audience laughter]

I am not making this up. I am living in a state wherein many bodhisattvas are following me around. [audience applause] This morning during the "news review" session — you might wonder what that is. It was a common activity in the army and at the surveying school. Since not everyone then had access to a newspaper, a student representative would be selected to read the morning newspapers and then review the headlines and important news with everyone else. This morning I had a "news review" session. Who read the news to me? The bodhisattvas. I was shown a news item that read "the xxx Temple was turned into rubble." A certain temple which, in the past, had some connection with us, was destroyed in a fire. I am telling everyone of this incident which, of course, has not yet happened, and I hope I can have this verified in the future. Anyway, I have already read about it in a future newspaper. [audience laughter] The bodhisattvas showed me this newspaper item of the temple being consumed in a fire. I learn about many events in the future through the "news review."

For example, in Taiwan during one particular "news review" session, I was shown the China Times. Then, suddenly, the China Times disappeared and turned into a xxx Daily. What could that mean? How can the China Times disappear? I cannot disclose the answer to this because there are implications concerning a nation. The reading of future newspapers is a kind of divination into the future. The newspapers that you read are current ones that report events that have just happened. The ones that I read are sometimes ten years into the future. Actually, the negative criticism written about me in the newspapers is previewed by me courtesy of the bodhisattvas. [audience laughter] The people who slander me have printed "Sheng-yen Lu" in such offensively large print! [laughter and audience laughter] Actually by the time the little, slanderous booklets were being printed, I had already read the contents. How could I not know? Through the same means, I found out about the fire that destroyed the residence of one of our students. I also had read about that beforehand in the "future newspaper." But how could I talk about it beforehand? Although I know of many future happenings, what good will their disclosure serve? Just think about this, how can I not know of certain things that are going to happen? But how or to whom should I divulge it? It is not possible to print such things in the newspapers! Even if I told these things to people who are intimate with me, (the tight-mouthed ones,) no rumors would be created. So the ones who are qualified to leak the news do not do so, while the ones who have no knowledge at all fabricate rumors. [audience laughter]

This clairvoyance into the future is not always pleasant, but the bodhisattvas have told me that they cannot show me the good news exclusively. Nor is it appropriate for them to show me just the bad news. The bodhisattvas were at a loss what to do. So I told them, "Do it anyway you want! Just show me whatever future happenings you want me to read." [laughter] So, the fact is, when they show me a newspaper from several years from now that contains an article that reprimands me, I have to be sad for several years before it becomes a fact in this reality. [laughter and audience laughter] What a snub! [audience laughter] Therefore it is not always pleasant to know of future events! Sometimes the bodhisattvas do not want me to know of certain events because they do not want me to get worried. Anyway, my philosophy is to flow and be free. Although fate exists, one has to have Self-Mastery, no matter what fate has in store for one.

My Guru, Thubten Taerchi, has written for me the verses [now hanging in the dining area of the Rainbow Villa]. He is teaching me through the verses to abide in the state of Freedom! The first verse urges me to propagate and uphold the proper Buddhadharma transmitted by Buddha Shakyamuni. The second verse encourages me to cultivate to the highest realm of Pure Light. The third verse points out the Nature of Equality shared by all beings who have arisen out of the Sanskrit seed syllable "hum." The fourth verse states that Tantrayana employs the Wisdoms of the Buddha to bring auspiciousness to all sentient beings. The putting together of the first word from each of these four verses forms the name he gave to me: Thubten Tsu Ju [Thubten Freedom] — to be in Freedom. I am aware that I could teach you these methods of psychic vision or psychic hearing, but such abilities can bring much unhappiness. What use is it to know of inevitable suffering in advance? Although you might have good intentions to help others, can you really help others alleviate their pain when it is sometimes predestined by fate and karma?

The most important task one can engage in is to practice the Buddhadharma. When one engages in the "actual practice" and attains Realization, one's psychic abilities will develop naturally. Buddhist practitioners will ultimately attain

Self-Realization and understand the Ultimate Truth of the Universe. When one attains Self-Realization, one transmits this method of awakening to others, enabling others to achieve Realization. This continues until everyone attains Perfect Enlightenment in both body and mind. A Buddha is one who has attained Perfect Enlightenment himself and can help others to attain Perfect Enlightenment. The purpose of "actual practice" is to attain Perfect Realization in body and mind, then to help others to achieve the same goal. When one achieves Perfect Enlightenment, every single action one carries out in the world brings tremendous value to others.

How does one attain Realization? One has to practice and gain a radical understanding of the Truth of the Universe. In the next several days, I will discuss these individual aspects of practice. In other words, I will explain how one can experience the different levels of the Dharma Taste. [audience applause]

The question is, "Do transcendental powers arise when one attains Realization?" Of course, they do. In the condition of Realization one can get in touch with other energies in the Universe. It is something like coming into contact with electricity. Before Realization, one is like an insulated body and not aware of other dimensions. With Realization, one automatically knows of karma and fate. For example, I have related to you this incident from one of my past lives. In that lifetime, I was an important Lama at the Portola Palace in Tibet. During that lifetime, a woman who was the proprietess of a metal shop on Octagon street in Lhasa made accusations against me. In this lifetime, she [the same female student who made the false accusations] is repeating her previous behavior. These events are karmically entwined and fated to happen. One cannot escape from them. The Buddhas and Bodhisattvas expressed to me that this was the way it had to happen because of the underlying karma.

During another lifetime, I was an abbot at the Golden Mountain Monastery in Mainland China. Master Sheng Fa [of the local chapter in Edmonton, Canada] was an administrator at the Monastery during that lifetime and was known as Dharma Master Kuang Miao. Individuals with affinity will meet again. During that lifetime, he got rid of me [audience laughter] and succeeded me as the abbot at the Monastery. Well, what really happened was that Impermanence had beckoned to me. Do you think an abbot can stay forever as an abbot? Do you think one can eternally be an executive? There is nothing in the phenomenal world that stays forever unchanged! Only Arhats, Bodhisattvas, and Buddhas who have reached Enlightenment and abide in the Realm of Non-birth and Non-death live in the Eternal Condition.

When you interpenetrate time and space, you will have knowledge of your past and future lives. You will have a clear understanding of the workings of karma and the causes and consequences of interrelated events. There is a karmic basis to the coming and going of events and the transmigration of individuals. Such being the case, how can one cling to any phenomenal condition? When, through the practice of Buddhism, you reach Realization and Enlightenment and abide in the Inherent Perfection, you will not grasp onto anything in the phenomenal world, becoming happy or sad over it. At such a stage, you are completely Sovereign and attain Freedom, as stated in the verses written by Guru Thubten Taerchi. Do you want to attain Freedom? If you do, you have to work on your practice seriously. You will then enjoy the Dharma Taste and transcend your problems. If you do not want Freedom, then you will continue to have problems and experience the cycles of birth and death. Freedom is the most valuable thing in life! Or do you think that antiques are the most valuable things in life? I was given a gift of some antiques by a student who had inherited them from her husband. In the future, I will give these antiques away to others. Valuable antiques are not to be owned forever by a single person. They are to be passed from one generation to the next!

The Buddha has made it very clear: Is there anything in the material world that belongs inherently to one? Only one's karma will follow when one departs from the world. You think that the acquisition of antiques and money is a worthwhile pursuit and you work desperately to accumulate them in this life. You keep yourself busy, working every day including Sunday. You even wish that there were eight days to a week so you could make more money. [audience laughter] At the end, you cannot take any material thing —money, antiques, houses, cars — with you when you pass on. You have spent your life acquiring things for nothing. What is the most valuable thing in the world? Freedom! When you embark on the path that starts with Faith and Comprehension, and engage in Practices that lead ultimately to Realization, you will understand the Ultimate Truth of the Universe. This is what is most valuable in life. How can you not choose this pathway which is a shortcut which will return one to the Source Condition?

I have found this life of mine very meaningful because I am able to achieve and abide in Self-Mastery. No matter what happens, I abide continuously in an Enlightened condition that is full of Bliss. My body is filled with a Luminosity and Radiance that is empowered by the Buddhas and Bodhisattvas.

The Four Noble Truths

We know that Buddha Shakyamuni began and ended his preaching with the teaching of the Four Noble Truths. The Four Noble Truths are known as Suffering, Accumulation [of Suffering], Extinction, and Path. When I was giving a discourse on the *Heart Sutra*, I also commented on this topic — "There is no suffering, no origination of suffering, no extinction of suffering, and no path." There is a mistake in regard to the order of these Four Truths. Perhaps the translator slipped and got the order mixed up. The proper order should be: Accumulation, Suffering, Path, and Extinction. Rendered this way, its meaning is: Accumulate all the Sufferings and go quickly to walk on the Path to enter into the Extinction of Suffering [Nirvana].

Life is a process of suffering because of its inherent nature of Impermanence, of transformations. Ordinary people cannot tolerate Impermanence. To them, the sudden disappearance of an acquaintance who was with them the day before is a source of pain. However, an Enlightened Being realizes that such is the way things are and thus he or she will be able to accept the transformations. The Buddhadharma recognizes that Impermanence or transformation is an inherent characteristic of the laws of transmigration and karma. The Four Noble Truths taught by the Buddha point out that when one contemplates on all sufferings and thus enters into the spiritual process, one will reach Nirvana. Upon Realization, the Four Noble Truths of "Accumulation, Suffering, Path, and Extinction" are transmuted into the condition known as "Permanence, Bliss, Identity, and Purity." "Permanence" is residing permanently in the True Condition, which is tantamount to the state of Self-Mastery. "Bliss" exists because of Freedom. "Identity" refers to the True Self, which is infinitely expansive and is not the egotistic self. "Purity" refers to the untainted and unqualified nature of the True Condition. So the Four Noble Truths also mean "Permanence, Bliss, Identity, and Purity" — a condition of Freedom and Bliss wherein one is continually identified with the Pure, True Self and recognizes all phenomena to be a transcendental game of the Universe.

The first teaching that the Buddha gave was this doctrine of the Four Noble Truths, which includes the concept of Impermanence. In the statement exclaimed by the Buddha — "Between Heaven and Earth, only I am the Most Supreme" — the "I" refers to the infinitely expansive Universal Consciousness which is also the True Condition. You must remember that this "I" does not refer to a single individual. Actually the most important significance of the teaching of the Four Noble Truths lies in its transformation from "Accumulation, Suffering, Path, and Extinction" to "Permanence, Bliss, Identity, and Purity." Various points of view arise as to how one can best effect this transformation. Here also lies the cause of the division of the Buddhadharma into the three existing Vehicles, with each one adhering to its own "Right View."

Hinayana Buddhism adheres to the Right View of Impermanence and proposes Renunciation as the solution. Mahayana Buddhism adheres to the Right View that the Absolute Reality is one that transcends "subjectivity, objectivity, all phenomenal worlds, and time" — the same view as set forth in the *Diamond Sutra*. Mahayana Buddhism also advocates the concept of Six Paramitas (Six Perfections) as the means to achieve this goal. Vajrayana Buddhism adheres to the Right View that there is inherently no separation between oneself and the Buddha. You are the Buddha and I am the Buddha. This Truth is realized when the Offspring Light and the Mother Light merge into each other. Vajrayana Buddhism also holds the view that, through the blessing or "grace" of a Realized Being, one can directly experience this Condition wherein one and others are inherently the same as the Buddha.

This concludes today's discussion on "Practice and Realization" and "The Four Noble Truths." Yesterday I discussed "Faith, Comprehension, and Impermanence." I hope you all gain a tacit understanding from these discussions.

Om Mani Padme Hum.

Third Day:
May 5, 1993

Masters, fellow cultivators, good afternoon. Today is the third day of this discourse on An Overview of the Buddhadharma. On the first day, I discussed "Faith" and "Comprehension." On the second day, I discussed "Actual Practice" and "Realization." These four topics of Faith, Comprehension, Actual Practice, and Realization comprise the four major steps of the Buddhadharma. With these topics already discussed and, as today is such a fine day, perhaps we can all go outside and have a picnic or climb the mountains! [audience laughter]

On the other hand, because An Overview of the Buddhadharma is such an important subject, we will continue our discussion today. Indeed, life is very short. During our daily lives, besides paying attention to activities that make our bodies and minds healthy, we also need to focus more on cherishing the valuable Buddhadharma. As part of our everyday life, I hope that each of us can go and spend some time with Nature. From water and mountains, one may experience the Truth of the Buddhadharma, for Truth is not confined just to reading sutras, chanting, keeping a vegetarian diet, or abiding by the precepts. It is possible for one to find the revelation of the Buddhadharma in any human activity in which one engages. A very important point is that each of the steps of Faith, Comprehension, Actual Practice, and Realization can be demonstrated in and integrated with one's daily activities.

Therefore, in practicing the Buddhadharma, one should find one's heart gradually expanding rather than contracting. Integrate every single speech, every action, and every aspect of your life with the Buddhadharma. "Experience" and "demonstrate" the Buddhadharma in your daily life. The more one expands one's heart and releases the ego, the more radiance will shine through. On the other hand, if one's heart becomes narrower or one's self-grasping tightens, then darkness will take over. It is very easy for one to become sidetracked from the right path and take up a wrong viewpoint. Therefore, on this Saturday, we will participate in our regular group cultivation at 8:00 p.m. and, on Sunday, we will go out and climb the mountain behind the Rainbow Villa. I assure you that you will be gasping for breath when you climb to the top. [audience laughter] Mountain climbing is good training and also good physical exercise. When you view the magnificent mountains, the earth, and the flowing waters, you will find that the beautiful sceneries of Nature are permeated with poetry and Dharma Taste.

The Modern Doorway into Buddhism

After understanding the four concepts of Faith, Comprehension, Actual Practice, and Realization, how does one then enter the door of Buddhism? Where is the doorway? There are different opinions as to which doorway to enter. Some people feel that one should enter through the doorway of "Theories." By this, they mean that one should first gain an understanding of the profound Buddhist theories and knowledge. Other people feel that one should enter through the doorway of "Actual Practice," engaging first in practices (such as the True Buddha Tantric Dharma) and ethics (observing the precepts) to acquire a pure awareness. Thus the two approaches may be termed "theory" vs "practice." Which approach should one attempt first? Do you have any suggestions? Chinese are very familiar with the idea of taking a "dual approach." [audience laughter] I remember this aphorism from the Chinese classics, "One should combine theoretical understanding and practical application in any undertaking." We all know now that one should approach both theory and practice simultaneously.

At the time of the Buddha, however, there was an emphasis on the approach of "practice." Many scriptures have noted that the Buddha himself emphasized that "actual practice is more effective than a wide exposure to theories alone." As pointed out by the analogy I gave yesterday, if one only attends Buddhist lectures and does not practice, then one is likened to an expert cook who does not eat the dishes prepared and, therefore, starves. In such cases there is practically no enjoyment of the Dharma Taste. This is why the Buddha emphasized "actual practice" over a "theoretical approach." Even so, my opinion is that we should proceed simultaneously with "theory" and "practice."

During the time of Buddha Shakyamuni, after the disciples came back from collecting food offered as alms, they would listen to the Dharma teachings and then disband. One would find a spot on the mountain top, another would sit halfway up the mountain, someone would sit at the foot of a hill, while someone else would sit under a tree. Everyone would engage in the actual practice of meditation. When the next mealtime arrived, someone would announce that it was time for everyone to go out to receive food offerings from the almsgivers. What the Buddha taught at the beginning was that sitting meditation was very important. The attainment of "inner stillness or stability" is the most important link in the whole process of practicing Buddhism.

To take a "theoretical approach" is to study the Buddhist sutras, to comprehend their meaning, and to savor the Dharma Taste. In the end, an inner radiance will shine forth from one's heart. When one reads, applies, and penetrates deeply into the treasury of sutras to achieve a true unification, one may actually see the manifestation of the Bodhisattvas on the pages. An infinite wonder may be found in the sutras. When one reads and see the subtle point, one will not just nod in agreement, one will actually shine forth with an inner radiance. This is the key to the reading of the sutras.

In China, since the Sung Dynasty, many repentance texts have come into existence through the editorial effort of numerous Buddhist masters. Prior to the Sung Dynasty, there was Emperor Wu of the Liang Dynasty who also contributed to the creation of some repentance texts. Such repentance liturgies, of course, offer certain benefits as they involve both the reading of sutras and the practice of bowing. The purpose of participating in a repentance liturgy is to become cognizant of one's errors and truly repent them; otherwise, one is merely going through the motions of reading and bowing and, therefore, only scratching the surface of the Buddhadharma. Of all the pathways, the repentance liturgy is probably the simplest one because it only requires reading of text and bowing.

Some pathways have been reduced over the years to very simplistic forms. For example, the modern version of chanting only encompasses the chanting of Buddha's name. The rationalization for this may be summed up in this claim, "A single Buddha epithet encompasses the whole Buddhist canon." Modern men favor simplicity and detest hard work in their practice. They welcome the idea of attaining Buddhahood through chanting the name of Amitabha. There were originally sixteen steps of visualization of the Amitayus [Boundless Life] Dhyana Sutra that accompanied the chanting, but this has been reduced to just the chanting of the epithet. If a single chanting of "Namo Amitabha" indeed encompasses the Buddhist Canon, one might as well replace the whole of Buddhist scripture with just these two words, "Namo Amitabha." The Buddhadharma has undergone great transformation in the hands of modern men.

In the past, the Zen school also consisted of many profound and lofty teachings, but it is now reduced to just the form of Zen riddles. Many of the wonderful "Ways of Inquiry" from the past have been lost. Many Zen masters today have not achieved Enlightenment themselves. When they give teachings, as shown by some of their shows on television, they can only talk about Zen riddles.

So where is the true doorway to the Buddhadharma? In truth, many students of Buddhism waver from one to the other doorway. Have you found the one doorway for yourself? The doorway adopted by the True Buddha Tantric Dharma is one of "Actual Practice." You may visit other Buddhist centers around the world and you will not find another school that will offer you such exquisite and detailed explanation of the practice. Included in the True Buddha Tantric Dharma are all of the pertinent elements: teachings of mantra, mudra, visualization, bowing, offering, the Four Immeasurable Vows, armor protection, Vajrasattva practice, the Fourfold Refuge, and the entering into Samadhi. Where else can you find a system as complete and detailed as these teachings?

Most Buddhist monks can only advise to read the sutras and chant the Buddha's name. When you ask them how to do meditation, they will tell you, "Be patient." [audience laughter] If you press them for an explanation, they will only tell you that meditation is not a simple matter and cannot be hurried. Perhaps chanting is the only actual practice ever done by some of these old masters, so how can they teach one how to enter into Samadhi? Then, before you can get an answer from them, they pass away! Why are they unable to teach you? Perhaps they themselves have never entered into Samadhi. It is not easy to attain Samadhi. Today you have come to hear me; today you have found the right teacher! [audience applause] I have trod on the path and experienced Samadhi and I can teach you how to realize it.

If you were to ask these old masters, you would find that some of them practice the "non-supine" sleep posture; that is, they assume a sitting posture even when they sleep at night. However, in the middle of the night, their heads droop and saliva starts to drool. Sleeping while sitting up is an extremely hard task! It is not right to force oneself to go through such hardship.

The crux of meditation is not how long one sits, but whether one is able to enter into "stillness." Do you know who is noted for meditating the longest? The Eminent Master Hsu Yun (Empty Cloud). One time he was getting ready to cook some potatoes and decided to meditate first. When he awoke from his meditation, mold was growing on the potatoes! He had lost track of time while meditating. Of course, his was a very skillful type of meditation, but is this what true meditation is supposed to be? In true meditation, although the "ego is transcended," there should still be awareness. This is known as "conscious meditation." Samadhi or "stillness" is marked by "awareness."

There are many times when people awaken and cannot remember having had any dreams. Would their sleep then qualify as meditating? Say that one lies down at 11:00 p.m. and the next time one opens one's eyes, morning has arrived.

One is not even sure if one has had any sleep at all. How come it is morning all of a sudden? [laughter] What a skillful meditation! Then one takes a look at the calendar. It was the first when one went to bed, how can it be the thirtieth now? One has been sleeping for a month! [laughter and audience laughter] This is a skillful meditation that is characterized by the "forgetting of time." One has forgotten about the passage of time and one has had no dreams during the interim. You know there was a Taoist by the name of Chan Hsi Yi who was famous for his "sleep practice." He could sleep without interruption for several years. It would be nice if I could do that too. [laughter] Master Hsu Yun could enter into a very deep meditation. There was a time in Thailand when he did not emerge from his meditation for more than ten days. Even the king of Thailand went to bow to him, to pay respect to his accomplished skill. Although Master Hsu Yun had lost track of time, his skill in meditation was excellent. However, when we practice meditation, what matters is not how long we can sit, but whether we can achieve "conscious Samadhi." This is very important. When one attains "conscious Samadhi," one will obtain the Dharma Taste. Without "conscious Samadhi," there is no Dharma Taste. [audience applause]

The "Theory" Approach

While the "theory" approach consists of studying the scriptures, the "practice" approach consists of actual practice, such as the True Buddha Tantric Practice. One may combine both approaches and treat them equally. However, if one has more affinity with the "theory" approach, one may choose that doorway. Or, if one prefers the doorway of "practice" one may choose that approach.

I would like to offer a few of my opinions here. Sometimes it is very difficult to gain a comprehension of the theories, as the Buddhist Canon is both vast and profound. Buddha Shakyamuni often said, "The Dharmas I have taught are like the earth in my palm, while the Dharmas I have not taught are like the great land." The Buddha preached for forty-nine years, and what he touched upon only amounted to a few grains of sand when compared to the whole Buddhadharma, or Truth, which is as vast as the Earth. That being the case, my teaching today will only amount to a few pinhead-sized specks, which will be gone when I blow some air on them. [audience laughter] How can one learn all the Buddhadharma, which is as vast as all the land, when what the Buddha taught in forty-nine years only amounted to a hand's grasp of earth? Therefore, the number of theories is vast and the "theory" approach is very difficult. The "practice" approach is relatively easier.

One might presume that the theory approach is simpler. Actually it is not simple at all! Just ask yourself if you know how your eyes can see things. You will say, "I just open my eyes and I can see things." Seeing seems such a simple act, but the mechanisms involved are not simple at all. I am asking if you know how the reflection and refraction of an object enters your eyes to stimulate the optic nerves, which send signals to a certain part of your brain, and if you know how you are suddenly shown an image and are thus able to perceive the shape of the object? You may not understand the hidden mechanisms involved. Similarly, the waving of my hand also involves some very intricate mechanisms. [Grand Master Lu waves, audience laughter] How and why is my hand waving like this? You tell your hand to wave and a certain part of your brain receives that message. Do you know which part of your brain does this? Although modern medical technology is very advanced, there is still a great deal we don't know about the mapping of the brain and its functions. When the intent is perceived by the brain, do you know which part of the brain orchestrates the motor nerves and, subsequently, all the movements of tendons, bones, blood, and muscle to make your hand wave? You do not know any of this! [laughter and audience laughter] I am asking you about the workings of your own body and none of the mechanisms is simple!

When you eat, you open your mouth and, with the chopsticks, move food into your mouth. The food automatically enters the esophagus instead of the trachea. If your autonomic response is slow, and the food enters the trachea by mistake, you will choke. When the food passes through the esophagus into the stomach, the stomach begins to churn and digest the food. Do you know how the muscular layers of the stomach wall move? Are the movements longitudinal, circular, or oblique? Why is the digestion of food necessary? If you have not made a study of it, you do not know. Food passes through the duodenum to the small intestine and then the large intestine. Secretion and absorption take place both in the stomach and the small intestine. Do you know how the large intestine moves and functions? You know how to eat large pork intestine [a popular dish among Chinese], but you do not know how the large intestine functions! The large intestine contracts and pushes waste to the anus. [audience laughter] From the moment the food is ingested to the moment it is excreted, it has undergone great transformations. How many people study these functions and understand them in any detail? How is food broken down by the aid of enzymes into amino acids, fatty acids, and simple sugars that are absorbed through the intestinal walls? The processes of metabolism and transportation are also involved. The transportation system is made up of arteries, veins, and capillaries, as well as exchange at the cellular level. You know that cells are the units that make up the human body. Do you also know what is inside a cell? [Someone replies, "Life."] I also know that it has life. [laughter and audience laughter] Of course cells have life. Perhaps someone who is a doctor or nurse will understand these mechanisms better. Do not feel ashamed if you don't know all these biological mechanisms. As a matter of fact, I also do not know them all. [laughter and audience laughter] My point is that it is very difficult to understand the theories of the Buddhadharma, just as it is difficult to understand all the mechanisms in one's own body. Most people only put food in their mouths and do not care what happens to it after ingestion. They do not, in fact, know all the subtle mechanisms involved in the process.

The same thing may be said about the theories and doctrines of the Buddhadharma, the Truth of the Universe. It is difficult to understand Truth through a dissociative study of the Universe. On the other hand, if one participates in the actual practice, if one experiences it, then one will gradually know what the Dharma Taste is and what the subtleties are. One can only truly know the subtleties of the Truth by identifying with it and experiencing it.

Many doctrines are found in the Buddhist scriptures. These doctrines are also expounded by many people who do not necessarily have the experience of Dharma Taste. Even though they know where to look for the Dharma Taste, they cannot taste it. The most important thing is "eating" and getting nourished. If one postponed eating food until one completely understood the mechanisms involved in the various biological and chemical processes of digestion, one would die of starvation. In one's lifetime one might be able to read the whole Buddhist Canon once, thrice, or even one hundred times, but could one understand every doctrine in it? It might take many lifetimes before one could understand everything in the whole Buddhist Canon. One may read the scriptures day in and day out, from youth to old age, but one will not experience the Dharma Taste unless one starts doing actual practice. One cannot taste the Dharma without penetrating the meaning of the doctrines. However, it is possible that one could die before one could penetrate the meaning of the doctrines! Therefore, do not bother with how a dish is prepared, eat it first. We will eat the food first — we will start with the actual practice.

The Buddha said that "the benefit of actual practice surpasses that of a wide seeking of knowledge." Who was most famous for having been exposed to the most doctrines? This was Ananda, one of the ten chief disciples of Buddha Shakyamuni. However, he was the last of the disciples to attain Realization. Mahakashyapa had a great dislike for Ananda. [audience laughter] Among all of the disciples, Mahakashyapa had a horrid temper and was the one most easily aggravated. He was very skinny and had an extremely angular face. In front of the Buddha, Mahakashyapa was very respectful, but sometimes he would act on his own will and ignore the Buddha's words. The Buddha would call to him, "Do not stay so far away! Come and spend some time at the Bamboo Grove Vihara. Eat a little bit more food to keep yourself nourished!" Mahakashyapa would not listen. He had strong will power and liked to stick to his ascetic practices. When he saw Ananda, he would fly into a rage! [audience laughter] He felt that Ananda was too greedy. Ananda was fond of good food and beautiful clothes. When he saw a piece of beautiful clothing that belonged to the Buddha, he would steal it and put it on himself. [audience laughter] When the Buddha was away, he would sit on the Buddha's chair and lecture the younger disciples. He was also very fond of women. [audience laughter] Ananda's desires were the strongest among the disciples. In reality, the Buddha greatly praised Mahakashyapa, despite his terrible temper and frequent absence from the Buddha's company. The Buddha considered Mahakashyapa to be an adept of actual practice who had attained the greatest level of Realization among the disciples. How about Ananda? He was the last to achieve Realization. [audience laughter] Mahakashyapa was not the only one who disliked Ananda; many other disciples also disliked him. This was because Ananda had been an attendant of the Buddha for a long time and people were jealous of him. [audience laughter] There was also some competition going on among the disciples.

The "Practice" Approach

As soon as one enters the doorway of "practice," one must cultivate the "purification of body, speech, and mind." This is to enable one to attain Enlightenment, to transform the energy in one's body, and to realize Emptiness. Ultimately one will obtain the Rainbow Radiance. Actually, as long as one achieves Enlightenment and the Clear Light, and realizes Emptiness, one will automatically understand the Buddhist doctrines. Although one has not studied or researched the sutras, one will be able to penetrate their meaning. The Sixth Patriarch Hui-neng was almost illiterate, yet, after engaging in actual practice, he opened his mouth and out came the expounding of the Buddhist doctrines! [audience applause] After the Fifth Patriarch Hung-jen transmitted the formulae for Enlightenment to him, Hui-neng fled to live among the hunters. He stayed for over a decade and, during those years, Hui-neng put the teachings of Hung-jen to actual practice and was able to achieve Awakening. After Realization, the words he expounded were the Truth of the Buddhadharma. Therefore, one does not have to be a scholar to understand the Buddhist doctrines. By focusing on one practice and practicing it wholeheartedly, one will also be able to understand the Buddhist doctrines.

This brings us to one of the issues of "practice." Should one learn many practices or concentrate on just one practice? It is better to cultivate just one practice at a time. The learning of many practices is tantamount to "seeking a wide knowledge"! When one concentrates on a single practice at a time and penetrates that practice deeply, one will arrive at Realization. This Realization will enable one to understand and penetrate all other practices. As long as one achieves Enlightenment through actual practice, one will understand all the Buddhist doctrines. That is why the approach of "practice" surpasses that of "theory."

Many of the older generation Buddhists today are very well versed on the Buddhist theories and doctrines. They can tell you the contents of each sutra but, when asked if they have done any actual practice or have attained Realization, their answer would be "no." This is the flaw of a purely theoretical approach. Pursuing many practices at the same time also has its problems. I have recently written an essay for the True Buddha News criticizing a certain contemporary Buddhist monk who admitted that he had not achieved Realization. We do not have any dark clouds here today! [audience laughter] This Buddhist monk claimed that he practiced Zen, Pure Land, and Tantrayana and confessed that he had not yet achieved any yogic response or Realization. Strictly speaking, he does not practice Tantrayana as he only chants the Great Compassion Dharani and the Ten Minor Dharanis. There is something wrong when he cannot obtain any yogic response even with "the Tantrayana" practiced "his way"!

Some people claim that their school is an amalgamation of eight different schools. Do not make the mistake of thinking this makes it better than others. You would become totally confused if you entered such a school. If you had to practice doctrines alternately from the Zen, Pure Land, Tantrayana, Vinaya [disciplines], Madhyamaka, T'ien-tai, Lotus Sutra, and Hua-yen schools, you would be completely confused! It is better to concentrate on one practice and penetrate deeply into it. If you do otherwise, you will not achieve Realization — even when you are sixty or seventy years old. If that happened to me, I would find the whole situation laughable and embarrassing.

Perhaps one has been pursuing other doorways, such as "money," "authority," or "power." None of these is a Buddhist doorway. Such pursuits are the behavior of ordinary people of the samsara world. Isn't there something wrong when a monk becomes involved in business deals?

Therefore, the most important thing in practicing Buddhism is to concentrate on one single practice and to penetrate it deeply. [audience applause] I have made this recommendation before: a young person can afford to look into different schools to hear more teachings; a middle-aged person should stick to just one practice and concentrate on it to reach Enlightenment; an old person should seek rebirth to a Pure Land. As one gets older, one does not have much time left and one should therefore concentrate on a practice that will lead one to be reborn to a higher realm. These are very important points. Indeed, focusing on one single practice is better than doing many practices at the same time. There was one student who sent me one hundred U.S. dollars, requesting one hundred different kinds of empowerments. He wanted empowerments for all the practices I have mentioned in my books. One should seek empowerment only for the practice that one will do, unless one is a master in this school. A master in this school might seek to receive many empowerments so that he or she could, in the future, give others the same empowerments. General students, however, should focus on one practice. As long as one achieves spiritual response or Realization in doing one particular practice that results in the opening of one's heart, one can immediately see the Light and the Truth of the entire Buddhadharma.

In the past I had trouble understanding the sutras. To be honest, my wisdom was not that developed. Before, when I read the *Diamond Sutra*, all the paradoxes were enigmas to me. [audience laughter] I could not figure out what it was about. Today, when I open the *Diamond Sutra*, I can penetrate deeply into it and understand its charms and meanings. I can open any sutra now and completely penetrate its meaning. [audience applause]

Thus, inherent in Realization are the other three steps of Faith, Comprehension, and Practice. While one may choose either the approach of "theory" or "practice," the approach of "practice" is better. Understanding the Buddhist doctrines does not necessarily result in Realization, while actual practice can definitely lead one to Realization. When one attains Realization, one will automatically understand all doctrines. [audience applause]

Integration of Practice with Daily Activities

Many students have been coming here for several years to learn to do the practice. There was one time when several were asked by someone outside the school what they had learned from me. One student replied, "Master Lu did not teach me anything." Did this hurt my feelings? Let me use this story as an illustration. One of the students of the Zen Master Bird Nest had been following him for many years. One day this student packed up his belongings and bade farewell to the Zen Master. The master asked, "Where are you going?" "I am going to look for another teacher." The master asked again, "Why are you going to find another teacher? Aren't you doing very well here?" The student replied, "You have not taught me any Buddhadharma in all the years I have been here." Zen Master Bird Nest then extended his leg and plucked out a hair. (Too bad, I don't have hairy legs!) [audience laughter] The Zen Master pointed to the hair, "This is Buddhadharma." The hair from the leg was the Buddhadharma. Do you comprehend? At that moment, the student suddenly had a breakthrough and understood what Buddhadharma was. If that student I mentioned earlier had packed up and come to say good-bye to me, I also would have plucked out a whisker [audience laughter] and told him, "This whisker is the Buddhadharma. Do you understand?" Buddhadharma is interwoven with everything in one's daily life and it has to be experienced! Everything is a manifestation of the Truth! After listening to the teachings, instead of going home and forgetting about them, one has to apply the teachings to one's normal life and daily activities — this is Buddhadharma.

Therefore every gesture of the teacher is a Dharma teaching. [audience applause] Every word uttered and every action performed by Buddha Shakyamuni was the Buddhadharma. Described in the sutras were the daily rituals of the Buddha, which indicated that walking, living, sitting, and lying down could also be intimate experiences of the Buddhadharma. Many people are not aware that to practice Buddhism is to have a sacred orientation to everything in one's ordinary life. Buddhadharma is not some special technique that is only taught to one special person. Its transmission is not based on any special "price." There are other teachers who would confer upon you special methods or exclusive empowerments if you made a huge offering. We have a Taiwanese folk saying to describe such practice, "One has a grand opening every three years and money made at each opening lasts three years." Sometimes some of these special methods are not authentic. There are people who use this form of practice solely to make money. At the time of Buddha Shakyamuni, such practices were forbidden by him.

Seeing the Mountain as a Non-mountain

We know that, as soon as one enters the door of the Buddhadharma, one's perception of the world will undergo a transformation. In the past there was a Zen Master who explained it this way. Before his entrance into Buddhism, he saw a mountain as a mountain and water as water. After entrance, he saw a mountain as a non-mountain and water as non-water. After a while, he achieved Realization and he again saw a mountain as a mountain and water as water. What do these three stages mean? One has to contemplate and experience them.

Recently I have started to learn Chinese painting. My teacher is Mrs. Au Moolan from San Francisco. Mrs. Au learned painting from Chao Shao-an, a very good Ling-nan style painter who has had many teachers himself. I have taken up lessons so I can paint when I get old and have nothing else to do. [audience laughter] The two activities I have decided on are music and painting. I can entertain myself with a musical instrument and my own voice — which probably will not generate any income. [audience laughter] Painting is better. I can exhibit the paintings and publish albums of my paintings. Mrs. Au came and stayed for a week to teach me.

We know that we see a mountain as a mountain and water as water but, after I started painting, I found that a mountain was not a mountain and that water was not water! [audience laughter] Water could become a mountain in my paintings and vice versa. [audience laughter] You could also say that in my paintings a cow becomes a horse and vice versa. [audience laughter] In the process of painting, one's consciousness undergoes transformations. When one enters the door of the Buddhadharma, one also sees with a different perception. Therefore I am not learning the "meticulous" style of painting, which takes a long time and much study. I am learning the "essence" style, which creates renderings that do not look exactly like the objects portrayed but which capture their essence. In "essence" painting, one is painting with one's mind. If an exact reproduction is wanted, one can learn to use a camera instead of learning to draw. Why would one want to draw in an exact manner that does not express any spirit? When one draws an object, one wants to express the unique quality and the invisible spirit of that particular object. A really good painting does this. What I am learning from Mrs. Au are her techniques of brush strokes and mixing colors. In the future, I hope you will come and lend me support. [audience laughter and applause] "Essence" style paintings are very simple, with the essence of a painted object sometimes expressed in one or a few strokes.

The practice of Buddhadharma is the same as the art of painting. Before beginning, one sees a mountain as a mountain and water as water. One knows that a mountain is stationary and water is fluid. A painter who captures the fluidity of a mountain and the stillness of water is one who is able to see into other dimensions. It is the same with practicing Buddhism. After practicing Buddhism for a period of time, one no longer sees a mountain as a mountain and water as water. Why? This is because one becomes awakened to the fundamental essence of all beings.

One day I came upon an album of paintings by the painter Yang Shan Sheng. After looking carefully through it, I passed it to Mrs. Lu. Mrs. Lu also looked through it and then remarked to me, "About his paintings, I'd rather have a slice of toast." What she meant was that she thought one could get more flavor out of a piece of bread. This was because Mrs. Lu does not understand paintings. [audience laughter] We cannot blame her. Yang Shan Sheng does not have to be offended by her as she really cannot understand. [audience laughter] His paintings have the essence of "seeing a mountain as a non-mountain and water as non-water," although there is also in them the more conventional element of "a mountain as a mountain and water as water." What struck me, however, was that the paintings of a skillful and experienced painter such as he could resemble those drawn by me, a kindergartner in painting. [audience laughter] Several of my exercise sheets had such terrible paintings on them that I had to reapply ink to erase what I had originally drawn. When I perused Yang Shan Sheng's album, I found that there was no difference between those few scrawlings of mine and some of his work! [audience laughter] I told myself that I should not throw away those few precious sheets, as such works were also found in Yang Shan Sheng's album. [audience laughter] When I ran into Master Lian-teng, I commented to him, "Yang Shan Sheng is a great painter. It is strange that his album contains painting that look like a few big brush strokes or just pouring ink onto papers and allowing them to dry." Master Lian-teng said insightfully, "This is because at the stage of Ultimate Realization, a mountain looks like a mountain and water looks like water again." [audience laughter and applause]

We have here Master Lian-jun of Indonesia who is also a painter of ink and color. The subjects of her paintings are shrimps, crabs, swallows, pines, cranes, flowers, and birds. At my house I have some of her paintings. She paints very well and some of her paintings have garnered her awards. She studies her subjects every time before she draws them. For example, if she wants to draw a painting of crabs, she will buy many crabs and observe them crawling around before drawing them. One time her husband said to her, "Fortunately you don't draw tigers. We would be in trouble if you bought a tiger." [audience laughter]

Whether one enters the door of the Buddhadharma through "theory" or "practice," there will ultimately be the awakening to the realm of "as-is-ness." After crossing the threshold, transformations start to occur which lead to the realization of one's "innate freedom" and the entering into "as-is-ness." In the realm of Emptiness, when one's ego expands to embrace all, there will be a spontaneous manifestation of one's Original Face. The Original Face will also manifest itself in such a person's paintings. There is an important link between practicing Buddhism and painting! Have you heard of "Zen paintings"? When a Zen master paints, he or she enters completely into the state of total purity wherein the egotistical consciousness and mind are transcended. Such a non-strategic painting is an excellent rendering reproduced from within, and it transcends both time and culture.

Understanding Suffering and Renunciation

After entrance one, of course, has to understand the meaning behind the Buddhist doctrines of the "Ten Dharma Realms," or the ten states of existence which include the "Four Holy Realms" and "Six Ordinary Realms." One must recognize the inherent sufferings found in the six ordinary realms of existence: devas, human beings, asuras, hell beings, hungry ghosts, and animals. When one understands these realms and becomes aware of the fundamental nature of "Impermanence," there will arise in one a desire to seek renunciation. At the realization of the inherent emptiness of all phenomena and that nothing exists independently, one becomes an Arhat. [audience applause]

The sufferings inherent in the six realms are, in fact, very clearly manifested to us. Take a look at the hospitals. Although huge hospitals have been built with charity in mind, if I were to name them, I would have named them differently. For example, Taipei General Hospital or Tzu Chi Charity Hospital would be a subsidiary of the Hell Realm of Namo Ksitigarbha Bodhisattva. [audience laughter]

In my view, hospitals are realms of Hell. In your eyes, hospitals are hospitals, staffed with many white-cloaked angels [audience laughter] who are in fact bad demons and yakshas, with knives and implements in hand, to cut and fix people up! Indeed, inside the hospitals are the hells of brain opening, kidney transplant, liver dissection, and eye gouging.

Truthfully, I have visited the Realm of Hell. There I saw a student of mine whose two legs had been pierced through by a nail. I had not heard from this student for a long time. We looked into each other's eyes and he started crying. I asked him, "How come you are here? Could it be that you have died?" [audience laughter] I asked him, "Are you dead?" I was not speaking Indonesian although in Indonesian, the morning greeting of "se la ma ba gee" sounds almost the same as "are you dead" in Mandarin. [audience laughter] While shaking his head, the student sighed and said, "I am in Hell." When I came back to this world, I made an investigation. It turned out that this student had actually been admitted to the hospital during that time. His legs, for some unknown reason, had suddenly developed atrophy and severe cramps. He could not move his legs, as if they were pinned down by a nail. In the Realm of Hell, I had indeed, seen his two legs nailed together. He was already experiencing punishment in Hell although he was still alive. Are hospitals then not part of the Realm of Hell?

Understanding Karma

We need to understand the principle of karma and reincarnation. This is a central idea in Buddhism. We have done many wrong deeds. Do not think that there is no retribution. One does not have to wait until one goes to Hell to receive retribution. Even while living, one is already suffering punishments from Hell when one's body becomes ill. Illnesses are the manifestation of one's negative karma. Do not think that hells do not exist. Some people say, "There is practically no such thing as Hell or karma! It is just a fabrication of men to persuade people to do good!" When you undergo brain surgery, you are entering into the hell of brain opening! When you have cirrhosis, removal of a kidney, or any other illness, the negative karma accumulated from numerous past lives are manifesting in you. It is quite horrible.

The Simplest Precept

That was why, at the beginning, the Buddha taught us the simplest way of practicing Buddhism: "Avoid all non-virtuous actions and execute all virtuous deeds." The avoidance of non-virtuous actions is passive while the execution of virtuous deeds is active. The avoidance of non-virtuous actions refers to the observing of "precepts."

In the beginning, there were not as many stipulated rules. The only precept was "to avoid all non-virtuous acts." One was urged to actively "pursue good deeds" and to meditate under a tree to enter into the "Pure Consciousness." Later on, many precepts came into existence. Why? When the students made a certain transgression, a rule was set up to provide guidance. As the number of transgressions increased, the number of rules also multiplied. The purpose of the rules was to retrieve one's mind to transform it into the One Mind and to cultivate stability. Without the rules, one's mind would become dissolute. However, if one is completely and freely grounded in stability, and one's mind is able to expand and contract freely, these precepts serve no purpose, as such a person already lives in the state of "as-is-ness" whereby all self-will is completely surrendered.

Stability

"Discipline, Stability, and Wisdom" together are known as the "Three Non-outflows" or the three requisites for achieving the state of "Non-outflows," wherein one is liberated from all troubles. One must gain an understanding of these three concepts after entering the doorway of the Buddhadharma.

The first requisite is "discipline" or "precepts," which I discussed yesterday. "Stability" is the next concept of the "Three Non-outflows." How is stability generated? Tomorrow I will discuss some of the meditation techniques and illustrate how discipline can generate stability and how stability can generate wisdom.

Stability without wisdom is tantamount to "foolishness." Wisdom and intellect without stability turns one into an "arrogant maniac." Therefore, in our practice, we have to cultivate both stability and wisdom.

Whether one practices exoteric or esoteric Buddhism, the most important key is still to develop a stability or "stillness." A stabilized and profound state of meditation leads one to

Enlightenment. Therefore, it is paramount that one learns to develop this stability or stillness. Without stability, one cannot tap into the source of all powers or obtain the wisdom associated with Truth. Without stability, one will absolutely not be able to obtain any Dharma Taste in this life. Whether one adopts the approach of "theory" or "practice," the ultimate union with the Truth or the Buddha still requires the engendering of stability. The cultivation of stability or stillness is a very important key in the spiritual practice of Buddhism.

Therefore, the goal of meditation is to enter into a true state of stability or stillness. I have written in my books that this involves the processes of first retrieving all wandering thoughts and focusing them into one point, then returning this one point to zero. What is this zero? Is it Emptiness? Zero can be described as a state of Emptiness, a spontaneous and natural state of "being," a kind of liberated condition. It is not, however, the nihilistic kind of Emptiness that negates everything. The Buddhist Emptiness is a liberated and natural condition that is totally undifferentiated or unqualified. Although it is a state that defies verbal description, my explanation is that the Emptiness state is spontaneous, liberated, free, and a condition wherein everything arises as the play of consciousness. [audience applause] Tomorrow I will go into the methods of how to enter into the state of stability in our meditation.

In my discussion today, I have pointed out that the approach of "practice" surpasses that of "theory," and that focusing on one single actual practice is superior to gaining a wider, surface knowledge. In other words, engaging in one single in-depth practice is better than pursuing multiple practices simultaneously. Through the practice of Buddhadharma, the transcendental state of consciousness will become manifest and be integrated into and demonstrated in every aspect of one's daily life. When there is an ultimate identification with the True Condition, one attains liberation and freedom, as well as obtaining all the powers mentioned in the Buddhist sutras.

The Issue of Taking Refuge

There is also the issue of "taking refuge" in the practice of Buddhism. Someone has asked me, "When should I take refuge? Should I wait till I have first gained some knowledge of Buddhism?" Taking refuge may appear to be very simple, as one may go and sign up for taking refuge whenever one wants to. In fact, it is not a simple matter. Just consider the aspect of the selection of a guru. If you choose a guru with a wrathful temper, you could be beaten to death by him. [laughter] If you choose a greedy guru, all your money could be handed over to him. If you choose an ignorant and foolish guru, you would not learn any practices from him. Therefore it is not a simple matter. Sometimes people fill out the registration cards to take refuge when urged to do so by certain masters, but they do not have any sort of understanding about the guru himself. When should one take refuge then? A person might ask, "I am a Christian, may I take refuge?" This is also a problem, as he or she might not know anything about Buddhism. Another person might say, "I have just started worshiping at temples. May I take refuge?" He has just started to become superstitious, [laughter and audience laughter] so this is also a problem. He might think, by taking refuge, he will receive money and the bestowal of fortune from me, and that all his disasters will vanish, no car accidents will happen to him, and everything will be auspicious. [laughter and audience laughter] Therefore, the appropriate time to take refuge becomes an important issue.

In whom and in what is one taking refuge? We know that one takes refuge in the Triple Jewels: Buddha (Buddha Shakyamuni), Dharma (the teachings of Buddha recorded in the Buddhist Canon), and Sangha (the holy sages and monks who represent the Buddha). In Vajrayana Buddhism, one also takes refuge in the Vajra Master who is the embodiment of the Triple Jewels. One must get to know one's Vajra Master well. Of course, when one gets to know the master well, one might want to return the refuge diploma, [laughter and audience laughter] because the Vajra Master may not necessarily turn out to be a good one. "To take refuge" or "not to take refuge" is the question.

In our school, the door is open to everyone. My principle is, as long as one engenders the thought to take refuge in me, I will take one as a student, whether one is Protestant, Catholic, or Muslim. The arising of the thought to take refuge in me indicates an affinity between oneself and me. I want to assure my students that I am a knower and an actual practitioner of the Buddhadharma. I have attained Realization through actual practice. [audience applause] Can one later leave and take refuge in somebody else? My answer is a soft "yes." [spoken in a lower voice. Laughter and audience laughter] I have laid in the open everything about me and the True Buddha Tantric Dharma for anyone who wants to take refuge to learn, to understand, to experience, to practice, to realize, and to become Enlightened. One will not go wrong in taking refuge in me! If one wants to take refuge in another guru later on, I will not object, as there are some very qualified gurus around. I cannot claim that I am the only "best teacher," as there are also many high adepts in the world. My advice is that, before taking refuge, one should still investigate to find out as much as one can about another guru.

I have often suggested, however, that after taking a certain guru to be one's teacher, one should not subsequently go around slandering one's teacher. If one decides later that one's teacher has deficiencies in his knowledge of the Buddhadharma and that he has not attained Realization, one should still be respectful towards him, for he must have some other virtues. It is most important that one learns to appreciate the virtues and overlook the shortcomings. [audience applause] If one only focuses on the guru's failings, one will absolutely not be able to obtain any transmission from the guru and thus not be able to succeed in one's practice. The reason is very simple. When all one can see is the negative in one's guru, one will lose respect for him, as well as for the teachings that he could transmit. Therefore, after entering into a guru-disciple relationship, it is necessary for one to focus only on the guru's virtues and to learn from his indefatigable spirit, his various outstanding achievements, and his subtle skills. The Buddhadharma transmitted by one's guru will be sufficient to nourish one for the rest of one's life.

Therefore, you have not made a mistake in coming to take refuge in the True Buddha School. As I explained earlier, the guru here has a full understanding of the Buddhadharma, a full experience in actual practice, and a full Realization. Fullness in these three aspects are more than enough to sustain you. [audience applause] If there are other things that you want, it is your own business. [audience laughter] If you want to find another guru who is more fun and interesting, this is acceptable as it all depends on your affinity with this other guru.

However, one should take refuge in a guru who has an infinite and expansive heart, [audience applause] a limitless wisdom, an infinite stability, a limitless Enlightenment, an inexhaustible knowledge of Dharma, and all kinds of infinite qualities. [audience applause]

When you gain a good understanding of the true Vajra Master and take refuge in him or her, you will receive the very concrete blessing of lineage transmission whereby you will naturally succeed in your practice.

Om Mani Padme Hum.

"Mountain is Non-mountain"

(An addendum to the third day's teaching of An Overview of the Buddhadharma, given by Grand Master Lu at the True Buddha Tantric Quarter on May 14, 1993.)

"Mountain is mountain, water is water." Then, "mountain is non- mountain, and water is non-water." At the end "mountain is mountain, and water is water." After listening to the third day's teaching, some of you are still puzzled about this riddle . Therefore, I will use another analogy to illustrate it, so that it may be more easily understood.

This riddle describes spiritual development in terms of three stages. The first stage is when one is still an ordinary being; the second stage is when one is in the midst of spiritual practice; and the third stage is when one has attained Enlightenment. Talking about mountains and waters all the time may not be very clear to you; a better analogy might be one using the example of a practitioner and a beautiful lady. This is an analogy I like to use, and one I hope you will respond to immediately, with a clear understanding.

At the first stage, before his entrance into Buddhism, when a man sees a very beautiful lady, he feels that the beautiful lady he sees is a beautiful lady. He is enthralled by her. This is the phase of "seeing mountain as mountain and water as water." A beautiful lady is just a beautiful lady and one is instantly entranced by her beauty.

At the second stage, one has already started practicing and is practicing the Skeleton Visualization. In this second phase of "seeing mountain as non-mountain and water as non-water," a practitioner sees a beautiful lady and feels that she is just a skeleton. This second stage signifies a segregation between him and the lady. In his eyes, a mountain is non-mountain, and water is non- water — they have all turned into skeletons.

At the third stage of Enlightenment, "mountain becomes mountain again and water is water again." What does this mean? In this phase, when a man sees a beautiful lady, he still sees the lady as beautiful, but his heart remains totally unmoved. It is true that the lady is beautiful, but one is already beyond enthrallment. This is "seeing mountain as mountain and water as water" again. [audience applause]

Because I was using the symbols of mountain and water, some of you could not make head nor tail of the analogy and are unable to get the meaning of this riddle. However, when I use the analogy between a practitioner and a beautiful lady, you get a clear picture right away! At first, you are completely enthralled when you see the beautiful lady. Then, after entrance through the door of the Buddhadharma and practicing the Skeleton Visualization, a woman is not a woman anymore but a skeleton appearing to be a woman. When you become Enlightened, you will still appreciate the lady's beauty but will not be influenced by her or her beauty. From these three simple examples, you can understand the three phases of spiritual development.

Actually, in the first stage or condition, one's heart is being enslaved by one's environment. Ordinary beings are easily influenced by the environment. If today's sky is dim and gray and it starts to rain, one will be in a bad mood. When it is bright and sunny, one lights up. This is a condition wherein one is entirely under the influence of one's environment. One has allowed oneself to be enslaved by one's surroundings.

In the second stage or condition, after one embarks on the path, there is a distancing between oneself and one's environment. There is a separation between one's heart and the surroundings. One tries one's best to avoid being disturbed by the sights and sounds of one's environment by hiding deep in the mountain to do cultivation. This is a segregation between one's heart and one's surroundings.

In the third stage or condition, one's heart has risen above one's environment. Regardless of the environment, of whether it is a good day or bad day, rainy day or sunny day, one's mind is always open and cheerful. [audience applause]

When you reach the third stage, no matter how great the external pressure is, how much cheering there is outside for you, or how much slandering exists, you abide in the same state of mind. This is the condition of an Enlightened person who has transcended his environment.

First, there is the enslavement of an ordinary person's heart by his environment. Second, there is the separation of heart and environment during the process of cultivation. Third, one's cultivated heart can totally decimate the influence exerted by one's surroundings. These are the three stages of "seeing mountain as mountain and water as water," "seeing mountain as non-mountain and water as non-water," "seeing mountain as mountain and water as water again."

This should be very clear now. Since some of you told me that you could not understand the analogy of the mountain and water, I have used the analogy of a man and a woman. This is the simplest explanation; do you understand now?

It is the same with the practice of the Buddhadharma. When you truly arrive at the condition of pure awareness, freedom, and sovereignty, every word and action exemplifies that of a Buddha. What shines through then is not a conventional light, but a kind of natural luminosity. It has nothing to do with: "Whose temple is the biggest?" "Who has the most students?" "Who is the wealthiest?" "How many people can one control?" It is a realm of the Buddhas and Immortals which completely transcends the conventional world.

Fourth Day:
May 6, 1993

Masters and fellow cultivators, good afternoon. [Audience returns greeting, "Good afternoon, Grand Master."] Today is the fourth day of this discourse on An Overview of the Buddhadharma. Over the last three days, I have covered the topics of Faith, Comprehension, Practice, and Realization, Theoretical versus Practical Approaches, as well as the Three Non-outflows. The term "Non-outflows" means liberation from kleshas [emotional afflictions]. The Three Non-outflows are the requisites for achieving liberation from emotional afflictions, and are a key topic in the study of the Buddhadharma. After the Three Non-outflows, I shall discuss the Six Pararmitas, Seven Factors of Enlightenment, the Eightfold Noble Path, and the Ten Transcendental Tathagata Powers.

These topics may be arranged in numerical order: Three Non-outflows, Four Noble Truths, Five Roots and Five Positive Agents, Six Paramitas, Seven Factors of Enlightenment, the Eightfold Noble Path, and the Ten Transcendental Powers of the Tathagata. This would be one system of structuring the Buddhadharma. However, if one often reads the Buddhist sutras, one realizes that, among all these Buddhist terminologies, the topics of my discussion today — "Stabilization" and "Wisdom" — occupy the most crucial position.

"Stabilization" and "Wisdom"

"Stabilization" and "Wisdom" are the two wings that can carry one to Enlightenment. Aided by these two wings, one may soar to the Four Holy Realms [of Arhats, Solitary-Buddhas, Bodhisattvas, and Buddhas]. Therefore, Zen meditation (as a method to engender "Stabilization") and "Wisdom" may be considered to be the most important focal points of all Buddhadharma.

At the time of Buddha Shakyamuni, there was a monk by the name of Assaji, who was studying under the Buddha. One time, while Assaji was listening to the Buddha's teaching, some words of the Buddha's went straight to his heart.

What were those words? They were, "The arising and disintegration of all phenomena are dependent upon causes and conditions." Assaji kept repeating this sentence to himself as he continued along the road. It was a statement that would bring profound insight if one could penetrate its meaning!

Which Came First, the Chicken or the Egg?

I remember when I was a child, one of my teachers gave our class a question to argue among ourselves. We became completely involved in the debate. What were we arguing about? I believe you have all pondered it before. The question was, "Which came first, the chicken or the egg?" We know that after an egg is incubated, a baby chick emerges. When the chick matures into a hen, she lays eggs. This is a very simple cycle and also a very simple fact. So, when our teacher asked us to debate this question, some students answered "chicken," while others said "egg." On the one hand, "chicken" seemed to be the right answer, because the chicken had to be there first to lay the egg. On the other hand, since the chicken had to grow from the egg, "egg" seemed to be the correct answer. I now pose the same question to you. What would your answer be? [A student replies, "Reincarnation!" Audience laughter] Reincarnation? He is bringing up the subject of reincarnation. Reincarnation is surely what Buddhism teaches. [audience laughter. Another student replies, "Whoever answers first is right!"] Oh, whoever answers first is right? [laughter and audience laughter]

All Phenomena Arise and Disintegrate Reliant on Causes and Conditions

Among the disciples of the Buddha, there was one named Shariputra. Before he met the Buddha, Shariputra also pondered a question similar to the one we have just considered. The father of Shariputra was a very famous Brahman scholar. Therefore, ever since his childhood, Shariputra had been exposed to all kinds of literature and rituals of the Brahman teachings. We know that in Hinduism, the creator God of the Universe and of men is the Great Brahmadeva. Shariputra was familiar with the Brahman teachings and he did not doubt the scriptures. What perplexed him was, "If the Great Brahmadeva created men, then who created the Great Brahmadeva?" He could not answer this question, although he contemplated it greatly. Christianity also teaches that men were created by God. If God created Adam and Eve, as well as the Paradise of Eden, then who created God? Therefore, when one seeks the cause behind such events, one ultimately draws a blank. Although Shariputra was a man of high intelligence, he could not find an answer to the question which so perplexed him.

"Did the chicken or egg exist first?" "Men were created by God, then who created God?" The Great Brahmadeva of Hinduism is the same God as the Allah of Islam, the Jehovah of Christianity, and the Jade Emperor of Taoism. The first statement of the Bible is, "In the beginning, God created the Heaven and the Earth." Who, then, created God? Just as Shariputra was contemplating his question, the monk Assaji happened to walk by. Wagging his head, Assaji pondered aloud, "The arising and disintegration of all phenomena are dependent upon causes and conditions." As soon as Shariputra heard it, he immediately grasped the meaning of these words. Give the statement from Assaji some consideration and see if you can also deduce an answer to the question, "Which came first, the chicken or the egg?" The answer is: neither the chicken nor the egg. All phenomena arise and disintegrate reliant upon causes and conditions. What gave rise to the Great Brahmadeva? Causes and conditions. What gave rise to men? Also causes and conditions. "Causes and conditions" is the profound answer that covers all bases.

Do not spend too much unnecessary time in trying to find the solution to a dead-end question! After all, "causes and conditions" gives rise to the chicken, "causes and conditions" gives rise to the egg, "causes and conditions" also gives rise to the Great Brahmadeva! Isn't this right? Men also came into existence through the coming together of various causes and conditions! The arising of every phenomenon is reliant upon causes and conditions. Therefore, all phenomena arise due to causes and conditions, and all phenomena extinguish due to causes and conditions.

After Shariputra comprehended the answer, he went immediately (along with MahaMaudgalyayana) to the Bamboo Grove Vihara to find Buddha Shakyamuni and to take refuge in him. The Buddha leaned over to Shariputra and spoke into his ear, "Today I have finally found someone who can tacitly understand the Universal Truth that I have realized." You did not know the Buddha had spoken this to Shariputra, did you? [laughter and audience laughter]

Among the ten chief disciples, Shariputra is considered to be the first-seated because of his ability to intuit the meaning of "causes and conditions" or "interdependency." During an earlier time when he was meditating under the bodhi tree, the Buddha had also awakened to this same truth behind "interdependency." The Buddha contemplated the Twelve Links of Causes and Conditions until he finally obtained a tacit understanding of it. Therefore, anyone who is capable of understanding the meaning behind the statement, "all phenomena arise and disintegrate dependent on causes and conditions," understands the Buddha and the Truth. This is why Shariputra is known as the disciple with the highest wisdom.

Chih [Cessation of Thought] and Kuan [Visualization]

Although the Scriptural and Vajrayana schools differ in their approach to the matter of meditation and the generation of stability, they ultimately arrive at the same goal. The methods used by the Scriptural schools are known as the "six wonderful gates." These are, breath counting, breath following, chih [cessation of thoughts], kuan [view or visualization], gate returning, and gate purifying. In Vajrayana Buddhism, "visualization" is utilized to engender "stability." There are many kinds of visualization. I have given a detailed explanation of this subject in *A Complete and Detailed Exposition on the True Buddha Tantric Dharma*, wherein I clearly delineate the various kinds of visualization techniques a True Buddha practitioner may employ to enter into Samadhi. In Zen, the methods used are "chih" and "kuan." Zen masters often seize opportune moments to give instruction on these two methods.

Once, an old Zen master took a young apprentice with him on an outing. In the open wilderness, they saw a flock of wild geese flying across the sky. This old Zen master often used whatever was on hand to teach his students. He asked his apprentice, "What do you see?" The apprentice looked up and said, "Oh! The wild geese are flying." He saw the wild geese flying. This answer sent the old Zen master into a rage, and he gave the apprentice's nose a painful squeeze. Then he asked again, "What do you see?" The student replied, "Oh, they have flown away." [audience laughter] The old Zen master raised up his hand and brought it down hard on the apprentice's head. You know, some of these Zen masters are very ferocious! Equipped with cudgels and lion's roars, they beat and growl at their disciples. If one does not "hear" the teachings, the Zen master will take out his cudgel and start hitting the student on the head. This will certainly bring one's mind to a stop as one passes out from such treatment! [audience laughter] While hitting this apprentice's head, the old Zen master asked again, "What do you see?" This time the student replied, "Now there is nothing. It only hurts!" [audience laughter] His nose hurt, and his head also hurt. The student was left to contemplate the whole incident when he went home.

The teaching style used by this Zen master is one of the "stimulating" kind that employs hitting, pressuring, kicking, and reprimanding to quickly jolt into sparks the minds of his students. In the "present," one observes the wild geese flying. When the wild geese fly away, the "present" moves into the "future." The observation of such a transition signifies that one still has thoughts. A Zen practitioner has to learn "chih" which is "cessation of thoughts." If the master asked you what did you see, what would your answer be? [A student replies, "Nothing." Audience laughter] This is a smart answer, but he would still hit you because you are lying! [audience laughter] You are committing a falsehood, since the wild geese are clearly flying in the sky. During the course of an instruction, one may witness the master and student hitting each other back and forth. [audience laughter] The old master's knuckles come down on the student as he asks, "What do you see?" The student responds by punching the master. [audience laughter] Let me tell you, the old master is actually pleased when the student returns the punch. It indicates a state of communion! [audience laughter and applause] So, if you see two Zen practitioners rallying back and forth with kicks and fists, you know they are doing the right thing! [audience laughter] Such a scene does exist in real life, when two practitioners actually slap each other — the two are abiding in the Condition of Realization, wherein nothing needs verbalization! It is a state of "chih."

The first skill to acquire in meditation is "chih" — to put a stop to the arising of all thoughts. Why would you slap me back? Because you realize that there is nothing to be verbalized. To claim that one does not see anything is false. There is nothing to be verbalized because no thought has arisen. A Buddhist practitioner has to be able to stop the chattering mind. Achieving Zen is to become unattached to the present when "the wild geese are flying," the past when "the geese have flown away," or even "how painful it is." [audience laughter] Here also lies the reason for using the "jolt tactic" of cudgel and lion's roar. Inherent in this tactic is the secret of Zen!

The first requisite for cultivation of stability is to stop thoughts from arising. The mind of man is constantly in a state of churning. Day in and day out thoughts ceaselessly move around in circles. If one can quiet down for even one brief moment, one will realize what a turmoil one's mind has been in. Now, if anyone here has no troubles, and possesses a mind completely free of turmoil or worries, please raise your hand. [A brief pause] You all have worries! I was the only one who had his hand up just now. [audience applause] It is not that I am not involved in any human affairs. Actually many matters require my attention. You have heard of the popular Taiwanese songs, "Who Knows What's In My Mind?" and "My Heart is Tied Up in Knots." [audience laughter] Last night it was raining, and I thought of the Taiwanese song "Tonight the Rain Falls Again!" [audience laughter] So, there are many matters that can trouble one's mind. All human beings, from heads of state to pawns, have worries. To be free of worries is to be able to view worries as non-existent and to transcend them. Today you regard all these worries as having a separate and independent existence, and you tinker with them, one after another. One trouble feeds into the next, forming an interminable chain. You have to put a stop to these reactive thoughts! Use your sharp sword of wisdom to cut through in one stroke! "Chih" is to cut through.

People of the highest wisdom are able to make an instantaneous severance and put a stop to their worries. From that point on, they abide in a state free of reactive thoughts. This is the state of Self-mastery and Freedom. [audience applause]

What is one to do if the thoughts will not stop? One finds oneself sitting there, doing the meditation and chanting to oneself that one has "to cut away the worries." This thought that one has "to cut away the worries" is a form of worry in itself. [audience laughter] What is one to do? Actually some of the visualizations used in Vajrayana practice can be very complicated and cumbersome. The methods of visualization used in our True Buddha Tantric Practice are of the simplest kinds. With visualization, the simpler it is, the better it can be carried out. Do not presume that performing visualization is an easy task. Some people say, "It is very easy to do visualization. I am able to perform the most complicated visualization." Try visualizing a round moon, blue in color, with a trace of cloud beside it. It takes some people a long time to visualize the color blue. If one has not experienced the moon in a certain color, one might have trouble visualizing it in that particular color.

There was a student who came to tell me that he could

not visualize colors at all. Purification is associated with white, magnetization with red, subjugation with blue, and enhancement with yellow. He said he could not visualize the associative colors. So I asked him to go and look at more colors! He then told me that he was color-blind. [audience laughter] A color-blind person, of course, will have difficulties visualizing colors. To him, red becomes blue and blue becomes red. Therefore, even the visualization of colors can sometimes be difficult.

Today, in our Vajrayana practice, I teach students to employ the simplest methods. First visualize a single moon disc, then a seed syllable. The seed syllable next rotates to transform into one's Personal Deity. One then performs the visualization of "the merging of the Personal Deity and oneself." The Personal Deity enters into oneself, and one also enters into the Personal Deity. Why this kind of esoteric visualization? It utilizes the principle that "one thought can be replaced by another thought." One is relying on the simplest visualization to stop other thoughts from arising. This is one technique for stopping thoughts.

When one is unable to stop thoughts from arising, one resorts to the method of visualization. When a very lucid visualization is achieved, one will enter into the state of "no thought." As one abides in the state of no thought, there may come the intrusion of an arising thought, upon which one returns to the process of visualization. This method is the dual employment of "chih" and "kuan." It is the best method of entering into "stability" or "stillness" in meditation.

I have previously taught the "breath counting method." With this method, one co-ordinates one's breathing with the mental chanting of "Om, Ah, Hum" or with mental counting. In the former case: when the breath is inhaled, it is "Om;" when the breath is held in the body, it is "Ah;" and when the breath is exhaled, it is "Hum." This is one way of breath counting. Another is for one to count "one, two, three, four, five, six" during inhalation and repeat the same numbers during exhalation. Because chanting and number counting are very simple, easy, and powerful in arresting the arising of thoughts, many people use the breath counting method. It is an excellent method to enable one to enter into "stillness" or "stabilization" in meditation.

In "breath following," one's mind follows and focuses on the sensations of the spontaneous in-coming and out-going breaths. In regard to the "six wonderful gates" of the Scriptural schools, we have covered the "breath counting," "breath following," "chih" and "kuan," (which are the Zen methods I just discussed.) The remaining two are the "gate returning" and "gate purifying" methods, which I will discuss at some time in the future. These are the methods used by the Scriptural schools.

Among these methods, I consider "chih" and "kuan" to be the most important. Besides playing a significant role in Zen meditation, "chih" and "kuan' are also related to many methods we use in Vajrayana practice. There is even the further division of "chih" and "kuan" into "major" and "minor" categories as devised by the Chih Che Daishi of the Tien-tai School. That is why there is the term "Tien-tai chih and kuan method." "Chih" is cessation of thoughts and "kuan" is visualization. During the process of visualization, wisdom is engendered. In Vajrayana, the following visualization techniques are also used: Flame Samadhi, Skeleton Visualization, Unclean or Impure View, and Stabilization of Ecstasy and Emptiness.

Zen and Vajrayana — Different Paths to the Same Goal

Although the practice of Zen ignores the cultivation of the body and focuses completely on the "spiritual aspect," while the Vajrayana practice places equal emphasis on the cultivation of "body" and "spirit," the ultimate goal for these two schools is the same. In other words, the paths of Zen and Vajrayana eventually become one. Although Zen practitioners do not engage in the practice of Energy Yogas, during the process of complete translation of the egotistical consciousness into the Condition of Emptiness, and when the cessation of thoughts occurs, the energy in the entire body will naturally return to its source.

There was this one method we used in the past. There is a particular point inside the body at the third-eye chakra. When one quiets down completely, the whole body's "ching," "chi," and "shen" [generative, vital, and spirit energy] become concentrated and return to their source at that one point. It is a very natural phenomenon, requiring no maneuvering of one's own. Therefore, at this moment when the entire body's "ching," "chi," and "shen" become concentrated at that single point, the same goal achieved by Vajrayana practitioners is arrived at by Zen practitioners. In the cultivation of the Energy Yoga (a Vajrayana practice), the practitioners first develop a full and vigorous chi to open up the central channel, then they bring all of the chi in the body to one single point. This turns out to be the same mechanism that is at work when a Zen practitioner truly enters into a state wherein the self is transcended. Although Zen does not engage in the practice of "chi, channel, and light drops," at the moment when the egotistical mind is completely transcended, the energy in the entire body also returns to its source. This is why the two paths eventually become one.

Flame Samadhi and Others

The Buddha taught us to meditate and use the Skeleton Visualization method to enter into Flame Samadhi. By igniting his inner fire to incinerate the self during visualization, the Buddha could enter into Flame Samadhi, a fruition of fourth level Arhats.

In the beginning, although the Buddha also taught many other different practices, the highest level of achievement attained by most of the disciples who were Arhats was through the Flame Samadhi. Therefore, the highest Realization attained by the Arhats was achieved mainly through the practice of Flame Samadhi. This is accomplished by first kindling the inner [psychic] fire. This fire is then led to ignite the whole body to burn away all obscurations, all unwholesome habitual tendencies, and all emotional afflictions, until a state of total purification is reached. The Realization of Emptiness through incineration of the self by inner fire is known as Flame Samadhi. Realizers of the Flame Samadhi are fourth level Arhats.

At the very beginning of our spiritual practice, it is not feasible to instantly abide in Emptiness. We usually start out by training to concentrate our consciousness to one-pointedness. In one of my earlier books, Highest Tantra and Mahamudra, I explained that the most effective methods to bring the mind to one-pointedness are also the simplest methods. Such methods should be clear, distinct, and focused, and they include the Vajra Chanting Practice [an inaudible recitation with the lips closed and the tongue slightly moving] and the Treasure Vase Breathing Practice. "Chih and Kuan" is another method. Furthermore, there is the method known as "Termination of Linkages." In this practice, as soon as one sits down, one empties one's mind completely and opens oneself totally to the Earth, wind, atmosphere, and the whole Universe. Such a method is practiced by people who have extraordinary wisdom and are able to merge with Emptiness as soon as they sit down to meditate. All these methods are tools to help one enter into "stability" or "stillness" when one meditates!

Only "No Self" Can Enter Into Stability

Why did I discuss the statement through which Shariputra was able to intuit the Truth? "All phenomena arise and disintegrate reliant upon causes and conditions." Actually the most important truth one can learn from this statement is that of "No Self." An Arhat is able to attain awakening because he contemplates on "Impermanence," generates the desire of "transcending the samsara," and then reaches the realm of "No Self." Inherent in the statement, "all phenomena arise and disintegrate reliant upon causes and conditions," is the concept of "No Self."

Here I shall point out to everyone that one must have an understanding of "No Self" when one practices meditation; otherwise, one is unable to enter into the state of "stability." Give this matter some reflection. As soon as one sits down to meditate — even before entering into "stability" — thoughts start to arise. A thought emerges, such as, "Who owes me money?" One's mind drifts to the issue of money. Some people have never experienced "stability" in meditation because as soon as they sit down, such thoughts as "who has reprimanded me or offended me" start to surface.

Let us use some simple illustrations. Yesterday's sun was just as bright as today's, but did anything happen to annoy you? On my way home yesterday, it suddenly started to rain. My car had been very clean, but its sides soon got splashed by other cars passing mine. A car in front of me was moving very slowly and, as I sped up, my windshield got splashed and dirtied. The thought surfaced that I would have to wash my car again, and I could not help thinking what a nuisance that was. [audience laughter]

Did anything else bother me yesterday? Well, yesterday's teaching, as well as that of the first two days, went quite smoothly but, while I was going over today's topic of Samadhi, it occurred to me that I had had already discussed this topic before. To avoid repeating myself, I should present this topic from a fresh angle, but I could not think of anything new. [audience laughter] This is also a nuisance. After all, I do have to face everyone, don't I? [audience laughter]

Then I reflected on something that had happened earlier during the teaching. I had in my hand a small piece of paper on which were jotted some of the key points of yesterday's discourse. The windows were wide open and a breeze was coming in, causing the paper on the table to flutter. That was why I had decided to hold it in my hand. You know, I gesticulate quite a bit with my hands when I talk. Because of my "note sheet," one of my hands became immobilized. [audience laughter and applause] Therefore, I found myself wondering what I was going to do with the next day's "cheat sheet." When I cheated at school, I used to hide the text book under my seat, and the cheat sheet was written on my set square. [audience laughter] I thought to myself, "Now I don't have a set square, and this paper is so flimsy, what am I going to do?" Good thing there is no draft today, so I may use both of my hands. Such considerations as these arose in my mind!

I also thought of the following: Before I go to bed, at around 11:00 p.m., Mrs. Lu usually makes some snacks for me. But, for the past four consecutive nights, my midnight snack has been just a bowl of plain boiled noodles, without any variation. [audience laughter] I was getting annoyed. [audience laughter] Plain noodles again! [audience laughter] Finally today she brought from home some Taiwanese meat stuffings which will impart a little flavor to the noodles! Last night, at around 11:00 p.m., Mrs. Lu and I went to QFC to do some shopping. We picked up a few items: four packages of beans, each containing ten different varieties, and a packaged whole chicken to use for making chicken broth. I was standing next to Mrs. Lu in the poultry section. First she picked up one chicken and, after looking at the price tag, she remarked, "Four dollars, too expensive." [audience laughter] And she put it down. Right there and then, I felt frustrated, "So I don't even deserve a four dollar chicken?" [audience laughter] Really, [to Mrs. Lu] how much was the second chicken you picked up? [audience laughter] The second chicken was three dollars. The difference in price was one dollar, and she bought the second chicken. In my mind, I had this troubling thought, "Why did she buy the cheaper one for me? Am I not the honored and revered guru?" [audience laughter and applause]

Then we went to buy some bread and bananas. We actually still had three bananas at home, but they had already turned black. [audience laughter] So I bought a few green bananas. When we got home, I peeled one of the green bananas and started eating it, along with a bowl of noodles. Then Mrs. Lu asked me, "The banana is still so green, why are you eating it?" [audience laughter] As she questioned me, I became annoyed. "We have been together for so many years, don't you know that I love green bananas?" [audience laughter] Isn't it so! I do not care much for over-ripe bananas, although Mrs. Lu prefers them because she thinks they are more fragrant that way. I like green bananas because they have a "different" taste to them. They have a unique texture and flavor which I don't know how to describe. [audience laughter] I do not care for the taste of over-ripe bananas; I prefer the greener kind.

So, just in one single evening, many thoughts such as these rage through one's mind. If one becomes bogged down by these thoughts, how can one not have troubles? As spiritual cultivators, we know that all these things which I have just mentioned are as small as sesame seeds. But sometimes small matters the size of sesame seeds can cause a riot! Some married couples fight over small matters like the ripeness of bananas. [audience laughter] You know that it makes no sense to fight over a banana peel, yet a little garbage can, indeed, start some big fights. There is really nothing more insignificant than such matters, and we have to be able to let them go. One must learn to let go of the insignificant as well as the significant graspings. After all, there is fundamentally nothing in this world that should disturb one's mind. "All phenomena arise and disintegrate dependent on causes and conditions." Nothing exists inherently and independently — this is the essence of Emptiness. When you realize this, nothing will trouble you.

Do you know the license plate number of my new car, a Mercedes Benz? I was afraid to purchase a Mercedes 600 because it would bring questions to some people's minds. I was criticized for five whole years for driving a Rolls Royce. So, although the Mercedes 600 is a very nice car, I was afraid to buy it. [laughter] I picked the Mercedes 500 because it is not the top of the line. This way I would have some peace and quiet and be free from criticism for a while. But a different sort of trouble arose. When the license plate arrived, it was "546" — which sounds like "I have died" in Mandarin. [laughter and audience laughter] A shiver went up my spine when I looked at the number! [audience laughter] So, what do you do when you are given such a number? Let me tell you, you look at it from another angle —"Everything is fine!" [The number 546 can also sound like "everything is fine!" in Mandarin.] [audience laughter and applause] So, many troubles are self-created because we believe that they are inherently troublesome. Now you should think of them as inherently empty, that "everything is fine!"

Nothing Inherently Exists — No Matter and No Thought

As Buddhist practitioners, we have to learn to enter into "stillness." I have discussed two very important formulae for this, "no matter" and "no thought." One must realize that everything is inherently empty of a separate existence, then one may enter into Samadhi. How can one enter into Samadhi when one's mind still grasps certain matters as if they inherently exist? One cannot. One also must empty one's mind. When the self-contracted mind is transcended, one will obtain the Dharma Taste. At such a moment, the "ching, chi, and shen" will return to their source. "No matter" and "no thought" are the most important formulae to enter into Samadhi in meditation. If one is unable to transcend both the objective world and the subjective mind, one will absolutely not be able to enter into Samadhi.

In the beginning, the Buddha told us that to become liberated from emotional afflictions (the accomplishment of an Arhat), one must realize the inherent emptiness of the "self." The "self" is the source of all emotional afflictions. All emotional afflictions of sentient beings exist because of the "self." I now realize that Sheng-yen Lu is not Sheng-yen Lu, and Lian-sheng is not Lian-sheng. By releasing the mind into the condition prior to the "self," emotional afflictions are transcended. Where do emotional afflictions come from? From wanting to save one's own face. To put it simply, when one sees through the "self," when the "self" becomes crystal clear, when the "empty nature" of the "self" is understood, one will no longer have emotional afflictions. Today, you have not yet awakened to this realization, so of course you still have troubles and want to fight to save your face. Where is one's face? You have troubles if you must fight for this face of yours! In conceptual realization, one abandons the self and is no longer attached to it. To understand "no matter" and "no thought" is to know the "fundamental emptiness of the self."

It is true that you have been wronged and have many frustrations. I also have many frustrations. Sometimes we all feel that we have been wronged. Take for example all our volunteers who have donated their services to the housekeeping and the patrolling of the grounds. Every day, after the teaching is finished and most people have left, these volunteers stay behind to pick up the garbage, clean the bathrooms, vacuum the floors, and tidy up the place. Since these chores are not performed in my presence, the volunteers think to themselves, "It's been four days and the Grand Master has not noticed us at all. We might as well quit. We have worked so hard, yet the Grand Master has not even come by to speak a few words of appreciation to us." [audience laughter] As a matter of fact, behind each ceremony are many nameless volunteers who have put in a lot of hard work. Because their contributions have not been recognized, they might not want to volunteer next time. Their frustrations are justified. In the True Buddha School, there are many unsung heroes who have contributed their efforts, while encountering many frustrations, such as being misunderstood or even slandered. But all of these troubles can be liberated if the "egotistical self" is released! Otherwise, one will have frustrations, will cry and shed tears, slap oneself, and bang one's head against the wall. [audience laughter]

Sometimes other thoughts occur to me, such as, "I have not indulged in any pleasures in this life. My days are spent energetically in writing, propagating the Buddhadharma, and in cultivation. Why have I attracted so much criticism and slandering? I might as well quit, go back to Taiwan and resume my land-surveying post with the military. I will apply to the Defense Department for my old position of Lieutenant Colonel. [audience laughter] In one stroke I will write off everything I have done. All this toil and sweat has earned me such harsh, mean criticism." Then these thoughts also occur to me, "Such happenings are very ordinary. I do not have to become self-oriented and self-grasping. Even if someone else has gotten the credit for my work, this is fine, too. I am cultivating the realization of the release of the self, and I will not engage in a struggle concerning my reputation. Nothing really exists independently and we all share in the harvest. This is realization of the inherent emptiness of the self."

The "release of self" is what one is cultivating in the practice of Buddhism. If you feel that the credit from your work belongs to you, then you are "abiding in the self." Such a person is not practicing Buddhism, but cultivating how to conduct oneself socially and to pursue prestige in the ordinary, conventional world. To practice Buddhism is to "release the self." Therefore, the first realization attained by the Arhats is "Emptiness of Self." If you want to enter into "stillness" or "stability" in meditation, there is no formula other than that of "no matter, no mind, and no self." If you do not have the determination to learn to "release the self," then you will absolutely not be able to enter into the Four Holy Realms.

That is why today I can make this statement, "I will not forsake any one sentient being." What kind of "mind" is this? This is the mind of "the release of self"! The Egotistical Self is transformed into the Infinite Self and all sentient beings have become "I"! When the sentient beings are at ease, I am at ease. When the sentient beings are not at ease, then I am responsible! Every sentient being is "I." As long as sentient beings benefit through my work, then it is tantamount to "I" getting the benefit. There is no difference between the sentient beings and "I." [audience applause]

Do not engage in conflicts over the Limited Self. "All phenomena arise and disintegrate dependent upon causes and conditions." All phenomena will transform and disappear. This is the truth of "Emptiness." The holy teachings of the Tathagata on the Supreme Enlightenment starts with the realization of "Emptiness of Self" and extends to "Emptiness of Dharma."

"There is inherently no separate existence of I, others, and all sentient beings." This "not forsaking any one sentient being" is an extension of the identification of "I" with "sentient beings." Subsequently, renown and status belonging to others also belongs to "I." Whatever offered by "I" to be enjoyed by others is shared by everyone. This "I" is the Infinite Self, and absolutely not the personal Limited Self. Be sure that you realize this is what you are learning in the practice of the Buddhadharma.

The Oriental Buddhist concept has spread far and wide, and it differs from the concept of an individual Divine God. The views of Buddha Shakyamuni differ from those of the Great Brahmadeva. Christianity, Islam, Taoism, and many other religions reflect the views of the Great Brahmadeva, but the view of the Buddha is a transcendental one that reflects the understanding of "no separate existence of self, others, or any phenomenon between the two." That is why the Buddha whispered into the ear of Shariputra the statement, "You have tacitly understood this Universal Truth that I have realized."

The goal of meditation is to arrive at one-pointedness and then return to "zero," the undifferentiated and unqualified Emptiness. It is a progression from the realm of coarseness to realms of subtlety, more subtlety, and the finest subtlety, until one finally transmutes into Emptiness.

The highest wisdom, or Complete Enlightenment, attained by the Arhats is the realization of "Emptiness of Self." The Buddha has taught that "all phenomena are impermanent," "all phenomena are empty of a self," and "Nirvana is marked by tranquility and stillness." The understanding of these three truths constitutes a real yogic response, a Yogic Communion.

In Tantrayana practice, there is a visualization that involves the moon disc and seed syllable. The Sanskrit or Tibetan seed syllable is visualized to gradually fade, disappearing from the bottom up, until it finally completely disappears at the highest point. At this moment one enters into the realm of Emptiness. This visualization of the seed syllable is an example of the most subtle kind of visualization.

Psychic Heat and Treasure Vase Breathing Practice

In Tantrayana or Esoteric Buddhism, there is the Psychic Heat Practice, an inner fire practice, that enables one to enter into the Flame Samadhi. In the future, I shall discuss the inner fire practice and explain certain key points that are related to the physical body. This is because the central channel is actually disconnected at two places: between the throat and the third eye, and between the root chakra and the navel chakra. The formula to bridge these two gaps, transforming the central channel into a whole and connected entity, is only explained to students who will engage in this practice. Again, I will teach this sometime in the future. Apart from this formula concerning the central channel, one still must be able to maneuver all the essence in one's body until it is concentrated at two points — this is the focusing of the light drops. The visualization associated with this practice has to be very clear.

We all have chi [vital energy] in our bodies. For example, one's temper flares when one is hit; this is an indication of the chi. Blushing upon seeing a member of the opposite sex is an indication of the chi in one's body rushing to the face. When one is mad, blood rushes to the brain. This is also chi. However, the chi involved in each of these cases is just the ordinary kind of chi. In Tantrayana practice, one transforms this ordinary chi into the "wisdom chi." What is "wisdom chi"? "Wisdom chi" is conscious chi that can be directed and controlled by intent. Such conscious chi may be developed through practice. There is also chi in the air that one breathes. When one breathes in, chi fills one's entire body; when one breathes out, one becomes deflated. Between the incoming breath and the outgoing breath, one may actually feel the chi moving within the body. Prior to the generation of the inner fire, if one can control this chi and direct it anywhere inside the body with one's conscious mind, then this chi is known as "wisdom chi." To develop this conscious chi, one must practice the Treasure Vase Breathing Method. First visualize oneself transforming into a treasure vase. After the chi is inhaled, direct it to fill up and merge with every part of one's body, all the way to the cellular level. Continue this until all the skin pores and the outermost layer of skin are completely filled with this chi. The whole body, like a treasure vase, completely envelops this treasure vase chi, which is transformed into heat.

When one possesses this wisdom chi, one may consciously direct it into one's hands and then project it away from one's hands. One may also direct it to fingertips, toes, throat, forehead, crown, or any part of the body. This is the cultivation of chi. [Grand Master demonstrates directing chi to his fingers while the audience applauds.] Through this cultivation, the wisdom chi becomes one's "truck." "Truck," as in a truck that is used to transport cargo. Did I pronounce the word "truck" correctly? Children often make fun of my English. [laughter and audience laughter] I thought perhaps I had pronounced it wrong again. [laughter] This truck inside one's body is used to transport the "light drops." What acts as the road, the "freeway"? The central channel is the freeway. Actually, there are many other channels in one's body besides the central channel. Chi is the truck, and the vital essence in one's body is placed on the truck and transported by it. The "five chakras" may be considered the five rest stops, or cities, along the freeway, through which run important line communications.

In this type of Tantrayana practice, one must first develop the chi. Even if one has an unblocked central channel, signifying an open freeway, one still needs the transportation vehicle, the truck. Without the chi, one cannot transport anything. So, first cultivate the chi.

How is the inner fire developed? The inner fire is generated from the stability or stillness associated with meditation. When this inner fire is kindled, it can be used to temper the light drops. When this inner fire is used to burn the light drops, vital essence is produced in the body. When this vital essence is elevated, one becomes the Buddha. When the physical light drops of an ordinary person are elevated, they will finally translate into the essence of Buddhahood. This is what the Tantrayana practice of chi, channel, and light drops is about.

One has to develop the capability to maneuver this chi throughout one's whole body. This way, one will not suffer illness and one's body will become strong and vigorous. When one maneuvers the chi and the inner fire to circulate throughout the entire body, all emotional afflictions and obscurations will be completely eliminated. One's central channel will transform into a bright road with the generation of the Clear Light. One will see the Clear Light. When one uses the truck to move and transport the vital essence along the central channel, one will reach the realm where one realizes one's Buddha Nature, where there is no more out-flow or leakage of physical or subtle light drops.

The Consort Practice

Many Tantrayana students engage in the Consort Practice, and I dare not claim that none of our students engages in this practice. A person may feel that he is capable of doing the Consort Practice but, at the end, as a result of the Consort Practice, a child is born. [audience laughter] My God! [audience laughter] What kind of Consort Practice is this? This is just ordinary conjugal relations as practiced by couples. How can it be called the Consort Practice? It is an error to mistake the "married life" for the Consort Practice. An authentic Consort Practice will not give rise to the conception of a child. The birth of a child is an indication that there is still leakage of light drops, or vital essence. Such false claims of Consort Practice constitute an infraction of the precepts and may cause one to descend to the Vajra Hell.

The Consort Practice does exist in Vajrayana Buddhism. One cannot deny its existence in the past in the Highest Tantra Section of Tibetan Vajrayana. However, the practice was so greatly abused that almost everyone started engaging in the Consort Practice. No wonder there are so many lamas! [audience laughter] Even here in the state of Washington, there was a great Tibetan lama who engaged in the Consort Practice with an American woman, and she gave birth to a little lama! Now the child is training to become a little lama in Nepal! Such a happening did occur, but it was not the Consort Practice! Calling such activity the Consort Practice is a grave infraction of the Vajrayana Precepts.

The minimum requirement for Consort Practice is to first develop the transport vehicle, one's conscious chi. One then elevates the light drops, placing them in the truck and sending them to be accumulated at the five chakras. This way, all the light drops are centralized at the five chakras. When there are no longer any light drops at the root chakra, one may practice the Consort Practice and enter into a Great Stabilization of Ecstasy and Emptiness.

Padmasambhava himself had five female consorts. During the Consort Practice, he would enter completely into the Condition of Emptiness and abide in the Great Stabilization of Ecstasy and Emptiness. This is a kind of stabilization that can transform Ecstasy into the Condition of Emptiness. "Ecstasy is Emptiness; Emptiness is Ecstasy." [audience applause] This is a practice that benefits both participating parties. During the process of such a practice, there is no longer any movement of light drops, just the movement of chi. Through the movement of conscious chi, Ecstasy is generated and transformed into the Condition of Emptiness. When the point of complete Emptiness is reached, it then gradually transforms back into Ecstasy. At the apex of Ecstasy, the condition transforms and reverts to that of Emptiness. The stability resulting from the cyclic movements between Ecstasy and Emptiness is known as the Great Stabilization of Ecstasy and Emptiness.

Not many people have knowledge of the techniques of the Consort Practice; there are also very few who are qualified to engage in this practice. Yet many people still claim the Consort Practice as a pretext. Do not trust such pretexts, as they can lead to the conception of babies. We who can "see" the energy, can immediately see whether or not someone is qualified to do the Consort Practice. We can ascertain whether there is sufficient chi, whether one can maneuver the chi, and whether the central channel is open. When a person does not have a transport vehicle, a "truck," and one's light drops are leaking, how is one then qualified to engage in the Consort Practice?

I have offered a clear explanation of the prerequisites for entering into the Great Stabilization of Ecstasy and Emptiness. The first requirement is the possession of a full and sufficient chi. One must be an adept in the practice of Chi Kung, and be able to maneuver the chi to ascend or descend. With a "truck" in the body, one may elevate the light drops. There are techniques that involve movements of the head and body, as well as the legs. There is a certain posture the body must assume for the elevation of the light drops. These instructions are taught to one by one's guru. If one does not possess the knowledge or the ability to do such a practice, one is actually doing what the Chinese proverb calls, "building a cart behind closed doors." Or, in this case, building a truck behind closed doors. [audience laughter] Except, in this case, a baby, rather than a truck, is produced.

This is the difference between the Buddhadharma and conventional practices. If one does not know how to relinquish one's egotistical self and enter into the Condition of Emptiness, one will experience only "pleasure" and not Emptiness. Herein lies the problem! Therefore, the practitioner has to first realize the Nature of Emptiness and then, during the practice, co-ordinate it with the other element, Ecstasy. Padmasambhava likened this process to that of "taking the pearl from the tongue of a poisonous snake."

There are some people who claim that if you pay them a certain sum of money, they will open your central channel for you. With one's "freeway" open, one can drive one's truck around. Did the Buddha ever say anything to this effect? Can someone else open one's central channel for one? As one's central channel is in one's own body, one must open it oneself. How can someone else open it for one? "How can you be so naive as to believe that it can be done by someone else?" [spoken in Taiwanese to audience laughter] It is possible for me to give you a little boost of energy, but you yourself still have to maneuver the chi to transform it into the conscious chi. This is a key point. One still has to do one's own cultivation. [audience applause]

The Highest Wisdom

When one reaches the realm wherein one has completely released one's Egotistical Self, a state of free expansiveness and weightless buoyancy is engendered. Thoughts will come to a cessation. One's body and mind can either expand to become very huge or contract to become very small, shifting between macrocosmic and microcosmic perceptions. What I mentioned the other day — gliding along with the snowflakes or hiding amid the stamens of a flower — can become a reality. In the twinkle of an eye one can travel to places thousands of miles away. One will be completely free, totally unstained, and unperturbed by any phenomenon. This is a very important realization. One is able to experience all of this when one enters into meditative stabilization.

When one is able to instantly appear at a location thousands of miles away (the siddhi of fleetness in running), when one has knowledge of happenings from other lifetimes (the siddhi of knowing other lifetimes), when one can view scenes from far away (the siddhi of divine vision), when one can hear sounds from far away (the siddhi of divine hearing), when one has knowledge of all kinds of happenings in the Universe (the siddhi of mind-reading), when one truly arrives at the state of non-outflow without any leakage of light drops (the siddhi of non-outflow).... In other words, when one possesses these six siddhis or transcendental faculties, won't one then be a Buddha? [audience applause]

So, one must first cultivate the precious chi in one's body. Without the conscious chi, one cannot engage in the Internal Practice which I will be teaching in the future. After this, one must develop the inner fire and use it to incinerate the light drops, transforming them into crystallization. One then transports the crystallized light drops on the truck along the freeway to each of the five chakras, opening them up, transforming them into the "Five Fierce Deities." After this, one may go on to practice the Highest Tantra Practice and the Great Perfection Practice.

Breath counting, chih and kuan, and the various visualizations used in Vajrayana Buddhism are employed to cause a shift in one's attention from coarseness to subtlety, until it reaches and abides in the state of cessation of thoughts. In the process of bringing the mind to one-pointedness, one is able to kindle the inner fire and attain the Flame Samadhi. Even visualizations such as the Skeleton Visualization, Impure Visualization, the Merging of Personal Deity and Self, and the Emptiness Visualization can bring one into a meditative stabilization. From such disciplines comes stabilization; from stabilization, wisdom is engendered.

What is wisdom? Wisdom is the light that illuminates and allows one to see and understand. Albeit invisible to physical eye, wisdom may be experienced. Inherent in wisdom is the Dharma Taste of meditative stabilization. Like a precious sword, wisdom can enable one to make swift decisions, keeping one from entanglements in all one's undertakings. The chih [cessation] in Chih Kuan Practice refers to the cutting through of all neuroses using the precious sword of wisdom. As a result, one is able to handle even very subtle situations with perfect finesse and ease and attain the "subtle fruition."

The Buddhadharma wisdom is a transcendental wisdom and not the conventional kind of wisdom. Conventional wisdom is what enables one to do business in the world and make a living, such as using one's intelligence to develop computer software. The Supreme Wisdom of the Buddhadharma belongs to the domain of Supreme Enlightenment and is concerned with the true meaning of existence and the Truth of the Universe. [audience applause]

We know there are five aspects to the Buddha Wisdom. The first aspect is called the "wisdom of ultimate reality," which is the basis of all things and can be experienced as the realm of

Dharma Taste. The "great mirrorlike wisdom" signifies the reflective aspect of this wisdom, which allows one to observe, analyze, and realize the innate fullness. The third aspect is the "wisdom of equanimity." After Buddha Shakyamuni attained Enlightenment, the first sentence he spoke (while still under the bodhi tree) demonstrated this equanimity aspect — "The great Earth and sentient beings all have the Buddha Nature." The Buddha Nature only seems hidden in them because of contamination and obscurations. The fourth aspect is the "wisdom of discriminatory awareness." Through discriminatory awareness, one gains an insight into the true nature of all phenomena. The fifth aspect of the Buddha Wisdom is called the "all-accomplishment wisdom." It enables one to carry out all of the karma yogas. These are undertakings which help bring sentient beings to Enlightenment and yet allows one to remain free from all attachment to the results.

The Buddha Wisdom cannot be verbalized, nor can it be expressed entirely through the actions and interactions of others. It is, however, completely merged with a spiritual cultivator's body and mind. Each movement, word, and deed of the spiritual cultivator is impregnated with this invisible wisdom.

Throughout the process of acquiring stability, one must have wisdom. In learning about wisdom, one also must have stabilization. Therefore, the cultivation of stabilization and wisdom go hand-in-hand. The two are entwined and cannot be separated. Earlier sages have remarked that stability is like an electric bulb, while wisdom is the electricity. For the light bulb to light up, it requires the existence of both the bulb and the electric current. To illuminate, one needs both stabilization and wisdom.

Among the Six Pararmitas [the six virtues perfected by a Bodhisattva in the course of his development] are meditative stabilization and wisdom —both deemed by Buddha Shakyamuni to be the most important virtues. Stabilization and wisdom belong to the domain of the inner world, while the remaining four Paramitas are more externally oriented. Together with Discipline, Stabilization and Wisdom constitute the Three Non-Outflow Studies.

Regarding the Practice of the inner fire, the formula for its success lies, of course, in achieving stabilization (i.e. achieving a concentration of the mind). This is a practice that requires co-ordination of consciousness, visualization, and body posture. One has to know the proper body postures in order to kindle the inner fire to incinerate the light drops.

When my guru, the Rev. Monk Liao Ming, taught me this practice, he stipulated that I restrict the teaching of the body postures to students of the Internal Practice. Prior to the transmission of the Internal Practice, only Tantric practice rituals are taught. So, in the future, students who want to learn the Internal Practice must first cultivate the chi, then the inner fire, then the opening of the middle channel, followed by the opening of the five chakras (which is the Practice of the Five Fierce Deities). Afterwards, they may advance to the Highest Tantra Section [the esoteric level] and Great Perfection [inner-esoteric level].

I have explained the Internal Practice of Energy Yoga using the metaphors of freeway, truck, and cities. The five chakras are the cities. One should now have a clear picture of what the practice entails. Very few people today can give a lucid explanation of the Buddhadharma and Tantric practice. [audience applause] I am able to enter into meditative stabilization and observe some of the eminent Dharma masters and monks, and to find out why some of them have such great power. I then understand, "Oh, he has the backing of the Great Brahmadeva, and he was a deva before. No wonder he is so powerful now." Many people have asked me the whereabouts of their ancestors. When I meditate, I can travel to the realm of Hell to investigate, to learn if that particular ancestor is now in the realm of Hell and the cause behind it. This does happen. In the Ksitigarbha Bodhisattva Original Vow Sutra, the maiden Kuang Mu, who was a previous incarnation of the Ksitigarbha Bodhisattva, asked an Arhat about the whereabouts of her deceased mother. The Arhat told her that her mother was still in the realm of Hell and communicated to her the causes that had led to the mother's state of suffering.

All the Buddhas and Bodhisattvas enshrined behind me do exist! When you attain realization, you will be able to perceive them. One evening, I came here alone to invoke the deities and sing praises to them. I beat the drum and started chanting their epithets one by one: Namo the Fundamental Teacher Buddha Shakyamuni, Namo Kuan Yin Bodhisattva, Namo the Crystal Light Medicine Tathagata, Namo Amitabha, Namo Chia Lan the Revered Temple Guardian, Namo the Revered Guardian Yang Chun, Namo Golden Mother of the Jade Pond, Namo Four-armed Kuan Yin, Namo Green Tara, Namo Manjusri, Namo Padmasambhava, Namo Ksitigarbha Bodhisattva, Namo Yellow Jambhala, Namo Ucchusma, Namo Cundi Buddha Mother, Namo Padmakumara, Namo Achala, Namo Red Jambhala, Namo Four Deva- kings, Namo Mahasthamaprata, Namo Earth Mother, and the Namo Goddess of Auspiciousness. Afterwards, I went upstairs to bed. In my sleep, a local Earth God came to me and said, "You neglected to chant my name." So, the next morning when I awoke, I went downstairs to sing the praises one more time, making sure that I included the local Earth God this time. The hurt feelings of the local Earth God were then soothed. [laughter and audience laughter] Every one of these deities is alive! Not one of them is a fabrication! Can I meet with the Buddhas? Can I meet Ksitigarbha Bodhisattva and Buddha Shakyamuni ? I am the one who knows Buddha Shakyamuni the best! [audience applause] All I need to do is to enter into another realm, and I can see him. I only have to enter the state of meditative stabilization, the realm wherein the Egotistical Self is transcended and released, and wherein the realm of Emptiness is realized. Then I can invoke the Buddhas and Bodhisattvas with my intent, and I can see them. You will also be able to do this in the future. As long as you use your wisdom and enter into the authentic meditative stabilization, you will also become a Buddha. In the future, everyone will become the Buddha! [audience applause]

Om Mani Padme Hum.

Fifth Day:
May 7, 1993

Masters, fellow cultivators, good afternoon. Today is the fifth day of this discourse on An Overview of the Buddhadharma. The subject of today's discussion is the Six Paramitas.

On the second day, I discussed the Four Noble Truths which is, in fact, one of the most profound and subtle doctrines Buddha Shakyamuni has taught us. Immediately after his Enlightenment, the Buddha taught the Four Noble Truths. Towards the end of his life, the Buddha also taught the Four Noble Truths.

Although the Four Noble Truths are commonly referred to as "suffering, accumulation, extinction, and path," the correct order should be "accumulation, suffering, path, and extinction." What are "accumulation" and "suffering"? The principal idea to understand is that accumulation of karmic obscurations and ignorance from previous lives contributes to one's present suffering. Accumulation is the cause while suffering is the consequence. After understanding the relationship between karmic causes and consequences, one must take up the "path" of spiritual practice. When one successfully reaches the goal of the path, one attains Nirvana, which is the "extinction of all sufferings and afflicting emotions." The doctrine of the Four Noble Truths, although seemingly very simple, has an extremely profound significance. In four key words, it concisely sums up the essence of the Buddha's teachings. During his lifetime, the Buddha taught his disciples to practice meditation, contemplate impermanence, take up renunciation and, finally, to release the self to reach the fruition of arhathood.

The Six Paramitas

The Six Paramitas [Six Perfections], the topic of today's discussion, refers to practices taken up by practitioners who want to go one step beyond arhathood. These practitioners are not interested in merely becoming arhats, they want to practice the Bodhisattva Way and renounce complete entry into Nirvana until all beings are saved.

Actually the whole subject matter of An Overview of the Buddhadharma contains an inherent systematic structure, and, after studying it this life, I have found that it can be approached in the following order: (1) The first step is to understand and actualize the concepts laid down in "Faith, Comprehension, Actualization, and Realization." (2) The "Two Gateways" or two approaches to the Buddhadharma: theoretical versus practical. (3) The Three Non-outflow Studies: Discipline, Stability, and Wisdom. (4) The Four Noble Truths: Accumulation, Suffering, Path, and Extinction. (5) The Five Roots and Five Positive Agents. (6) The Six Paramitas or Six Perfections. (7) The Seven Factors of Enlightenment. (8) The Eightfold Noble Path. (10) The Ten Transcendental Powers of the Tathagata. (12) The Twelve Links that constitute the chain of conditioned arising. By structuring this discourse of An Overview of the Buddhadharma in this numerical fashion from one to twelve, with the omission of nine and eleven, I hope you will find it easier to retain it in your memory.

Paramita literally means "that which has reached the other shore." The Six Paramitas, therefore, refer to the six kinds of methods or virtues that enable one to reach the shore of Enlightenment.

Actually, some of the elements of the Six Paramitas, the Seven Factors of Enlightenment, and the Eightfold Noble Path, have already been covered in previous discussions. For example, three of the Six Paramitas are Discipline, Stability, and Wisdom, which I have already discussed. Also, many factors in the Seven Factors of Enlightenment are very similar to the Six Paramitas.

So, I will devote most of the time today to the remaining three paramitas.

The Buddha spent many years teaching. For example, it took more than twenty years for the Buddha to teach the Great Wisdom Sutra (Mahaprajnaparamita-sutra). There was a verse describing the order and length of the major sutras.

Flower Adornment in the first twenty-one days,
Agamas took twelve years and Vaipulya took eight;

Twenty-two years in the Great Wisdom Teachings,
Finally, the last sutras were the Lotus and the Nirvana.

This verse means that the first sutra the Buddha expounded on was the Flower Adornment Sutra (Avatamsaka-sutra). Then the Buddha began the Hinayana teaching, which started with the Agamas and ended with the Vaipulya sutras.

Next the Buddha expounded on the teachings of the Great Wisdom (Mahayana), which include many sutras, over a period of twenty-two years.

The last sutras the Buddha expounded were the Lotus Sutra and the Nirvana Sutra. This is a list of the major sutras taught by the Buddha in his life.

Most of us here know that the Six Paramitas are: generosity (giving), precepts (discipline), patience or endurance, energy or exertion, meditation (stability), and prajna (wisdom). These six methods constitute the six antidotes for the afflictions in each one of us. We all know, I don't need to remind you, that the greatest enemy one faces in the world is oneself. The goal of practicing Buddhism is to first awaken oneself and then help other sentient beings to achieve awakening. The Six Paramitas work entirely towards the goal of attaining one's own awakening. Generosity is to cure one's greed, precepts are to cure one's undisciplined behavior, patience is to cure one's anger, energy or exertion is to cure one's laxity and slothfulness, meditation is to cure one's lack of concentration, and wisdom is to cure one's stupidity and ignorance.

Generosity

We will first discuss generosity. We know very well that generosity consists of giving in both the material and spiritual sense, as well as in a non-strategic way.

Regarding generosity, there is a very good question one may ask oneself in order to bring more insight into the matter. This same question is often posed by Zen masters to their students. "Is there anything that is yours?" You have to be able to come up with an answer to this question. [A student replied,

"Everything is mine."] Well, this is an excellent answer! Since nothing is yours, therefore everything is yours. This is a model answer that exemplifies a certain realization of the Tao. [laughter, audience laughter and applause] Generally a Buddhist practitioner will reply that nothing belongs to one, as this is what is often emphasized to one by one's guru. So, if you offer a view different from what is ordinarily taught and claim that everything belongs to you, you have attained a certain realization. You have realized that there is no separation between you and every phenomenon in the world; therefore, what belongs to others is also yours. This does not mean you are sanctioned to take things away from others! [laughter and audience laughter] It is true that when one achieves realization, one will engender this kind of view, that everything belongs to one. This is also considered a correct view.

Ordinarily, a Buddhist teacher teaches, "Nothing belongs to you, including you yourself." In the past, I did not completely understand the meaning behind this. A doctor friend of mine who owns a clinic in Taichung, Dr. Chou Tai-shou, the same pediatrician who cured my son, Fo-chi, of allergic gastroenteritis, used to give me the same piece of advice each time we met. When I was still living in Taichung, each time I ran into him, Dr. Chou would ask me to go with him to a Japanese restaurant or a sushi bar and drink beer. Each time, while he was drinking his beer, he would remark to me, "Only things that you eat and use are yours. Look at this food. It is mine only if I eat it. It is yours only if you eat it." He was pointing out that only things that one had eaten or used could be claimed as one's own; otherwise, nothing else belonged to one. Such a realization of his, albeit different from the Buddhist claim that nothing belongs to one, does indicate a certain level of maturity. At that time, I did not truly understand him. But now, thinking back, what he said was a very realistic statement. If an ordinary person can mature to understand the truth in Dr. Chou's statement, he or she will derive great benefits in life by putting it to use.

Many rich people have amassed for themselves a great

deal of wealth. When I used to do geomancy inspections, I had the chance to visit the homes of many rich people. What I found was that many of those rich folks had not really put their money to use. They were not living in luxury, and some were actually leading rather sub-standard sorts of lives. A rich man may live a "pauper's life." There are many such rich people who appear to be wealthy, but in reality they live like paupers. The truth about money is that it is merely pieces of paper if it is not used. If one just keeps looking at one's bank book, becoming euphoric when the account gains another digit and refusing to spend any of it, one is being controlled by one's money. That is why there is a certain grain of truth behind the words of Dr. Chou, "Only what you have eaten or used is yours." Things that you cannot eat or use are not yours. One may be very rich, but the wealth is useless if one does not put it to use. Today, as Buddhist practitioners, we have an even deeper level of understanding, and we know that nothing is inherently ours. With such an understanding, the paramita of generosity will manifest itself. Since nothing inherently belongs to one, then why not share what one "has" with other sentient beings? This is generosity. Generosity is to take out all you have and offer it to be used by other sentient beings. [laughter and audience laughter] Many of you will be unable to let go of all your possessions. The ability to let go and give is an external manifestation of one's evolution to the state of "self-release."

I remember a particular incident from my childhood. When I was in grade school, I used to run the hundred meters dash. Those of you who have run the hundred meters dash, how fast can you run? Well, San Yuan [to Master Richard Yan], how about you? [audience laughter] About twelve seconds? That is not bad. But, if you had to do it now, wouldn't you be rolling like a ball? [laughter and audience laughter] I used to be able to do it in twelve seconds. Now, I don't know how long it would take me. [audience laughter] Let us have a hundred meters dash event one of these days and find out. In any case, when I was in grade school, I was indeed able to run a hundred meters dash in twelve seconds. I was the shortest one in my class and yet I was the first one to finish the dash every time. As soon as I finished, I would return to the classroom to look for food to eat. Children get hungry very easily. In those days, every student brought a lunch box to school. When the teacher turned his back to us, we students would sneak some food from our lunch boxes and put it in our mouths. When the teacher turned his back again, we would immediately start chewing. [laughter and audience laughter] So, although the lunch period was scheduled between the fourth and the fifth periods, almost all of our lunches would be gone by the second period. That time, as soon as I returned to my classroom, I thought of eating my lunch. Our lunch boxes were kept inside our desks. Among my classmates, there was one student by the name of Chou Kuo-chang who was very tall and often bullied me. I can still recall his face clearly! [audience laughter] That one time I suddenly had the strong urge to find out what was inside his lunch box. I went over to his desk and opened his lunch box. Wow! There was a soy-pickled egg in it! A food item of high cholesterol! [laughter and audience laughter] I looked around the empty classroom and an idea came to me. I could save my own lunch to eat later during the lunch period. For now, I would eat his first. I picked up the egg and started chomping away. Then I finished all the delicious pickled vegetables and went on to eat a few more mouthfuls of rice. Afterwards, I replaced the cover of his lunch box and returned it to its original spot. Then all the other students came back to the classroom and returned to their own seats. At that moment, I was secretly very happy. [audience laughter] I was in a very good mood because I was able to save my own lunch for later by finishing off half of his first! [laughter and audience laughter]

Then came the third period, and a loud scream resounded in the classroom. It had come from Chou Kuo-chang. [audience laughter] Honestly, the scream made me feel good. To this day, I can still remember very well this scream of his. [audience laughter]

This incident is in fact an illustration of an ordinary mind that is without any spiritual awareness. Generally speaking, a person without spiritual awareness is often reluctant to part with his own possessions, but very generous with other people's. [audience laughter] This is true, isn't it? Everyone is watching out for the big "number one" by placing one's own benefit before other's. One might even totally disregard others by violating other's rights while keeping a close guard on one's own. This is because one lacks the Bodhisattva's heart: Bodhisattvas are different; they know how to give. Ordinary people are concerned with private interests, while Bodhisattvas are completely selfless. In walking the Bodhisattva Way, the Bodhisattvas do not just share with others, they even sacrifice everything they have for others. As Buddhist practitioners, it is very important that we learn to give up private considerations. In fact, after practicing Buddhism and generosity, you will be able to see beyond someone's actions and know how much of it is motivated by private or public concerns. You will see through the various facades and karmic relationships in the undertakings of the sentient beings, and you will not become entangled and go along with those who perform unwholesome deeds. To a person who has not engaged in any Buddhist practice, eating another's lunch is not only acceptable, it is even pleasurable. I was, of course, very happy at the time. Prior to that incident, it was I who would scream when being bullied by him. That one time, I could hear him scream for a change. [laughter and audience laughter] It was definitely a different experience.

However, things are different for me today. After becoming a Buddhist, I can only have a heart that is totally open to sentient beings and without a shred of personal concern. One has to constantly reflect on how much of one's mind is on oneself or on others. Only by constantly engaging in such an introspection can one engender the heart of generosity. [audience applause]

There is a story about a previous incarnation of Shariputra, of which you might have heard. Although this is a story, it does tell us something about the challenges a Bodhisattva faces. Sixty kalpas ago, Shariputra had not yet met Buddha Shakyamuni, but he had already engendered the desire to become a Bodhisattva and vowed to give up everything he had to help others. As soon as the devas learned of Shariputra's intent, they came to test him. A deva transformed himself into a young man, weeping bitterly on a roadside. Coming upon the wailing young man, Shariputra stopped to inquire and offered help. "My mother is severely ill. Only an eyeball from a young spiritual cultivator can cure her," replied the young man. Shariputra realized he, himself, was exactly the person the young man was looking for — a young spiritual cultivator who had just made the vow to take up the Bodhisattva Way. After all, he still would have one eyeball left after giving one up. Swiftly he gouged out one of his eyes and offered it to the young man. As soon as the young man got hold of the eyeball, he started stamping his feet, "You have made a mistake. This is from your left eye, what I need is an eyeball from your right eye." Wow! As soon as the first challenge was met, the second challenge surfaced. Wouldn't he be blind without either eyeball? Shariputra thought about his vow of total sacrifice and proceeded to gouge out his other eye. When the young man took hold of the second eyeball, he gave it a sniff and exclaimed, "What kind of eyeball is this? How could a spiritual cultivator's eyeball smell so foul! I don't think you are a true spiritual cultivator at all." He threw the eyeball to the ground and started treading on it with his foot. Although Shariputra was blind, he could hear the squashing sound coming from the trampling of his eyeball. He sighed, "How difficult it is to walk the Bodhisattva Way! I think I might as well go back to paying attention to my own salvation, without thought of others. I will just aim at becoming an arhat instead of a Bodhisattva." As soon as this intent came forth, the devas spoke to him, "Shariputra, please continue on with your cultivation of the Bodhisattva's Way. This was just a test from the devas to find out how strong your determination truly is."

From this simple story, one may begin to understand how

difficult it is to be a Bodhisattva. Just the paramita of generosity alone is not easy to carry out. Can one sacrifice oneself if faced with a challenge similar to Shariputra's? This story shows how difficult "giving" can be. In this world, one will come across many such incidents. The challenges of a Bodhisattva can be higher than the mountains and deeper than the seas. Therefore, the first paramita is to practice "giving."

We have here a thangka of Machig Labdron. She was the first lineage holder of Chöd, the Tibetan Body Offering Practice. Chöd was the major practice taught by Machig Labdron, and "generosity" is the basis of its teaching.

Now, among our students, there are some who have requested that I establish a charitable organization for the purpose of practicing generosity. Actually, people with clear perceptions understand that many charitable organizations are not what they purport to be. Someone approached me to give him permission to set up a charitable organization. I asked him, "What kind of charity work are you going to do? Tell me some of your plans." He proceeded to tell me that the first person to benefit from the organization would be himself, as he was unemployed and without any source of income. If that is charity, anyone can do charity! [spoken Taiwanese to audience, laughter] This kind of concept is totally wrong.

Another person approached me and said, "Grand Master, you can set up a large charitable organization without spending a single cent. All you need to do is ask students and other people to donate." This is not right either. Why should one not contribute a single cent? Set up that way, the organization should be called the "Charity Intermediary Company." Think about it, if you do that, you are just a mediator asking others to come to you, and letting you do the charitable work for them. Since you are merely a go-between and do not spend any money, the merits would go to the true givers and not to you. That is not charity. True charity consists of giving truly from yourself, including all of what you have. [audience applause]

Since the well-known Buddhist charity organization, Tzu Chi Charity, has produced excellent results, many other groups are trying to emulate them. Suddenly, many charitable organizations have sprung up. At the same time, instead of taking an active role in "giving," many people just wait for such organizations to do the job. If an intermediary takes from the public and returns to the public, it is still acceptable. If one fattens one's wallet from the public coffer, that is greed, and this will cause one to descend to hell. Many "charitable" organizations use the following strategy: they appeal to the public to send them the money, then they keep seventy percent for themselves and use only the remaining thirty percent for actual charitable work. This is where the flaw is. Groups who keep only thirty percent for themselves and use seventy percent of the revenue for charity are not as bad. Obviously, there are "charitable" groups which satisfy their own greed under the pretext of charity. True charity or giving is: when one collects ten dollars from the public, one adds two more dollars to it from one's own pocket, and uses the total twelve dollars on public welfare. In our school, we can do this kind of charity with a heart of total giving. Do not think of not spending a single cent and using only other people's money. Many will ask others to donate money to them to build temples. This is wrong. Such funds are not public welfare funds but private welfare funds, with only a very thin line between the latter and complete avarice.

The key to the important issue of generosity or giving is provided by the answer to this question: "Is there anything that belongs truly to you?" As Buddhists, we know that nothing inherently belongs to us, and everything ultimately is ours. When one reaches the state wherein the limited ego is completely released or transcended — a state wherein nothing is one's and yet everything is one's — any giving or generosity then becomes true charity.

Precepts

The second paramita is "precepts," which I have already discussed. To abide by the Buddha's precepts is to walk on the Bodhisattva Way and to follow the footsteps and teachings of the Buddha. It leads one to awakening and keeps one from falling back into samsara.

Patience

Regarding the third paramita of "patience," I have an inquiry here for you to contemplate: Who is slandering me? Such contemplation will lead to an understanding of the highest level. You have to constantly remind yourself, "Who is slandering or making charges against me?" You might reply, "My neighbors are insulting me, the Grand Master is reprimanding me, my wife is scolding me, and my children are reproving me. Not only my superiors, people junior to me are also putting me down. With pressure from above and below, I am turning into a sandwich." The Japanese word for sandwich is San-do-yi-ji. English words incorporated into the Japanese language can sound quite stiff. One time I went to Pizza Hut and ordered by saying, "Give me Sandwich." Perhaps I had been studying Japanese sometime in the past because the employee could not understand my English. [laughter and audience laughter]

If one does not practice patience or endurance, one will frequently find oneself feeling as if one is a sandwich, because very few people in this world like to use kind words. Pay attention to what you hear; you will find that people who use malicious remarks greatly outnumber those who speak pleasant words. Although one should not speak ill of others when engaging in chitchats, the opposite is exactly what people like to do. No one likes to talk about one's own faults; it is always someone else's faults. There is a Taiwanese saying that nine out of ten mouths are foul-smelling. This does not mean halitosis, but that nine out of ten people utter words that are unpleasant, abusive, and judgmental. When surrounded by such slandering and judgments, one cannot help but feel like a sandwich. Buddhists have to be patient and endure such situations. It is a difficult task, but consider this: Who is there saying these malicious things about me? Who is there scolding me?

Such inquiries will lead one to realize the nature of the emptiness of the ego.

Where is the "I" of my past? It has gone into the past and is no longer here. Where am I now? I am here now at the Rainbow Villa giving a teaching. Will this current "I" turn into a past "I"? Definitely! The past "I" no longer exists, and the current "I" will become a past "I" and will also disappear. How about the future "I"? The future "I" is not here yet. So, who is there slandering me? One has to think constantly about the truth behind these questions. Do you realize that even "slandering" itself will also become a thing of the past and disappear? Since you, yourself, will disappear one day, how can the slandering exist on its own? The person who slanders you will also vanish. Fifty years, or a hundred years, from now, who is there to slander you? When you constantly think this way, you will not be tempted to go and commit suicide. [audience applause] I frequently reflect on this truth. Otherwise, I would have committed suicide a long time ago. [laughter] You have to think this way!

I ask myself, where was Sheng-yen Lu before he was born? He did not exist. Now Sheng-yen Lu is living in this world and some people are criticizing him, but will this Sheng-yen Lu vanish in the future? Definitely. The Emperor Ch'in of the Ch'in Dynasty[221-207 B.C.] no longer exists, neither do Confucius, Chuang Tzu, and Lao Tzu. Mr. Sun Yat-sen and Chiang Kai-shek are not here either. Sooner or later, Sheng-yen Lu will also disappear, isn't it so? Will the people who criticize him be here then? No, they also will disappear. Since everyone will disappear, is there really anyone who slanders one? The past no longer exists, the present will become the past, and the future is not here yet! By thinking this way often, I realize there is inherently nothing for one to endure, thus one rises above endurance. In fact, I sometimes feel grateful to people who have criticized me and am appreciative of the energy and labor they have invested in their endeavors. Endurance is therefore transformed into gratefulness and appreciation. At the highest level of endurance, one realizes that one needs not endure anything as there is inherently nothing to endure. [audience applause]

Many times people have accused me of putting forth fake light photographs. Is there any point in making a rebuttal? First of all, I do not own a camera. Those light photographs were not developed by me, as I do not have a dark room. Although I am often photographed by others, I do not take pictures myself. These light photographs were sent in by many, many different students. Some people have theorized that the photographs capturing the phenomenon of light were falsified by students in order to please me. However, we are talking not one or two students, but several thousand of them. So, how could all these photographs be fake? People can make whatever conjectures they like; we do not have to become upset because we have not engaged in any deliberate falsification. As for myself, I would find such a falsifying act despicable because what the True Buddha School emphasizes is authenticity. Such "doctoring up" of photographs is cheating and a breaking of the precepts. So, just let nature take its own course. If we happen to get a light photograph, that will be good. If we do not, that does not matter. In any case, we do not have to get upset when we hear such accusations — this is endurance.

Coming back to the issue of the True Buddha Tantric Dharma, I remember there was a student who once raised a question while we were all totally immersed in doing the practice. She asked, "Is it possible to attain Enlightenment by just making these hand gestures and chanting the mantras in front of the Tantric shrine?" Consider this: these are words from my own student! The True Buddha Tantric Dharma is the product of a labor of heart and mind that has taken more than twenty years to become crystallized. She just took a look and decided there was nothing to it because it was so simple. After viewing the video tapes on *A Complete and Detailed Exposition on the True Buddha Tantric Dharma*, one might exclaim, "Oh, I get it now!" Of course, after you watch the tapes, you get it. But, if you have not been shown it, would you have gotten it? Many of the intricate parts of the practice are a distillation of what I have learned over a course of more than two decades. After watching the tapes once, you are able to practice accordingly and claim it as your own. It is a simple process for you, but if there were no such instruction, would you have known it?

There is an itinerant entertainers' saying in China: a trade secret is not worth much after it is revealed but, if no one tells you, it will take you three years to figure it out on your own. A magician can make objects appear magically from out of nowhere. How it is accomplished is the magician's trade secret. Once, when I was a child, I became totally awed by a magician and started chasing after him to beg him to teach me. He asked me what I would like to learn. I said I would be satisfied if he would only teach me this one trick — to make money appear. [audience laughter] He replied that he would have no need to ply his trade if he could do that.

What I have discussed in *A Complete and Detailed Exposition on the True Buddha Tantric Dharma* are the keys to visualization, mudra, and mantra. Although students who have practiced for many years will notice right away the intricate points being disclosed, those who are exposed to such material for the first time may not be that impressed. When we hear doubtful remarks from the latter, we just have to be patient and practice endurance.

After spending some time in explaining how to do the practice for her, this student finally asked, "Why should I attain Buddhahood?" [audience laughter] I asked her back, "Why did you take refuge?" She said, "I was just doing what my friends were doing." So, she was being a conformist and following the pack! I explained to her that the fruition of Buddhahood is wonderful, a realm of ultimate bliss, peace, tranquillity, and perfection. She professed that she was not interested at all in such a realm. "Then what do you want to be?" I asked her. She replied, "I want to be a dog." [audience laughter] Oh, my heaven! It is terrible to run into this kind of student. To her, it is a good idea to be a dog, especially in the United States where the supermarkets are well stocked with all kinds of dog chow. When a poor foreign student with limited English first comes to the United States, he or she might buy many cans of dog food for consumption because they are cheap. [audience laughter] Indeed, dogs in America have a good life. They are well taken care of by their owners, who share beds with them, bathe them, blow dry their hair, clothe them in the winter, and stroll with them in the parks. Dogs seem to fare better in life than men, being fed without having to do any work. When she finished extolling the benefits of being a dog, I said, "You have not met any Cantonese yet." [uproar of audience laughter and applause] It is a fact that there are always both sides to an issue.

I have totally devoted and immersed myself in the study of Tantric practice. It is heart-rending to make an offering to others of the cream of what I have learned, and be turned down. When faced with the kind of attitude that some students have towards the Dharma, I just have to be patient.

As a founder of the True Buddha School, many people feel that I am highly revered and am constantly being paid homage to by 1.5 million students. They do not know that I also pay the same kind of homage to my gurus, although a few of them have said good-bye to me. In the past, I have experienced great inadequacy in front of my gurus, who would criticize everything that I did. Just recently, together with some of the masters from the True Buddha School, I visited Guru Thubten Taerchi in Hong Kong. I was given a seat next to Guru Thubten Taerchi while the other masters sat below us. As a distinction between the guru and the student, Guru Thubten Taerchi sat on two cushions while I sat on one. After we were seated, Guru Thubten Taerchi turned to me and said, "I need to reprimand you for something that you have done." He said that in front of all the students, without any concern about saving face for me, the founder of True Buddha School, the honorable guru, the Living Buddha Lian-sheng, the Flower Light Self-Mastery Buddha! [audience laughter] Guru Thubten Taerchi continued, "Would you define our relationship as one of guru and disciple or of friends?" I replied, "One of guru and disciple." "Very well, then, why have you made such a mess of the task I gave you last time?" Actually, I did not know the details of this task because after it was delegated to me, I delegated it to someone below me. [audience laughter] Right after I had gotten the telephone call from my guru, I immediately asked some of our masters and students to take care of the matter. At the same time, Guru Thubten Taerchi, being quite impatient, also had delegated the same task to another person. It took us two months to get the task accomplished, while the other party was able to report back to him in one month. As a result, he was unhappy with me for ten days and actually was considering whether he should have me "stripped," like someone having their martial prowess "stripped" in martial arts fiction. [audience laughter] Fortunately, he had a dream which made him change his mind. He did not disclose the content of the dream, but it persuaded him to keep me as his student. From what he said, I gathered that a certain Bodhisattva had appeared in his dream to tell him that I still had great reverence for him in my heart.

After ten days of displeasure with me, he had a change of mind, but he also decided to give me a lesson when I visited him. He said he had something to give me and, while extending both of my hands out to accept the item he was handing to me, he asked, "Is this the way you are supposed to behave?" He was neither smiling nor speaking softly. "Kneel down!" He ordered. Do you know then what this honored guru of yours, Living Buddha Lian-sheng, the founder of True Buddha School, the Flower Light Self-Mastery Buddha, did? I knelt down obediently. As soon as I knelt down in front of him, all the other masters and students who had come with me also got up from their seats and knelt down. One has to have complete faith in one's guru. I did not argue with him or try to justify that it was not my fault, as I already had delegated the job to my staff. There was nothing to rationalize.

In the past, when my other gurus reprimanded me, I just knelt down and repented for my error. I never tried to reason with them, because they already had their minds made up and would not listen to any of my reasoning anyway. Some of the experiences I had with one of my masters were quite miserable. He would raise up a hand to hit me and, if I tried to evade it, the other hand of his would come down even harder. [audience laughter] Now, Guru Thubten Taerchi reprimands me whenever it pleases him. He has been doing that for ten years and is still not tired of it. [audience laughter] He is the guru, and I just have to graciously accept his treatment of me. Honestly, what else could I have said at that time? I could not say, "Hey, if you scold me like this again, I am going to leave you." I could not have said that. In Vajrayana, the Samaya Pledge one makes at the time of taking refuge is sacrosanct. If one leaves one's guru, one will violate the Samaya Pledge. The Samaya Pledge is not any ordinary vow; it is the most important Buddhist vow that aligns one with the guru and the Buddhas and Bodhisattvas during the meditative state.

My guru can scold me and order me to kneel down, and I will do whatever he asks me to. I am completely one-minded, without any doubts, about my guru. If I feel even a trace of aversion or even a little out of tune with my guru, the channel between the guru and me will no longer be open; it will become blocked at my end, and I will not receive any lineage empowerment from him.

Afterwards, Guru Thubten Taerchi asked me to go up to the mezzanine. There he wrote a Tibetan mantra for me and asked me to be the successor to his lineage. So, what he had been doing to me was a test. First, he mistreated me to ascertain if I could endure the hurt. He had to kill me first to see if I could endure the death of the ego. If I still returned to him, then he would transmit the lineage to me. Several of my gurus have employed similar methods to test me. A Tantrist has to be patient with one's gurus and not argue with them. The education of a Tantrist is more vigorous than that of a soldier.

While studying under Marpa, Milarepa was physically beaten up by his guru. Marpa also instructed Milarepa to build a triangular shaped house, then ordered him to tear it down after its completion. The same sequence of events was repeated with houses of various other shapes: round, square, and semicircular. Not knowing the true purpose of the guru, a disciple might question the rationality behind such tribulations. Actually, through the hardship of the building and dismantling of the various shaped houses, the disciple was removing his own obscurations, as well as learning the various karma-yogas of purification [circular altar], enhancement [square altar], magnetization [semicircular altar], and subjugation [triangular altar].

My gurus were even more demanding. They scolded me, and ordered me to kneel and crawl around before passing the transmission to me. This is how a Tantrist earns his or her learning — by not retreating after taking refuge in a guru. While a practitioner of the scriptural school may turn back from the path without suffering any retribution, the Samaya Pledge in Vajrayana can cause a reneging Tantrist to fall into the Vajra Hell. As a Tantrist, could I have turned my back on my gurus? Lama Shakya Cheng-kung was very strict with me, Monk Liao-ming has beaten me, and now Guru Thubten Taerchi of Hong Kong has been scolding me for ten years, but I have not dared to raise half a thought, let alone a single whole thought, of receding from the path. The Samaya Pledge is not a vow to be taken lightly. In Vajrayana, a guru will put one through trials and tribulations to test one's patience. When one indeed proves to have an inviolate will to cultivate the Tao, the guru will transmit the authentic practice to one.

From Lama Shakya Cheng-kung, I received many empowerments as well as many trials. From Monk Liao-ming, I was given many "humiliations" — I cannot call them such, [laughter] as they were more like "blames" I had to take on. But he did tell me this, "The more blames you shoulder, the more disasters you meet, the higher your achievement will be." To be reprimanded in front of my students completely took away my facade, but I did not care at all about saving my face. Can a Buddhist worry about saving face? That day, in front of Guru Thubten Taerchi, more than ten masters and students were present. Those of you who were present, raise your hands now. [A group of students including masters and reverends raise their hands.] Quite a few, and not everyone who witnessed the scene that day is here. If, while my guru was scolding and blaming me, I had been concerned about losing my face and had decided to get up, declaring that I was going to quit and leave, I would have broken the Samaya Pledge. It would also have meant that I had not learned any patience. Since I have taken refuge in him, I would have to abide by the Samaya Pledge even if he were to beat me to death. This is the kind of determination I have. I deserve to die in the hands of my guru if he chooses to beat me to death. In fact, I would consider it an early deliverance and rebirth to the Pure Land of Ultimate Bliss, expedited by my guru. If I have outlived my purpose in this life, I can always come back in another life to continue helping the sentient beings.

As Buddhists, what we are learning from our gurus today are their good qualities. One day, when you become a guru yourself, if you have learned nothing except how to treat your students the way my gurus have treated me, your students will be in misery. Anyway, I do have faith and confidence in my own gurus. As long as I have taken refuge in them, I consider them as Buddhas. They can fix me up, scold me, help me fulfill my mission, or beat me to death. Such is the attitude a Vajrayana student should have. [audience applause] Otherwise, one should not go and take refuge. If you know you are taking refuge in the Vajrayana pathway, and you make the decision to take refuge in a Vajrayana guru, you have to have complete faith in the guru. By upholding an undoubting faith in your guru, you keep your Samaya Pledge intact. You also succeed in the practice of patience.

Energy

Next we will discuss the paramita of energy. Like sailing a boat against the current, one must have energy or exertion to forge ahead, or one will be driven back. To be energetic on the pathway is to be constantly mindful of the following question, "Is there anyone who can remain as zealous about attaining

Buddhahood as when the first aspiration is sparked? Who is that person?" Then you have to think of yourself and be mindful of your own initial aspiration. When you are walking, you have to ask yourself, "Why am I walking on this path?" When you are residing in your house, you have to ask yourself, "Why am I now residing in this house? What is the purpose behind it?" When you are sitting down, you have to ask yourself, "Why am I sitting here?" When you are lying down, you have to think, "Why am I lying here?" The goal of asking such questions is to bring the focus of your energy back to cultivation in every task that you undertake. For example, tonight you tell yourself, "Well, I am going to relax today. Tomorrow is Saturday and the day after is Sunday. It is the weekend, so go outside, tour, barbecue and go anywhere you like. Go to a movie, a store, any place you choose." [Grand Master spoke in English to audience applause.] However, when you walk into the movie theatre, you must think to yourself, "Why am I walking here?" When you are barbecuing, you have to think of this, "Why am I barbecuing?" When you are climbing a mountain and having a picnic, you must also ask yourself the same questions. This is "mindful walking."

Sometimes you will take a wrong path. "Wow, it is Friday night, now we can go see... go see what? Topless!" [Grand Master spoke in English to audience laughter.] Topless is strip-tease, and it is called "toppuresu" in Japanese. My mother is nodding. [laughter and audience laughter] I love to joke around. We have two tulkus living in the area whose names sound like "Topless" and "Chocolate." I have been calling them Topless Rinpoche and Chocolate Rinpoche. [audience laughter] When you are relaxing, whatever you are doing, you have to ask yourself, "Why am I walking on this track? Why am I going to a strip-tease joint?" This is to remind you to put energy back into the path and be aware that whatever you are doing can distract you from the proper path. In general, as a means of relaxation, you can go and watch a movie; but watching a strip-tease is not advised, as it will fan your lust and detract you from the path. Asking yourself such questions keeps you energetically focused. When you are focused, it will help you realize when you are doing something that you should not be doing. In addition, chanting [the Buddha's epithet or mantra] while you are walking is another way of keeping yourself energetically focused.

Whether walking, resting, sitting, or lying down, you have to be energetic. Even while lying down, you can continue to chant! Pray to your Personal Deity or guru to bless you with a good night's sleep that is filled with luminosity and without any undesirable dreams. In every undertaking, you can pray to your guru and Personal Deity to bless you. This is one way of keeping up the energy of spiritual cultivation.

Energy or zeal can sometimes bring forth wonderful and perfect creations. Take the True Buddha Tantric Dharma as an example. It is a result of my energetic studying of the Tantric Dharma. [audience applause] When I read the sutras, I always have a pen in hand. If I come across a wonderful or subtle line, I immediately circle it and write a comment beside it. Then I will find the key point of the chapter and underscore it several times. This is how I read books written by the ancient sages and Bodhisattvas. While marking the books, this thought has occurred to me: If the author of this book knew that there would be, in the future, a Sheng-yen Lu who would study this book with such zealousness, he would emerge from this book and utter to me, 'You are indeed my bosom friend.'" [audience applause]

This is how serious I am when I read the sutras. I study every single volume in the Buddhist Canon very carefully, underscoring passages and writing comments. I believe the writers, bookmakers, and people who have expounded on these sutras — sages and Bodhisattvas — would appear before me to tell me, "Finally there is someone who has studied my writings very carefully and commented upon them." This is how energetic I am in my practice. Many people on the outside are not aware of it.

The energy I put into my writing is just as great. I have completed my 105th book and am writing now the 106th. [audience applause] Many people criticize me, not knowing that I am actually very energetic about my practice. I write daily without a day's break. Even during this period, while this discourse is being given, I still spend each morning writing. If a person wants to succeed in whatever he is doing, he must be energetic and totally abandon himself to the task. You might say, "Rumor has it that Sheng-yen Lu is a swindler." A swindler would cheat you today and vanish tomorrow, but I have been grinding slowly on my writing pad every single morning, and have written 106 books! Is this the action of a swindler? I have dedicated all my energy from this life into the studying of the Buddhadharma. My heart and soul are totally devoted to the Buddhadharma. This is the paramita of energy. [audience applause]

Many students are also very vigorous and energetic in their cultivation, and devote themselves to chanting every day. Master Lian-ching, Go On-men, gives students lists of homework specifying the number of mantra chantings and prostrations. Also, Master Samantha of the Purple Lotus Society often gives homework to the students, specifying the number of good deeds one has to perform, the number of mantras one has to chant, and the number of copies of sutras one has to print for distribution.

I know many students are very energetic in their cultivation. However, many others are too relaxed. After taking refuge, they only go occasionally to group meditation and do not do any meditation at home. They find the daily practice to be a chore and drudgery, and cannot derive any pleasure from it. They even regret having taken refuge and having made the commitment to do a daily practice in their personal shrine. They would rather go and have a drink. When one harbors this kind of feeling, one will never be able to reach any fruition in one's cultivation. To be energetic in one's practice is to totally abandon oneself to the practice.

Many people are very serious and energetic when they first make the resolution to do spiritual cultivation. The Avatamsaka Sutra says that, if one can uphold this initial zeal, one will attain Buddhahood. [audience applause] When they first become Buddhists, many students make the following vows in front of Buddhas and Bodhisattvas, "I will support the True Buddha School and the Grand Master until the end of my life." "I will try my best to learn the Buddhadharma until the end of this life." "I vow to follow the Grand Master in this life as well as in all of my future lives." Well, in a few short years, their initial zeal is spent, and they are gone. [laughter] Therefore, it is paramount to remain energetic and uphold the initial zeal. When one does that, one definitely will attain Buddhahood. [audience applause]

By coupling initial zeal with perseverance, one will arrive at spiritual fruition. Otherwise, one is just a creature with a tiger's head and a mouse's tail, as the Taiwanese saying goes. This kind of fizzling out after a strong start is not unique just to our students; many masters also exhibit this kind of behavior. In the beginning, these masters came to me and spoke passionately, "Grand Master, I want to support you in this life and follow you forever. I want to pay homage to you and support the True Buddha Tantric Dharma..." I told them, "Don't rush it, let me take some time to observe you first." While I was still observing, the hot air was already leaving the balloon. Their initial zeal was excellent, but they have no perseverance. This is a flaw of human beings. I asked one of the masters, "Why are you like this now?" He replied, "I have become sick." "What kind of illness?" I asked. "Terminal illness," he said. After being diagnosed with a terminal illness, he completely lost his initial enthusiasm. The Avatamsaka Sutra states very clearly that the coupling of initial zeal with perseverance definitely will enable one to attain Buddhahood. [audience applause] To have zeal with perseverance is to be energetic. This energy is extremely important because there will be no spiritual accomplishment without it.

Meditation and Prajna (Wisdom)

The fifth and sixth paramitas are respectively "meditation" and "wisdom," and these I discussed yesterday. Together with generosity, precepts, endurance, and energy, they form the Six Paramitas. When these six virtues are given a full play and applied in all activities, they will enable one to reach the other shore.

After a Buddhist learns the Four Noble Truths and attains arhatship, he or she needs to practice the Six Paramitas to transform into a Bodhisattva. The Six Paramitas are practiced by Bodhisattvas on the Mahayana Path. At the beginning and end of his teaching mission, Buddha Shakyamuni taught the Four Noble Truths. The ideas pertaining to the Mahayana Bodhisattva Way were taught by the Buddha during the middle of his teaching career.

As Buddhists, you have to abide by the precepts of the Buddha, practice the Six Paramitas, understand the doctrine of impermanence, and know how to practice renunciation. Or, you may practice as a lay Buddhist. Whether one is a monk or a householder, there are skillful means which one may employ to attain similar spiritual accomplishment. When one practices the Six Paramitas, one is a Bodhisattva. A key point in the practice of the Buddhadharma is to transform oneself from an arhat to a Bodhisattva, then to achieve self-awakening and help others to achieve awakening. When one achieves perfection in awareness and activities, one arrives at the fruition of Buddhahood.

This ends my discussion on the Three Non-outflow Studies and the Six Paramitas. We will stop here today.

Om Mani Padme Hum.

Sixth Day:
May 8, 1993

Today is the sixth day of the discourse on An Overview of the Buddhadharma given here at the Rainbow Villa. The topics to be discussed today will be the Seven Bodhyanga (branches of Enlightenment) and the Eightfold Path.

Actually, during my year-long discussion of the Maha Prajnaparamita Heart Sutra, which I just completed two weeks ago, I gave an extensive commentary on the Eightfold Path. If you paid close attention during those talks, you will have realized that, in the Four Noble Truths which are "accumulation, suffering, path, and extinction of suffering," the "path" refers to the Eightfold Path. In the future, when you want to experience and actualize the Eightfold Path at a deeper level, you may go and read the transcript from my discourse on the Maha Prajnaparamita Heart Sutra.

The Seven Bodhyanga

We will first discuss the Seven Bodhyanga, which are branches of bodhi-illumination (Enlightenment). What are the Seven Bodhyanga? They also may be called the Seven Factors of Enlightenment. Like pillars, these Seven Factors of Enlightenment give support to seven kinds of wisdom. Where may one find reference to the Seven Bodhyanga? In the Amitabha Sutra. People reborn to Amitabha's Sukhavati continue to develop the Seven Bodhyanga. The seven rows of jewelled trees, together with the birds of Kalavinka and Jivajivaka which are mentioned in the sutra, enable one to experience these seven kinds of illumination. The Seven Bodhyanga are: Investigation, Effort (which was already discussed in the Six Paramitas section of this discourse), Joy, Mindfulness, Alert Ease, Samadhi (which was also discussed earlier), and Relinquishing.

Investigation

The key subject of my discussion today will be Investigation. It is extremely important to have this illumination in the process of learning the Buddhadharma, for one cannot learn and practice every single Buddhist practice which exists. The Buddhadharma knowledge is as vast as the ocean, and it is impossible for one to learn all of it, even if one devotes one's whole life to this endeavor. Therefore, one has to make an investigation into the Dharmas and select those Buddhist practices which are most appropriate for oneself. In fact, such Investigation has led to the division of the Buddhadharma into many different schools and sects.

In the past, a Buddhist monk may have decided that a certain sutra was the most inspirational to him, and he was able to obtain many insights from studying it. Thus he went and established a new school based on that particular sutra. Each of the ten best-known Buddhist schools has its own emphasis and orientation. For example, the Abhidharma School emphasizes the tenet of "egolessness." The Satyasiddhi School, which is based on the Satyasiddhi Treatise, emphasizes the nature of the emptiness of both "ego" and "Dharma."

Among the teachings of the many schools there also exist doctrines which are contradictory to each other. To my knowledge, for example, the Abhidharma School teaches that the Bardo state is a concrete state. In other words, the Abhidharma School believes in the existence of the soul which takes on a form in the Bardo state. On the other hand, the Satyasiddhi School emphasizes that there is no Bardo state, nor any existence of the soul. Thus these two schools contradict each other. One affirms the soul while the other negates it. What, then, is the Mahayana viewpoint regarding the question of the soul? The Mahayana view is, "Some have souls, and some do not." It may be hard for one to comprehend why there are three different viewpoints regarding the existence of the soul. One says the soul exists, one says the soul does not exist, and one says the soul exists but only in some conditions. How is one to decide which school's teaching is correct? Actually, what Mahayana means is that great sages or adepts do not have to pass through the Bardo state but can ascend directly to the realm of the Buddhas. The bypassing of the Bardo state skips the stage of the soul. In my case, when the day comes for me to depart from this physical existence, I will transform directly into the Rainbow Light and enter into the realm of the Buddhas. There will not be a transitional stage of the soul. On the other hand, Mahayana also teaches that greatly evil people skip the Bardo state too. When a person with heavy negative karma dies, there is no taking shape of the soul in the Bardo state because he will descend directly to the realm of the Hungry Ghosts. From these three different beliefs, one may choose the one that personally makes the most sense.

What, then, does the Ch'an (Zen) school emphasize? Ch'an emphasizes that "Enlightenment is attained when one glimpses into the Innate Nature." One becomes the Buddha when the Original Nature is intuited. This is the main focus of Ch'an.

The T'ien-t'ai School stresses the tenet of "One Mind and its Three Aspects." The three aspects are "the absolute, the relative, and the mean."

The Hua-yan school stresses the tenet of "Ten Divisions Six Appearances." In the future, if the opportunity arises, I will talk about the practice method of each of these schools. You may want to make an investigation into one of them, if it appeals to you.

There is also the Fa-hsiang School (Yogachara School) which holds that "everything experienceable is mind only."

The Pure Land School is the most popular school nowadays because it is the most convenient kind of Buddhism to practice. The Pure Land School teaches that, when one practices recitation with one-pointed concentration, one can also see into one's Innate Nature and attain Buddhahood. The Pure Land School is based on three sutras (the Sukhavati-vyuha, the Amitabha sutra, and the Amitayurdhyana-sutra), and on one treatise (the Rebirth Treatise).

There is the Vinaya School which stresses the importance of precepts and is based on the Four-division Vinaya. Disciplines (precepts) lead to stability, and stability gives rise to wisdom. When one becomes an adept in meditative stability, one can also reach Enlightenment.

There is the Three Treatises or Madhyamika School. The three treatises are, the Madhyamika Treatise, the Hundred Verses Treatise, and the Twelve-Points Treatise. Collectively, their main tenet is again the nature of the emptiness of the self.

There is also the Esoteric School. The True Buddha Tantric Dharma is an esoteric teaching. The teaching of the Esoteric School is mainly based on the Vajra Apex Sutra and the Vairocana Sutra. Within the esoteric structure, its first (or external) level of practice deals with purification of the body, speech, and mind. The second (or internal) level of practice deals with the Energy Yoga of "chi, channels, and light drops." When the body, speech, and mind of an ordinary being are purified, transmuted, and unified, one sees one's Original Nature and attains Enlightenment.

Altogether, these are the ten best-known Buddhist schools in Chinese Buddhism. One has to make a selection from among all these schools. Say we have here, in a row, ten noodle shops, and each one claims that its noodles are the best. So far, I have not heard anyone admitting that its noodles are inferior to others. They all claim that their products are the best and the price is reasonable. Some people like to try their luck by random selection. In fact, when any one of these noodle shops can fill one's stomach, the choice then comes down to the affinity or the causal connections one has with any particular shop.

Similarly, there are many different Buddhist schools and every school claims to be the best. In the Shurangama-sutra, when Buddha Shakyamuni inquired about the methods of practice of the twenty-five Bodhisattvas, he was told that some used the method of fire to attain the Flame Samadhi, some used the method of water to attain the Water Samadhi, while Kuan Yin Bodhisattva reported that he had used the Inner Hearing Method. Nowadays, some people still practice the methods of inner hearing and inner light vision.

During his lifetime, the Buddha frequently emphasized the cultivation of the Flame Samadhi and the Four Noble Truths. To succeed in the practice of the Flame Samadhi is to realize the fourth level of arhathood. There are also many great

Bodhisattvas who have arrived at Buddhahood through their own particular practice methods. One should therefore make a decision based on one's own preferences. Select the school for which one has the strongest affinity, and turn that into the root of one's Buddhist practice.

This is Investigation. You have to make an investigation and then make a selection. Which school are you going to pick today? [Audience replies, "The True Buddha School."] [laughter and audience laughter] Well, you have made the right decision! [laughter and audience laughter and applause] This is Investigation. To select the right Buddhist practice for oneself, one must use one's judgement. If one does not care, but prefers to wear a blindfold — just like the pandas, Green Hornet, Batman or whatever-man who all wear blindfolds around their eyes — one may try one's luck by groping around to find which school one will end up in. One might call it fate, but such "fate" may not be the best, as it is based on a blind decision.

Investigation means that one has to use one's wisdom to judge the right practice for oneself. It is the same with taking refuge in a teacher. One has to observe and make a wise judgement. Otherwise, if one does not care and just enters any tavern randomly, one might just end up as an ingredient for the "human flesh buns." In the Chinese classical novel, *Water Margin*, there are evil taverns that sell "human flesh buns." When one goes unawaringly into such a tavern, if the storekeeper happens to run out of raw materials, and sees that one is plump and tender and has a lot of grease, [laughter and audience laughter] one will be slaughtered and turned into snacks. Similarly, there are many false Dharmas which claim to be the true Buddhadharma. So be careful and don't jump on board a pirate ship, or enter into an evil tavern. Instead of enjoying a great meal, one ends up as somebody else's snack. To avert such a happening requires investigation into the Dharmas.

An Excellent Dharma

Why does one choose the True Buddha School? Why is the True Buddha School so excellent? One must be able to back up one's selection. All of you here have chosen the True Buddha School, and I commend you for your great wisdom and intelligent choice. But, what makes the True Buddha Dharma so excellent? You have to be able to tell. When one talks about the excellency of a dish, one may claim that it is all in the soup stock! The soup stock has been prepared using only authentic ingredients, without any monosodium glutamate. Food enhanced by MSG really gives me the shivers now. [laughter] The soup stock has been prepared by slowly cooking pork bones and dried seafood delicacies together in a double-boiler for three days and three nights. Sprinkled on top of the soup are some green onion, garlic, and a little bit of red carrot, Tagu Man [in Japanese]. [laughter and audience laughter] It is not just aromatic and flavorful, it is also colorful. What a delicious soup! It stimulates your appetite and you want more of it. The purpose is not to stuff one's stomach instantly. If you do that, you will not come back anymore. Instead, if you are given half a bowl of this excellent soup which has everything — color, aroma, and flavor — then you will want to come back for more.

An Outstanding Root Guru

Topping the list of the excellent qualities of True Buddha School is the Root Guru, isn't it? [audience applause] I am blowing my own trumpet now! [laughter and audience laughter] Yet this is the truth. You could ask the many masters and esoteric tulkus out there, "Have you been to Sukhavati, Amitabha's Pure Land of Ultimate Bliss?" Most of them cannot answer "yes." Very few people can talk about their visits to Sukhavati. Perhaps some exist, but very few. Most of them have not done any actual travelling there, although they can imagine how it would look based on the descriptions in the

Amitabha Sutra. There are many Buddhist monks and nuns who have gone to Sukhavati, but they have not made it back to tell us. [audience laughter] When they go there after they have died and passed on from the physical realm, they cannot communicate to us how Sukhavati looks, the names of some of the sites there, or what kinds of transportation exist there. Right? What is the population there? How large is the Pure Land? Only a guru who himself has actually walked on the path and returned can guide others to walk on the same path without getting lost. [audience applause] This is a very simple principle. If you have been to a particular city, you know how to get there and what the city looks like. If you have not actually travelled there, and all you have is just a tourist guidebook, you may still be able to tell others how to get there and what kind of architecture, sculpture, or museums are there, but it would be inferior information than that of someone who has actually been there himself. That is why the Root Guru of the True Buddha School is Ichiban. [audience laughter] Other Dharma masters are also quite good, but they are second-seeded [in Japanese]. [audience laughter]

A Buddhist master who has never travelled to Sukhavati himself can only describe the Pure Land based on the Amitabha Sutra, as spoken by Buddha Shakyamuni. The sutra describes lotus flowers as large as carriage wheels. What kind of carriage wheels are those? At the time of the Buddha, there were no cars or jeeps, just carriages and carts drawn by cattle and horses. So, what is the actual size of these lotus flowers as large as carriage wheels? Only someone who has travelled there and seen them can describe them. How many people can sit inside one lotus? You might feel confident answering "one," since there is always only one lotus throne to each Buddha or Bodhisattva in the Buddhist paraphernalia that we have seen. But that answer is wrong. The lotus flowers that I have seen in Sukhavati can accommodate from one to more than a dozen of people. Some seat one, and some seat more than ten people. The other Dharma masters will not be able to tell us the seating capacity of each of these lotus flowers, as they have not witnessed them first-hand. The True Buddha School is remarkable because its root guru has been to Sukhavati himself. [audience applause] We engage in actual practice to confirm and validate for ourselves what it is like in Sukhavati. Everything is clear at one glance. This kind of wisdom awareness is not derived from books. Other Dharma masters' knowledge of Sukhavati comes entirely from books, as they have not travelled there for verification. A remarkable root guru is the primary reason why the True Buddha School is so outstanding.

The Outstanding Empowerments

The second remarkable quality of esoteric schools is its rituals of empowerments. [audience applause] Do exoteric or scriptural schools perform empowerments? Well, one Dharma master of an exoteric schools has recently started to give empowerments. He also prepared a vase of "sweet nectar" to sprinkle on his students. Where did the water in his vase come from? From the faucet. When you go home, you also can go and get some water from the faucet and start giving empowerments to your children and grandchildren. Actually, if the sprinkling of water is all there is to giving empowerment, one might as well purchase a water pistol, as it holds more water and is more convenient to use. As each student approached, you could squirt the water pistol at each of them.

The bestowal of empowerments is absolutely not like that. The master has to first visualize the Wisdom Deity residing in the spiritual realm to enter into the water inside the vase. Next the master must visualize another Wisdom Deity appearing above the top of his head, and entering into his heart. Then, in one flash, the master transforms himself into the Wisdom Deity. Only after such a procedure may the water be used for the esoteric ritual of empowerment. [audience applause] Since esoteric empowerments appear, on the surface, to be very simple, this other Dharma master of the scriptural school decided it was much better than the school's regular ritual of taking refuge, so he borrowed it. Empowerment is not the same as sprinkling water for the purpose of purification. It involves the recitation of mantra, visualization, and the merging and communion with the Wisdom Deity. The integration of all these elements constitutes an esoteric ritual.

Before giving others an empowerment, one must have already received such an empowerment from one's root guru. This is just common sense. If a master of the True Buddha School wants to give an empowerment to other students, he or she should first come and receive the same empowerment from the root guru. [audience applause]

That Dharma master of the exoteric school does not have any Tantrayana lineage. Although he sometimes chants mantras, he does not have a Tantric guru, and he has not received any empowerment from any Tantric guru. His training and practice have always been exoterically oriented. Therefore, giving others an empowerment is an error on his part. In the esoteric tradition, empowerment is transmitted from one person who has received it previously from his teacher to the next, constituting a lineage. Its source can be traced. One does not suddenly, out of the blue, give others empowerments. It is a mistake to give another an empowerment that one has not previously received from the root guru.

I have explained before that, in Tantrayana, the Initiation Empowerment turns one into a Dharma Prince, a Buddha-in-waiting. Through initiation, the fruition of future Buddhahood is conferred upon one, and one becomes a successor to the Five Buddhas. Esoteric schools are remarkable for this "taking fruition as the path" approach.

In the past, someone asked the Ch'an master Pai-chang, "Who is the Buddha?" Has any of you read about this koan? Pai-chang's quick reply showed that he had already attained Enlightenment, "Who are you?" You are the Buddha! You yourself are the Buddha. In the past, students have asked me, "Grand Master, are you a Buddha?" I replied, "You are the Buddha!" [audience laughter and applause] Although this is a very simple inquiry, some people are unable to come up with the answer right away. Tantrayana is a direct pathway. When I give you an Initiation Empowerment, you become a Buddha, a Buddha-in-waiting.

I remember when I was applying for college, there was this one fellow student who told me that he was "in between being accepted." When pressed for a clarification, he told me that he was a candidate on the waiting list. As soon as a vacancy showed up, he could enroll. Similarly, all of you are on the waiting list to become the Buddha. What kind of Buddha are you? You are the Buddha-in-waiting. You immediately become the Buddha-in-waiting after the Initiation Empowerment. Esoteric empowerments are mysteriously profound. You must not slight yourself, you must become the Buddha. [audience applause]

The Remarkable Pure Land — The Realm of Eternal Rest and Light

An ordinary Dharma master of the Pure Land school will tell you that, through his chanting practice, he is going to Sukhavati when he dies. However, if he has not had any vision or experience of Sukhavati while alive, he cannot know for sure that he will be going there.

In our school, all preparations have been made. Your palaces and rooms have already been created for you; even your attendants are waiting there in the Pure Land for you. [audience applause] The manifestation of the Maha Twin Lotus Ponds Pure Land is already completed, and all its celestial palaces are ready for you to move in. The Maha Twin Lotus Ponds is a Pure Land established by your root guru, and it is located in the Realm of Eternal Peace and Light in Sukhavati. All True Buddha School students can go there in the future. Everything is prepared and ready.

The Pure Land Dharma masters urge you, "Go, go and seek rebirth in the Pure Land of Ultimate Bliss." Who are you going to look up when you get there? [audience laughter] You have to have some kind of plan, isn't this so? So, you want to find Amitabha. It is true that Amitabha is in Sukhavati, but you should also know someone personally there. Remember that your Pure Land is the Maha Twin Lotus Ponds located in the Realm of Eternal Peace and Light in Sukhavati. [audience applause] If you know where you are going, Amitabha will know that you are a student of the True Buddha School and will immediately assign a residence for you. [audience applause] If you are unable to tell him the Maha Twin Lotus Ponds, he will have to ask you which school you belong to, what kind of practice have you done, and many other questions. If, after half a day of questioning, he is still clueless as to where you want to go, he will say, "Well, I will just have to assign you to the borderland of Sukhavati!" [audience laughter]

Therefore one of the outstanding features of the True Buddha School is its remarkable Pure Land. Its Pure Land has already been established and has manifested.

The Remarkable Tantric Practice

In this world, can one find another Buddhist practice like the True Buddha School practice? You won't find another one. Someone told me, "Oh, there is a Dharma master who also teaches the same True Buddha Tantric Practice. It is exactly the same as what Grand Master teaches." Indeed? I was curious and wanted to meet with him. So, we did some investigation and found out that this Dharma master is actually a third generation True Buddha practitioner, kind of a "step-student," like a grandchild. How is that? Well, one of our students had given this Dharma master a set of True Buddha Tantric Dharma video tapes. After seriously spending some time in his room secretly studying the tapes, he is now openly teaching others our True Buddha Tantric Practice. [laughter and audience applause] Isn't this Dharma master a step-student True Buddha practitioner then? Holding the Teaching Mudra, he announced, "Oh, I have to hold this mudra, this is just too wonderful." I looked around and was surprised by the number of these step-students. There are, indeed, many Dharma masters now secretly learning the True Buddha Tantric Dharma. [audience applause]

Most contemporary Buddhist masters teach from books. I don't mean they use cheat sheets, but their teachings are entirely from the scriptures and scriptural commentaries. What would happen if you took away his notebooks when he was not looking? When he got to the podium and reached into his briefcase for the notebook, he would be completely flustered. [laughter and audience laughter] His face would turn ashen and he wouldn't be able to teach at all. Although he may have been teaching the same platitude for more than forty years, once that precious notebook is gone, he can't go on. This is because he has not had any direct or personal experience of the Buddhadharma. His knowledge is entirely from books. So, if you steal the notebook away from him, he has nothing to talk about.

There was a similar incident from my college days. It is embarrassing to bring it up. There was a physics professor in our surveying department who was also a professor at the Feng Chia University. The notebook he lectured from had grease marks all over it and reeked of fried bread dough. [laughter] Perhaps he ate his breakfasts of soy milk, fried bread, and sesame seed cake over it. One time we stole his book, and for a whole week he did not show up for class. That week became a period of self-study or goofing off for us. [laughter] Finally we took pity on him and returned his notebook. At the time, I was the head of the student body in the geology department, so I was completely aware of the whole incident.

Apart from the remarkable guru, empowerments, fruition, and Pure Land, the most remarkable thing about our school is its outstanding True Buddha Tantric Practice. [audience applause] When one decides to immerse oneself in the Buddhadharma practice, it becomes paramount to find the nuances that make the practice so exquisite. It is impossible to learn all knowledge; therefore, one has to concentrate on the subtle key points. One must not spread oneself too thin by covering the breadth of the Buddhadharma, but one must try to penetrate the subtle points deeply. One will succeed in one's practice when one is able to do this. This also has to do with Effort.

During my marksmanship training in the army, I had to learn how to handle the M1 semi-automatic rifle, submachine gun, carbine, light machine gun, heavy machine gun, and the canon. In fact I was known as a sharpshooter then. [audience applause] In learning anything, if one is careful and meticulous, one will figure out an ingenious way to tackle the problem and make progress. There is an interesting story about a student of archery, back in ancient times. At the beginning, the only thing his master asked him to do was to capture the tiniest spider and hang it down from the top of his window. He was then to focus his gaze on the spider every day for three years. How was this spider-gazing supposed to help one's marksmanship? This student was, however, very vigorous and disciplined, and he spent the next three years in gazing at the spider. Do you know what happened after three years? The spider became as big as a cart wheel. Earlier I talked about lotuses as big as carriage wheels, now it is spiders as big as cart wheels. When he went back to see his master, his master told him, "You have already learned all there is to archery. The next step is just to aim your arrow at the spider." He went home and aimed his arrow at the spider which now appeared to him as big as a cart wheel. When the arrow was released, wow, it took flight and hit right on the target. The diameter of an arrow is far bigger than that of a tiny spider, yet, with concentration, the spider can be shot down. When one devotes one's mind totally to a single task, one will be able to pinpoint its key subtlety.

How did I become a sharpshooter? First, I had to learn how to adjust the front sight of a gun. Due to individual sighting habits and idiosyncrasies, the sight of a gun needs to be adjusted before one uses it. After the sight device has been adjusted, repeated practice will develop an unfailing accuracy. If it is a gun one has not used before, then one might have trouble when first using it. This is the first key point. The second essential factor is, when the trigger is pulled, the gun must remain stationary. However, since the downpull of the trigger generates an upward rebound force, I always aim the sight of my gun right below the target. I raise the barrel of the gun until the sight is aligned with the lowest exposed rim of the bull's eye, then I pull the trigger. The gun will move upward slightly with the shell hitting right on the target. This is a secret. In addition to holding the gun very firmly, one's arm has to be fully extended. If one is using the ordinary kind of M1 semi-automatic rifle, which comes with a leather belt, the gun may be stabilized in a triangle by applying a circular grasp on the shoulder belt. There is also a psychological aspect to the art of marksmanship: one doesn't mentally announce to oneself that one is about to pull the trigger. Being that self-conscious, one's heart would beat faster, one's breathing would become tense and, at the critical moment, the gun would jerk upward. Therefore, the trigger has to be pulled in an "unconscious" way. With the mind totally focused on the target and the breathing quiet and smooth, when one pulls the trigger unconsciously, one hits exactly on target. It is a science as well as an art. With all this gun talk, it seems like I have turned into a military trainer and deviated from my talk on the Buddhadharma. [audience laughter] But, this actually has a great deal to do with the Buddhadharma!

Do not think I am teaching you how to kill! No. What I am teaching you is: everything has its subtle secret. When you are able to figure out this secret, then every shot of yours will hit the target, and you will become ever-victorious and attain high achievement. [audience applause] There is the art of balance and the science of rebound. To hit the bull's eye, you must aim right below it since the gun will jerk up slightly as soon as the trigger is pulled. Keep your breath smooth and steady, and pull the trigger without any deliberation or even subconscious awareness. Then you will hit exactly on target.

The True Buddha Tantric Dharma includes many such subtle keys and authentic treasures. Carefully study the video tapes on *A Complete and Detailed Exposition on the True Buddha Tantric Dharma*, as it consists entirely of the highest essence produced from a process of arduous and thorough distilling. Ordinary Dharma masters would not be able to offer you such a practice. [audience applause] An Investigation into Dharmas enables one to select the most remarkable practice for oneself.

Effort

Earlier, in the discussion on the art of archery, I brought up the importance of Effort. Effort also plays an important role in my painting practice. To improve my painting skill, I often go and look at other artists' work. I will stand in front of a painting, study the brush strokes, and locate its essence. Sometimes a seemingly casual placement of a dab of paint captures the exact spirit of the object painted. One must work hard if one wants to make progress on whatever one is studying. If you are studying painting, go and look at other painters' work, then get active and start experimenting yourself. When you integrate your hands, heart, and mind, your paintings will come alive. Do not be perfunctory in whatever you are studying. Approach Buddhist study the same way — vigorously using your body, mind, and heart — and you will definitely succeed. Effort is to learn and work vigorously to make progress on the path.

Joy

Joy is generally explained as the kind of joy generated and maintained in one's heart when one realizes what a precious thing the Buddhadharma is. It is easy for someone who appreciates and cherishes the Buddhadharma to have this sentiment, but does everyone who comes into contact with the Buddhadharma automatically sprout such a joy? Will one spontaneously exclaim, "What else in the world can be more important than studying and cultivating the Buddhadharma!" The truth is, before one experiences the subtle wonders of the Buddhadharma, one will not engender a profound joy in one's heart. Only after one obtains the profoundly wonderful Dharma Taste will one engender such joy, and appreciate sitting through long sessions of meditation.

Although I have emphasized the importance of making time each day to do the practice, many students really lack such motivation. Even if some students could find the free time, they would rather sit in front of the television. It seems that one's favorite television show always comes on during the time one may squeeze in a free moment. A practice each day then becomes a burden. What a pain it is that the Grand Master has asked us to do at least one practice a day! At first one manages to do so, but only with some effort. But, after several days, even that effort becomes too much. This is because one has not yet experienced the Dharma Taste. If one has tasted the Dharma Taste, one will have felt the Joy which is such a feeling of joy and rapture.

In my case, I meditate daily, although the meditation does not follow a fixed time schedule. Actually, I don't just meditate daily, I meditate continually throughout the day. This is a condition wherein one is filled with an extraordinary kind of Dharma bliss. Take this moment, for example, I am feeling a tremendous joy right now. This teaching is not a chore to me, and I do not find it tiring. In fact, while sitting here teaching, I am at the same time transporting and maneuvering the chi inside my body. Inside my body, a circle of conductivity goes on which generates an extremely happy feeling. This is the Dharma Taste.

The same thing happens when you meditate in a shrine. The vital force from the Universe will enter your body. When your body is filled with this pure, vital force, you will experience a solidifying or firming sensation. It is a very tangible and solid power that gives rise to bliss and euphoria. When you are able to experience this kind of bliss, you will love meditation. You must practice vigorously to reach this level. When the vital force descends into you, you will feel very happy and free. How can I describe it? Like swinging up and down on a swing? No, it is not quite the same. [laughter] Any other better analogies? Like being dazzled by great beauty? No, not quite. Like sinking your soul into a soft cushion? No, not that either. I can't explain it in words. [laughter] It is indescribable. What happens is the chi in your body keeps on circulating and moving and, during this circulation, an ecstasy is generated. This is Joy. This is Dharma Taste. [audience applause]

In Tantrayana, the so-called four kinds of stabilization ecstasy are actually a kind of Dharma Taste. When the "drops" at the thousand-petalled lotus (located at the brow-point chakra) melt and descend to permeate the channels and centers of the subtle body, a bliss is generated. This bliss is the Dharma Taste and corresponds to the four Tantric ecstasies.

References to Dharma Taste are also found in many Zen koans. For example, the fifth Patriarch Hung-jen asked the sixth Patriarch Hui-neng, "Where are you from?" "I am from Ling-nan which is to the south," replied Hui-neng. Hung-jen asked, "How can anyone from Ling-nan be qualified enough to attain Buddhahood?" To which Hui-neng replied, "Men may be classified as from the south or north, but there is no such distinction in the Buddha Nature." This is an answer with Dharma Taste.

After Hui-neng realized this Dharma Taste, he also liked to pose the same question to his students, "Where are you from?" The answer would reveal one's realization of the Dharma Taste. Now, let me ask you the same question, "Where are you from?" Would you say you are from Taiwan? [laughter and audience laughter] Or would you say you have no idea at all? [laughter and audience laughter] You have to come up at least with the answer of "somewhere nearby." The Dharma Taste lies in the word "nearby." It is apparent that you have travelled from faraway Taiwan, why then do you say you are from "nearby"? This answer appears to be nonsensical but, when one reconsiders it, one knows that it is an answer of Dharma Taste. What is most intimate to one? The Buddha Nature. I am the Buddha! The Buddha Nature and I are indivisible; therefore "somewhere nearby" is, of course, correct. Such an answer indicates an understanding of the Buddha

Nature. There is no separation between you and the Buddha Nature. "I am from `nearby,'" signifies that one has glimpsed into the nature of the mind. [audience applause] Such an answer scores ninety points on a scale of one hundred. It is an acceptable answer of Dharma Taste.

The Sixth Patriarch asked again, "Where are you from?" [A student replies, "From the Empty Space."] Isn't it too far away! [laughter] The Empty Space is so boundless, I would not know how to begin thinking about it. [audience laughter] Your answer is too broad and difficult for me to accept. [laughter] Another student of Hui-neng's gave this reply, "I have not come from anywhere." This is also an answer of Dharma Taste, signifying the indivisibility between the Buddha Nature and oneself. The "I" is the union of the Great Self and the limited self. Wherever the "realized person" is, the Buddha Nature is with him or her, so how can one be from anywhere else? When the Sixth Patriarch heard this reply, he announced, "Good, this is a good answer. You have received my transmission of the Dharma." To a third student, Hui-neng asked again, "Where are you from?" He often posed this same question to many different students. This time, someone replied, "Where I come from or go to makes no difference." Wow! This is also an enlightened answer. It indicates a realization of "non-coming and non-going" which is actually the meaning of the term "Tathagata." A Tathagata is a Buddha. Such words are words of realization. [audience applause]

In the Zen school, Dharma Taste is experienced through the exchange of dialogues. One party poses a question and another answers. When one gives the answer some thought, and senses the Dharma Taste in it, Joy will arise, and one will instantaneously instinctively understand the Buddha Nature. The intuition of the Buddha Nature brings Enlightenment. Pervading the exchange of Zen dialogues are the Dharma Taste and the revelation of one's realization. Through the dialogues, which are a unique tool of Zen, one obtains the Joy of Dharma, intuition, and realization.

In the context of Tantrayana, Joy is something very tangible. When the central channel is opened, one perceives the Clear Light. When the five major chakras are opened, one is linked with the Five Fierce Deities. When the heart chakra is opened, one immediately realizes the Bliss Body of Buddhahood. When the throat chakra is opened, one realizes the Emanation Body of Buddhahood. When the brow-point chakra is opened, one realizes the Dharma Body of Buddhahood. To a Tantric practitioner, the Joy is, at the very least, a very tangible and concrete sensation which one may experience during meditation.

In the past, there was one lineage holder who actually experienced, while meditating, the phenomenon of "the east wall meeting the west wall." We know this side is the east, that side is the west. Seattle is to the west while Spokane is to the east. If the east wall meets on the west wall, all the Buddha statues enshrined on the east wall here will meet on the Padmakumara statue at the opposite end of this hall. [laughter] The east and the west walls are separated by a distance. However, during meditation, one discovers that the east and the west have dissolved together. What kind of phenomenon is that? This dissolution has made the space dimension disappear. With the space dimension gone, one's body is also gone. The meeting of the east wall with the west wall means that the two have dissolved into each other to become "One Taste." When one is completely merged with the Buddha Nature, the phenomenon of One Taste is engendered. This is the underlying meaning behind the enigmatic phrase "east wall meeting the west wall." It signifies the evaporation of the space dimension, and a direct experience of One Taste, which is a complete dissolution of the limited ego into the nature of the mind. This is Joy, a joyful phenomenon associated with the experience of Dharma.

Mindfullness and Alert Ease

What is Mindfullness? It refers to the meditational practice of alternating visualization with the cessation of thought.

Next is Alert Ease, which requires some discussion. As a practitioner of the Buddhadharma, one's mind will take on the qualities of water — openness [fluidity] and clarity. The mind becomes cheerful and sees everything with a transparency. A Buddhist practitioner must not spend every day in grief and brooding, with a heart tied up in knots. One's train of thought should flow smoothly and easily without any obstruction. The three channels and seven chakras in the subtle body should be open. This is the Alert Ease that Buddhist practitioners should find themselves in. If one is constantly brooding, one's heart will be tied up in knots.

In the past, a person went to seek help from a Dharma master. The person said he was very weary, unhappy, and felt suffocated. That Dharma master only asked him in return, "Who is tying you up?" All of you today must keep this in mind, "Who is tying you up?" [A student replies, "I myself."] Right! You are the one who is tying yourself up. There is, in reality, no one else tying you up. Your feet are in good condition, your body is sound, and you are free! Who is tying you up? Why are you unhappy today? Nobody has tied you up. You can actually be happy and free from suffocation. Why indulge in unhappiness and brooding? You are free!

We who practice the Buddhadharma today have to learn to be free. We are all free. No one has tied us up. This is Alert Ease, the condition in which one must constantly abide while practicing Buddhism.

Samadhi and Relinquishing

In the scriptural schools, Samadhi is concentration, one-pointedness. In the esoteric schools, Samadhi is Zen meditation. One enters Samadhi and realizes Buddhahood; that is, one uses the highest level of consciousness to realize the truth of Emptiness and then attain transcendental accomplishment. This is Samadhi.

What is Relinquishing? According to Buddha Shakyamuni in the *Diamond Sutra*, "My teachings may be likened to the raft. If the Buddha-teaching must be relinquished, how much more so must be the misteaching!" What this means is that, like a raft that has to be relinquished when one reaches the shore, the Buddhadharma ultimately has to be relinquished.

However, during the path of cultivation, some practices have to be relinquished while others cannot. The decision has to be made with wisdom. Thus, in order to receive the bestowal of blessing from the root guru, one should not relinquish the Guru Yoga. [audience applause] To attain the merits of one's Personal Deity, one cannot relinquish the Personal Deity Yoga. [audience applause] To succeed in any general undertaking that needs the aid of the Dharma Protectors, Daka or Dakinis, one must not relinquish the Karma Yogas. [audience applause] How about other practices? You must employ your wisdom to make a decision. Along the graduated stages of the pathway, after achieving a yogic response on a certain stage, one will be ready to embark on the next level. Here one must decide which additional practice to take on, and which part of one's current practice needs to be given up. This is something which requires a thoughtful decision. [audience applause] This is the awareness of relinquishing.

Involved in these decision makings is a subtle challenge, because it is sometimes difficult for one to let go of a practice in which one has been experiencing yogic response. For example, say you have become so attached to the great joy derived from your response in the Four Preliminary Practices, that you have no desire for other practices. At such times, it is important to make a wise choice. Do you want to move on to the next level? How may you adapt your current practice to the new plan: which practices to keep, which to add, and which ones to relinquish? It is a judgment based entirely on your wisdom. This is the meaning behind the Buddha's words, "My teachings may be likened to the raft. If the Buddha-teaching must be relinquished, how much more so must be the misteaching!"

The Flexible Precepts

Here I would like to bring up the problem of precepts. When we first become Buddhists, we must abide by the precepts completely. However, precepts are alive and not rigid. A very important point is: how to employ the precepts in a flexible way. This again requires supreme wisdom. Precepts are not to be inflexibly clung to.

Some people say, "Do not kill." That is correct, so you stick to this precept and tell yourself, "I absolutely must not kill, not even an ant." This morning I saw a bee buzzing around in my room, I thought to myself, "Should I kill it? If I don't, I am going to get stung in a while when I work on my writing. This side of my face will be swollen and it will show up in the videotape of the discourse to be filmed this afternoon." [audience laughter] So, after some contemplation, I opened the window and shooed it out. I also used my supreme wisdom to make a decision. [audience laughter] To kill the bee is a very simple thing, as it will give me trouble if I don't kill it, isn't this true? Otherwise, I would be stung. Then, suddenly, on this sixth day of the discourse, a bump will show up on my lip. People will say, "Is there something wrong with the Grand Master? Why is his lip swollen? Did someone bite him?" [audience laughter] Unjust accusations would surface. Because of these considerations, I decided to open the window and shoo the bee out. In any undertaking, we have to think through the ramifications and make our decisions accordingly.

Buddha Shakyamuni has also faced the problem of "to kill or not to kill." A robber was going to kill five hundred merchants in a ship. In order to save the five hundred people, the Buddha killed the robber. This is a story from the Jitavaka. Has the Buddha broken the precept of "non-killing"? He has. He did this so that five hundred lives could be spared. It was a wise decision. If the robber started killing, and you told yourself, "I can't kill, just let him kill everyone else," [audience laughter] this would be wrong. If you had the ability to stop the robber from killing, then you must immediately decide whether or not you should kill the robber. In order to save those five hundred people, the Buddha also has killed. Therefore precepts such as "refraining from killing" are absolutely not inflexible. You might think that they are rigid, but they are actually flexible.

Take the precept of "refraining from alcohol or intoxicants" as another example. During dinner, a dish of sesame chicken is served. Since wine is used in preparing the dish, you decide not to eat any of it. Everybody else is eating the sesame chicken except you. That kind of behavior is eccentric. [audience laughter] One of the four methods taught by the Buddha as a means of drawing other people to the Buddhadharma is "participate in the same activity as other people." When everyone is enjoying this chicken, even if you don't want any of it, you should not show that you are repulsed by the sight of others eating it. It would be worse if you start crying! [audience laughter] You should not act that way even if you are abiding by the precept of "non-drinking." Actually, if you want to share the Buddhadharma with other people, why not share it while sharing the sesame chicken? Or you can tell the others jovially, "Go ahead and have my share of the chicken since I am not having it." If it were me, I would have gone ahead and eaten the chicken. [audience laughter] It would not have bothered me. [audience applause] Among the four methods of drawing others to the Buddhadharma is to join in the same activity with other people.

That is why, when you ask me to sing for you, I comply even though I am not very good at it. We had some dancing girls come to take refuge in the True Buddha School. This has happened because I have gone dancing and drawn them to the Buddhadharma. [audience applause] If you want me to go up to heaven, I will go up to heaven. If you want me to go into the ocean, I will go into the ocean and swim for you. Actually it is not easy to be the Grand Master. Yesterday, some students were trying out the parallel bars, so I also demonstrated a few movements on them. People were wondering if I was a capable chi practitioner. Seeing what I was able to do on the parallel bars at the age of fifty, they were impressed. [applause] Among our students, Sifu Wong from England and another student from Alaska are both kung-fu masters, so I joined them and showed a few hands. [applause] Sifu Wong demonstrated his Mantis Fist while I showed my Crab-style Fist. [audience laughter and applause] This is known as "joining in the same activity as others."

So, precepts are flexible. One of the stanzas in the Fifty Stanzas of Guru-devotion states that stepping on the shadow of one's guru is a transgression as grave as destroying a pagoda. However, yesterday, while several hundred of us were climbing up the hill at the Rainbow Villa compound, how could one avoid stepping onto my shadow? According to the precepts, one is finished when one treads on my shadow. [audience laughter] That was why I told everyone to disregard the precept under such circumstances. The trail was so overcrowded with people going up and down, if you did not step on my shadow, you were alienating yourself from me and not joining in the same activity. It is true that the root guru is venerable, and one should be attentive and courteous to him but, under the crowded conditions yesterday, even if you had not deliberately wanted to tread on my shadow, you would have no choice when others pushed you. [laughter, audience laughter and applause] This is why precepts are flexible, and this flexibility has to do with knowing when and what to "relinquish"!

Everything is fundamentally empty, devoid of a separate existence. This is what Emptiness means in the Buddhadharma. When one reaches Perfect Enlightenment, whatever one does is in accordance with the Universal laws. In this state, one is free and abides completely in a blissful and tranquil condition. It is a perfect and transcendental state that flows naturally and spontaneously.

People have accused the True Buddha School of advocating "shen tung" [miracles] and manufacturing a lot of hot air! Where is the hot air? If one eats a lot of beans, of course there will be a lot of hot air and noise! [audience laughter]

That would be "chi tung" [passing of gas] and not "shen tung" [miracles]. Everything is spontaneous and just "as is." To heal others, I just visualized the Life Force from the Universe flowing into their bodies to empower them, and they became cured. This was not deliberately done for the purpose of creating miracles. The outside talk which says that the True Buddha School and I like to emphasize miracles is therefore groundless! I am just living my life "as is." Wherever I go, whatever I desire just manifests spontaneously. If people want to insist that there is some kind of "tung," then they must go and manufacture it — all this "shen tung" has nothing to do with me. [audience laughter and applause]

In Buddhism, Emptiness is this freedom from, and non-attachment to a self. Earlier, I asked, "Where are you from?" The answer "from the Empty Space" which someone gave was quite correct. Emptiness exists everywhere; everywhere is Emptiness. The innate Buddha Nature is fundamentally the Empty Space. Where does one live? One lives in the Empty Space. Only a realized Buddha has this kind of insight. [laughter, audience laughter and applause] The truly great accomplishment is to abide peacefully and tranquilly in this state of Emptiness. In this liberated and free condition wherein one's mind abides in the true and universal law of Emptiness, "precepts" become unnecessary, and thus there are no "precepts" for one to break

The Remarkable Lineage

The lineage of our school is remarkable. Yesterday, after hiking down the mountain, we saw a rainbow colored aureole around the sun. Actually, the same auspicious phenomenon of a circular rainbow also could be observed around the sun during the consecration of the Pootee Lei Tsang Temple at Vancouver. I had not told the sun, "Please do me a favor, put a wreath around yourself!" [audience laughter] I did not do that at all. It could have been a windy or rainy day, but a rainbow aureole appeared. I did not notice it until others pointed it out to me. This spontaneous phenomenon is a sign of auspiciousness, a validation of the remarkableness of the True Buddha School.

We have all originally come from the Great Sun Tathagata (Mahavairocana) who exists in the realm of Emptiness. From the Mahavairocana emerged the Female Buddha with Buddha Eyes whose two eyes are the site of Ch'ang Chi Kuang T'u (the Realm of Eternal Peace and Light). These two eyes further transformed into the Maha Twin Lotus Ponds. Inside the Twin Lotus Ponds Padmakumara manifested. When Padmakumara incarnated into the human world, he became Sheng-yen Lu. [audience applause] Actually I have not come here alone, many Padmakumaras have also come here. All of you have an affinity with Padmakumara and are all Padmakumaras. [audience applause] In the future, all of us will return to the Maha Twin Lotus Ponds — the realm of Female Buddha with Buddha Eyes — which is equivalent to returning to the realm of Mahavairocana. Therefore, the authentic lineage of the True Buddha School is as follows: Mahavairocana —> Female Buddha with Buddha Eyes —> Padmakumara. This lineage is one hundred percent accurate. [audience applause]

The Eightfold Path

Next on the list is the Eightfold Path, a topic that has already been discussed by many other Dharma masters. During my discourse on the Maha Prajnaparamita Heart Sutra, I delivered a detailed discussion on the Eightfold Path, which is one of the truths of the Four Noble Truths. You may read up on that book when it comes out to get a more detailed treatment on this subject. Here I will just briefly list them: "correct view," "correct thought," "correct speech," "correct livelihood," "correct conduct," "correct zeal," "correct memory," and "correct meditation or absorption." Many Buddhists know that the Eightfold Path refers to the eight methods taught by the Buddha as the correct means to reach Buddhahood. By following the Path, one will not become distracted, fall astray, or end up in an "evil tavern."

I will reiterate what I have discussed today. The Seven Branches of Enlightenment are: Investigation, Effort, Joy, Mindfulness, Alert Ease, Samadhi, and Relinquishing. The Eightfold Path is: correct view, correct thought, correct speech, correct livelihood, correct conduct, correct zeal, correct memory, and correct meditation.

What I have covered so far are the most important topics in the study of the Buddhadharma. What the Buddhadharma encompasses is, of course, very broad. For example, each of the ten Buddhist schools has numerous texts of its own. When one decides on a certain pathway, after making an investigation, one should then orient one's life toward that goal. A Tantric practitioner should concentrate on Tantric practices, while a general knowledge of the other nine schools would be quite sufficient. When one attains Enlightenment, one automatically understands the theories in the other schools.

For example, in the past, I found the classical Chinese language to be very difficult. The Chinese Buddhist sutras are written in a much simpler language. The writing of *Liao Chai Chih I* [*The Chronicle of Ghost Stories*] —a classical work — is intricate and abstruse. In the course of my vigorous reading of the Chinese classics, I laid aside the ones that were difficult and first read the ones that I could more easily understand. Strangely, when I finished reading everything else and came back to *Liao Chai Chih Yi*, I found I could understand it without having first translated it into modern day language. I can now read the abstruse classics and understand the profound meanings behind each word. What kind of phenomenon is this? It is the same with Dharma practice: success in one single Dharma practice leads to success in all Dharma practices. In the past, I have found the *Diamond Sutra* to be an abstruse work. The analogy of the Dharma and the raft, to which I referred earlier, was beyond my comprehension. In the sutra, the Buddha says, "Anyone claiming that I have delivered any teachings is vilifying me." The Buddha taught for forty-nine years, why did he disclaim it? In the future I can also make this statement, "I have never discussed any Dharma at the Rainbow Villa. If you claim that I have done so, you are being slanderous." Is it really this simple? No, it is not. When you read and understand its subtle meaning, you will experience the Dharma Taste. Interwoven into its subtlety is the Dharma Taste.

Now when I pick up and read a sutra with which I had difficulties before, I find I can understand it completely. I know what the Thus Come One [tathagata] means. [audience applause] Why is this so? Because the state of mind I now possess is not the same as before. I am now abiding in a state of Realization. Through the deep and intensive practice of one single Tantric practice, I opened up my heart. When I use this heart (mind) of Realization to read the Buddhist sutras, I am able to intuitively understand their meanings.[audience applause]

If you want to read the entire Buddhist Canon and research all the Buddhist theories first before attempting any single practice, you might find that several lifetimes would be required. Although Hu Shih [a famous Chinese scholar] made a study of Zen Buddhism, he did not engage in any actual practice. In the end, what he attained was just the knowledge of Zen, and not any true Realization.

When you attain Realization, you will be able to intuit the meanings of all sutras. Therefore, achieving yogic response in one practice is tantamount to achieving yogic response in ten thousand practices. Devote yourself deeply to one single practice, and you will achieve great accomplishments. The key word, therefore, is "depth" and not "width," as attested by the following statements of the Buddha's. "The benefit of actual practice surpasses that of a wide seeking of knowledge," and "Engaging in one single practice is more effective than doing multiple practices at the same time."

Earlier, one of you called out, "One is many." Perhaps that is why yesterday at the exercise ground, that student only performed one movement each on the single and parallel bars. When he was pressed to go on, he responded, "One is many!"

[audience laughter] Since he sounded so convincing, how could I not believe him! [audience laughter]

The truth is, once one attains Realization, one will see clearly into everything as if it were transparent. Prior to Enlightenment (even though one may be engaged in many practices) things will still appear "opaque." Therefore, one should concentrate on one single practice at a time to penetrate it deeply. This is the principle behind the study of the Buddhadharma.

Om Mani Padme Hum.

Seventh Day:
May 11, 1993

The Three Types of Enlightenment

Masters, fellow cultivators, good afternoon. [audience applause] Today is the seventh day of this discourse on An Overview of the Buddhadharma, and today I will be discussing the Ten Powers of a Buddha. The Ten Powers of a Buddha may be regarded as the ten wisdom-powers which are developed in an Enlightened being. Several days ago, I discussed the meaning behind the term "Enlightenment." An Enlightened being is someone who has achieved awakening. What kinds of wisdom-powers does such an awakened being have? This is what will be covered in today's teaching.

"Enlightenment" does not happen easily. Generally, when the subject is brought up in conversations, people profess that it is something very far away and hard to attain. Therefore, when a person is able to present proof that it is possible to achieve liberation and Enlightenment in one lifetime, this becomes an extraordinary and powerful testimony. If I told people today that they could, without taking any test, achieve Enlightenment in one second and liberation in three seconds, I suspect the number of people coming to take refuge would be even greater than it is. [laughter] Is such a feat really feasible? I suppose so. All I need is a big cudgel! [audience laughter] With one blow to the top of your head, you will attain Enlightenment. With three blows, you will be truly liberated! [audience laughter] Other than this, I don't think there is any method that can enable one to attain Enlightenment in one second and liberation in three seconds.

Since I have been talking about "Enlightenment" for the past few days, you have probably grown so accustomed to the term that you think you are already Enlightened. [audience laughter] Indeed, you may be Enlightened in a conceptual sense — you have understood everything in these seven days of teaching, including the concepts of Impermanence, Renunciation, and Egolessness — the three bases of arhathood. Arhathood is what one achieves when one is Enlightened through the Buddhist Hinayana. Many of the disciples of Buddha Shakyamuni, among them the ten chief disciples and five hundred arhats, had attained Enlightenment through the practice of these three tenets: Impermanence, Renunciation, and Egolessness. In the future when people ask you, "What have you learned in Buddhism?" You can reply, "All things are impermanent; all things are without self; and nirvana is tranquility." That is Enlightenment. [audience laughter]

A pet term used by Buddhists nowadays as an answer to another's inquiry is to say that they have learned "egolessness." Well, egolessness, very wonderful! However, if I give you a punch, you will probably become mad and discover your "ego" again. [laughter and audience laughter] What happens to your egolessness then? Many people claim they are Enlightened. I had a student call me up on the telephone to tell me that she had become Enlightened. When I heard the word "Enlightened," I became panic-stricken. [audience laughter] Why? I was afraid that it was a false kind of Enlightenment. Sure enough, a couple of days later, she called to tell me that she had become "unenlightened" again. As "Enlightenment" is no easy matter, I have categorized it into three types. How strange! Isn't there supposed to be only one kind of enlightenment? Why are there three types? I shall explain.

The First Type: A Fraud

The first type of "Enlightenment" is achieved by swindlers who scheme for certain objectives. Such people announce, "I am already enlightened. I have become a Buddha." In many people's minds, a Buddha is a very high and transcendental being with great powers. And people are often gullible, so they go to make homage and offerings to this "Buddha," hoping to get some blessing in return. They figure that with the blessing from this "Buddha," everything will be auspicious and money will roll in. However, before one sees any money rolling in, this "Enlightened" Buddha has already "rolled" away. [audience laughter] The point is, as long as one calls oneself an "Enlightened being," one can also proclaim this mantra: "Om,

Money Coming Home." [audience uproar of laughter and applause] This is to get money by fraud.

Some of these swindlers also scheme for sexual gains. How is this done? They will say, "I am a Buddha. I have this Buddha flavor or power in my body. There is only one way for you to receive this Buddha chi from me.... By touching me, you can receive some of it, but even more by embracing! If you embrace me, all my energy will go to you, and you will become the Buddha and I will become human. [audience uproar] When I practice and recharge my energy, we can do it again." These are just exploits of swindlers!

A swindler will tell you that he is Enlightened and can open your central channel for you. How is that done? "Bring me your money, and I will use a broomstick to help you." [audience laughter] Having practiced Buddhism all these years, I have yet to find a tool which will open up someone else's central channel. A feasibility is to transport some of the chi in one's own body into another person to enhance the circulation of their chi. Other than that, what can one use? A bicycle pump and applying it on the rump? [audience laughter] Perhaps that is the way to do it! Anyway, after receiving this promised "central channel opening," one goes home. At first one indeed feels a stream of energy in one's body, but after a while, one can't feel it anymore. What is happening? Your teacher calls you back, "You have to undergo the same procedure once a month; otherwise, the drain will be blocked!" Well, that seems to make sense. This then becomes "Om, Money Coming Home." [audience laughter]

Spiritual evolvement is achieved through self effort. Never expect any person to bestow anything upon you. As a guru, I will transmit the teaching to you, but you still have to do the practice yourself. How to distinguish the truly Enlightened being from the fraudulent ones? There is one simple test. Beware of an "Enlightened" teacher who requests money from you. A truly Enlightened being knows that the whole Universe is his and there is no need for him to ask for any money. Something is wrong if this "Enlightened" person tells you, "This is how much you have to pay me before I can give you the empowerment or esoteric teaching."

Among the so-called "Enlightened," some are swindlers. Therefore one has to be careful and make sure that such a claimer does not harbor any greed. Greed indicates that such a person does not yet have a heart of equanimity. An Enlightened being is an embodiment of benevolence, compassion, joy, and equanimity. How can someone be Enlightened if he or she still has greed? The heart of an Enlightened being is as vast and infinite as the Empty Space, and the whole Universe belongs to him. There is no longer the need for him to ask for money from others; whatever voluntary offerings he receives is sufficient. Therefore, an "Enlightened" person who asks for money indicates that greed still exists.

One also should observe the behaviors of such an "Enlightened" being. Does he or she get mad unreasonably? It is true that a "Fierce Deity" also gets mad, but is the action justified? Unreasonable anger and capriciousness are unacceptable.

Sometimes a guru will also test his students. When he meets a student who claims that she has attained egolessness, this guru will say, "Fine, you have attained egolessness, will you marry me?" This student then thinks to herself, "How can a guru say such a thing? How can I marry him? I am only in my late teens, and he is so old, with skin all wrinkled up like an orange peel." [audience laughter] Actually the guru may not want to marry at all, but since she claimed that she had reached egolessness, he decided to administer a test by asking her to marry him.

"Greed, hatred, and delusion" repudiate true Enlightenment. An Enlightened person will speak with Dharma Taste and wisdom. One should be careful if the "Enlightened" person shows a lack of wisdom, acts disorderly, and harbors greed. Be meticulous in distinguishing if a person is Enlightened. As for me, I will sometimes say something foolish, but remember that "a man of great wisdom often appears slow-witted." [audience laughter and applause] I also sometimes speak ironically. Although I have no personal considerations, I will say words that appear to be self-motivated. Although I am a cultivated person, I will sometimes fly into a rage. These are sometimes necessary as tests or for educational purposes. At such times, you have to judge with your insight. As you know, a person of great wisdom sometimes behaves just like everyone else; only occasionally will his wisdom and Dharma Taste be revealed. As Buddhist practitioners, you must be very meticulous in making such distinctions.

If you discover an "Enlightened" person to be of infinite greed, hatred, and delusion, what should you do? If you have already taken refuge in him, leave him silently, and refrain from slandering him. That is why the selection of a Buddhist teacher should be done carefully. After taking refuge, treat the guru with respect and learn from his virtues instead of his shortcomings. It would be good if you could learn the Buddhadharma from him; if not, go and learn from someone else. When you find a suitable practice for yourself, concentrate on it and devote yourself deeply to it. Use your wisdom to observe and analyze the teacher's words and actions to determine if they reflect the Buddha's teachings. If they do not, you will be losing your money and wasting your time.

If someone asks you to take refuge in him, and he has nothing to teach you, then you know he is a fraud. In contrast, when you came today to take refuge in me, I offered you *A Complete and Detailed Exposition on the True Buddha Tantric Dharma*, a practice replete with subtle Dharma Taste that you may experience and which leads you to Truth and Wisdom. [audience applause]

The Second Type: A Madman

The first type of "Enlightened" being is a fraud. What is the second type? The second type is a madman. A madman is a mentally ill person. One can tell if someone is crazy by the way he behaves. However, not all lunatics are true lunatics, some of them only act like lunatics. One must also be able to distinguish these. For example, Living Buddha Chi Kung [a famous Enlightened Buddhist teacher in China] only acted like a madman and was not mentally ill at all. His crazy behavior was just his way of imparting the Buddha's teachings. Once, he was observed grabbing lice from his chest and depositing them on his back. Then he would grab lice from his back and put them on his chest. People asked him, "Why don't you kill the lice?" He replied, "I abide by the precept of non-killing." People then asked, "Why are you moving the lice around?" Living Buddha Chi Kung replied, "This way the lice are unaccustomed to their new environment." [laughter and audience laughter] You see, he knew what he was doing. He was teaching that there were expedient methods that one could use without resorting to killing the lice. [audience laughter]

We also have a similar problem here at the Rainbow Villa. We discovered that some rats had recently immigrated here. [audience laughter] So we told Reverend Hsiao Kuang to set up a trap using a five gallon plastic pail. Some peanuts were placed inside the pail which was placed against a wall. When the rats smelled the peanuts, they climbed up the wall and jumped inside the pail. After eating the peanuts, they found that they could not get out because the plastic pail was too slippery. [audience laughter] Reverend Hsiao Kuang then took them for a ride and deposited them someplace very far away — this way they were unaccustomed to their new environment. [audience laughter] We learned this from the Living Buddha Chi Kung. He might act like a lunatic, but he knew what he was doing.

One time, Living Buddha Chi Kung went into the Ling Yin Temple. After removing the statue of the Dharma Protector Wei-t'o from his shrine, he placed it on his own back and started running away. People stopped him, "What are you doing with Wei-t'o on your back?" He replied, "We monks are relocating the temple." People were satisfied with his answer. Actually he was taking Wei-t'o on a demon-subjugating mission. A scholar's house was plagued by demons. By placing Wei-t'o inside the scholar's house, Wei-t'o would manifest to subjugate the demons. Although Living Buddha Chi Kung behaved like a madman, he was a rational lunatic.

If someone is incoherent in his speech, or improper in his thoughts and actions, then that person is not Enlightened. In the case of Living Buddha Chi Kung, a truly Enlightened being, although he sometimes acted in an unconventional way, his thoughts were sane and rational. All of his behavior, though idiosyncratic, was motivated by "correct thoughts." A person who acts erratically, speaks incoherently, and harbors unwholesome thoughts is a true lunatic.

I remember there was a case of a very famous, contemporary monk. He became ill and was hospitalized. What kind of illness did he have? I don't know the exact diagnosis, but it had to do with a deterioration in his mental status. I did not personally witness the following episode, so it may not be one hundred percent accurate, but many people were there when it happened. Anyway, the monk was lying on the bed when a beautiful nurse walked into the room to give him an injection. His hand reached out and grabbed the nurse at places that I cannot mention. [audience laughter] In addition, when a beautiful nurse or one of his female students came into the room, he would pull his pants down. When this first happened, his attendants and students would say, "Our teacher is Enlightened!" What did they mean? They meant that their teacher had reached an "Enlightened" condition that transcended differentiation. Can such behavior as pulling down one's pants upon seeing a woman and grabbing at beautiful nurses be that of an Enlightened being? No, that was not Enlightenment. That is why he is now locked up and is no longer seen in public. If he were really displaying a mind transcending differentiation, why didn't he grab at the male doctors or pull down his pants when his male students visited? A true transcendence of differentiation would have been to pull down his pants regardless of whom he met. Was he afflicted with dementia? He may have been suffering from dementia, but he was still able to distinguish between the sexes.

I do not think that is a case of Enlightenment at all. The truth is, that monk had been suppressing his desires for a very long time, ever since he was young. As an eminent monk, he had always carried himself in a dignified way and surrounded himself with an inviolate aura of holiness. Then came the day he lost control of his mental faculties, and the floodgate to his desires was completely opened. It is a case of lunacy and not Enlightenment.

There are many lunatics inside mental institutions. Take a look at the patients in the wards; they can all see gods and ghosts. They are all agitated. Some claim that they are being chased, but we cannot see anyone pursuing them. Another will say that the Virgin Mary has appeared to him. Still another will be kneeling and praying, his whole body shaking, because he thinks Jesus has come. Sometimes he thinks it is the Buddha, and sometimes it is the Goddess Matzu. From morning till night, he has numerous "visitors" coming to talk to him. Let me tell you, he also thinks he is "Enlightened." Beware of so many "Enlightened" people. If this is Enlightenment, I would rather remain unenlightened. [audience laughter] To become Enlightened this way is to fly over the cuckoo's nest. [audience laughter] Although these patients may seem to have all kinds of extrasensory abilities, including psychic vision and hearing, they have no control.

The Third Type: Master of Tao

What is a truly Enlightened person? A truly Enlightened person is a "Master of Tao." Such a person lives in the present, and all of his actions are in accord with nature. Free, at ease and contented, he abides in "as-is-ness." Whatever happens to him will not make him wild with joy or grief. Nothing ever perturbs him. In other words, to him, nothing ever happens, so he is able to handle every matter skillfully with his penetrating wisdom. Manifesting through him is a profound, subtle, and non-deliberate virtue. His heart is pure, stainless, and transparent, hiding nothing — this is a very important point.

This condition of Enlightenment has been compared to a sunny untainted sky that stretches forever. The state of mind of an Enlightened person is completely transparent and filled with infinite bliss. He or she is neither gloomy nor depressed, for living amid the Dharma Taste is a wonderful and transcendental joy. As described in the High King Avalokitesvara Sutra that we chant, it is a condition characterized by "Permanence, Bliss, Identity, and Purity." "Permanence" is "to flow in synchronization with nature," to be at ease and to experience true freedom. "Bliss" is the infinite bliss grounded in Dharma Taste and in the absence of emotional afflictions. "Identity" is the "Universal Self," the source and its myriad manifestations expressed in earth, water, fire, wind, and space. "Purity" is complete purity and serenity.

Talking about this "Identity," someone remarked that during this discourse at the Rainbow Villa, the four elements of earth, water, fire, and wind have all come into context. Every day you have had to take a car ride to come here. You have come by land, by "earth," and not by "air." The tires of your automobiles have rubbed against the earth for forty minutes to bring you here and take you back. What about water? The other day we had some showers when the dark clouds gathered and turned into rain. What about fire? Yesterday afternoon, the temperature suddenly shot up, and we all felt hot and muggy. What about wind? Yesterday morning, the wind was so strong that one of our tents was blown away. Earth, water, fire, and wind are all here. They should not have bothered us, because our bodies, like the physical Universe, are made up of the same four elements. No separation exists between these elements and one's "self." This is "Identity." A state of well-being is attained when one yields to and meditates with the earth, water fire, and wind in the Universe and in one's body respectively. If these four elements are in harmony, one will not become ill and catch cold. [audience applause]

Many students arrived a little earlier for this teaching, and some have colds. I was somewhat worried that I might catch a cold from someone. If one of you coughed in my face just as I breathed in, several thousand viral germs would have entered my body. Although I am a chi practitioner, I would have been coughing for the last seven or eight days if my immune system were weak. How could I teach if I lost my voice? It is an uncomfortable thought. So, during these last few days, when you coughed at me, I immediately performed the Armor Protection and manoeuvered the chi to protect myself. [audience laughter and applause] After all, would a person who coughs uncontrollably in front of the video camera look like an Enlightened being? [audience laughter] People would say, "The Asian sickman! What kind of Enlightened being is he?"

What is a chi practitioner? In Taiwan we used to watch a puppet show called "The Chi Practitioner of the Golden Gourd Hut." [audience laughter] Tantric Buddhists are all chi practitioners or yogis. A yogi cultivates the chi to open up channels and elevate the light drops in the subtle energy body. When the chi is full, one's physical body and immune system will be strong and impervious to all kinds of illnesses. The goal of cultivation is to arrive at the "vajra indestructible body" that is immune to all afflictions. However, I should not boast. Fate decrees that one sometimes must experience a certain grave illness in one's life. If this is so, then there is nothing I can do about it. [laughter] I dare not boast, as each time I have boasted in the past, I was finished! [audience laughter]

"Permanence, Bliss, Identity, Purity." Permanence is to be eternally present. A person residing in "Permanence" is always at ease and lets events take their course. Although no noticeable features appear to distinguish one from others, one's inner world is filled with great Dharma Taste and infinite subtle "Bliss." One always identifies with the earth, water, fire, wind, and air, and each interacts, permeates, and combines with each other. One resides in "Purity" because one is totally pure of attachments. Such a person is an Enlightened person.

An Enlightened person is a Master of Tao, a Dharma Prince, a Son of Buddha. He or she is neither a lunatic nor a swindler, although the three superficially resemble each other. You have to be careful not to get them mixed up, as many self-proclaimed "Enlightened" persons use the Buddhadharma to swindle others. However, some truly Enlightened beings do act like madmen. Didn't I name one of my essays "Crazy Dharma King Sheng-yen Lu"? Although I sometimes act like a lunatic, I am rational, at ease with myself, always exist in the present, and am free. [audience applause]

On the conceptual level, you are all Enlightened, but you may not necessarily be Enlightened in reality. A person has approached me, saying, "Grand Master, I am already Enlightened. Can I tell you something very important?" So I asked him what was on his mind. Who would have thought that an Enlightened person would need a personal consultation? After half a day, it turned out that he wanted to know why the chickens at his house had been refusing to eat. Did he think I had something to do with his chickenfeed? I still don't know. [audience laughter] Therefore, pay attention, words of an Enlightened person will shine forth with wisdom. Such a person is an embodiment of wisdom and is without any traces of greed, hatred, or delusion.

Make a wise choice among the three types of "Enlightened" beings. One criterion by which to measure is that this teacher should be able to explain the Buddhadharma and its practices in a rational way. The True Buddha Tantric Dharma, for example, can only be presented together by someone who has, for a very long time, been profoundly involved in its study and practice.

The Ten Powers of a Buddha

(1) Omniscience

Today we will look at the Ten Powers of a Buddha. A Buddha is an Enlightened being who, first of all, possesses a "complete awareness." When someone came to see Buddha Shakyamuni, the Buddha would soon perceive the entire history of that person from beginning to end. This signifies a complete knowledge of the workings of the Universe. This kind of ability is one of the manifestations of the wisdom-power of the Buddha.

(2) Knowledge of the Karma of Every Being

The second power is "knowledge of the karma of every being, past, present, and future." This is really an extension of the first power. How does the Buddha find out about one's previous incarnations? Through bodily signs. Every person has signs on his or her body revealing past and future incarnations. This knowledge becomes available when one develops the Buddha wisdom. As I have said before, all of you are, in my eyes, "antiques" [audience laughter] although most of you are only within an age range from about twenties to fifties. What you have done in your past lives have left marks on your body, and it is apparent to me although I cannot casually divulge it. You may only be in your thirties but, if you lived to ninety in your last life, you would be a composite one hundred twenty years old. And if one includes all the successive lives prior to the last, you may actually be several thousand or ten thousand years old. Aren't you an antique then? An Enlightened being, whose Tathagata wisdom is developed, can read the history of transmigration through the bodily signs one carries. How many wholesome and unwholesome deeds has one done in one's previous life? How much hindrance and merit has one accumulated? All these things are revealed through signs on one's body.

(3) Knowledge to End All Illusion of Every Kind

A Buddha knows the ways to liberate oneself from illusion of every kind. What are these ways? As I have explained, one must observe "Impermanence" in all worldly phenomena, engender the desire of "Renunciation," and practice to attain "Egolessness." An Enlightened being with Buddha wisdom knows how to teach this path of liberation in a very lucid and succinct way. What I am teaching you today is this "knowledge to end all illusion and be liberated from emotional afflictions." [audience applause]

(4) Knowledge of the Desires and Moral Direction of Every Being

Next, a Buddha has "knowledge of the positive and negative attributes" of every being. Positive attributes are to be put to good use, while negative attributes need to be overcome. According to Vajrayana teachings, these attributes are habitual tendencies carried over from the previous life. If one was a chicken in the previous life, then one will have very strong desires in this life. If one was a snake that attacked everyone crossing its path, then one will have great hatred in this life. If one was a pig before, then one will have great delusion in this life. Thus these three animals serve respectively as symbols for greed, hatred, and delusion.

Such knowledge is not used for the purpose of discrimination. From a teacher's point of view, knowledge of an individual's habitual tendencies enables him to teach in accordance.

Among the disciples of Buddha Shakyamuni was a monk by the name of Kalodayin who enjoyed great popularity among women. As a result, he was always the one sent by the Buddha when opportunities arose to teach the Dharma to women. Unlike Shariputra, MahaMaudgalyayana, and Mahakashyapa, who distanced themselves from women, Kalodayin enjoyed the company of women, and women also lit up and agreed with him when he spoke. Thus he was the Buddha's ambassador to women's groups. However, Kalodayin ended up being murdered, largely because he became too intimately involved in someone's household.

Spiritual cultivators sometimes have to avoid becoming too much involved in other people's family lives. My own teacher gave me this precept, "Unless you are invited, do not casually call at somebody else's home." Today I would only go to your house if you invited me. I would not just drop in. This is to minimize secular involvement. In those days, Kalodayin often frequently dropped in to socialize at other people's homes. This particular propensity contributed to his murder.

Buddha Shakyamuni also had a disciple by the name of Dolanlanta. Dolanlanta was a shrew among the nuns. She was most disgusted with Mahakashyapa because he was so serious that his eyes never looked at women. In the morning, if Dolanlanta saw Mahakashyapa, she would shout abuses at him, "What lousy luck! I have to run into a heretic like you early in the morning." The Buddha had established "the Eight Pure Ways," the eight methods used by nuns to pay respect to the monks, but Dolanlanta would have none of them. She totally ignored that Mahakashyapa was a monk and a chief disciple of the Buddha, and kept on shouting abuses at him. But the Buddha was aware of her attributes. Instead of evicting her from the community, he used many ways to educate her.

So, in those days, the Buddha taught the students in accordance with their aptitudes. Since Dolanlanta was a fierce person, she would be the chief defender when the community was attacked. Sometimes being a shrew had its advantages — before the other party could utter a sound, she would already have shot them down with words in a rapid-fire fashion. In her place, a gentle or courteous nun would have lost. In arguing, these shrews are definitely useful. [audience laughter]

(5) Knowledge of How to Liberate Every Being

The fifth wisdom-power of an Enlightened being is knowing how every being can be liberated. This is also teaching in accordance with each being's aptitudes.

When a Buddha speaks, his words will transform into tens of thousands of "Dharma voices" and travel to faraway places. Once MahaMaudgalyayana flew to the Eastern Pure Land and yet was still able to hear, even from there, the Buddha's teachings. The sound of Dharma is very profound and subtle. Sometimes one kind of sound spoken by the Buddha can transform into ten thousand kinds of sound, to teach ten thousand different kinds of beings. This is the magnetizing power of the Buddha. [audience applause]

One time the Buddha disappeared from the spiritual community for almost three months. Nobody knew where he had gone. It turned out that he had traveled to the Trayastrimsas Heaven to speak on the Ksitigarbha Bodhisattva Original Vow Sutra for the Lady Maya. This was discovered by Aniruddha, one of the ten chief disciples, who had used his supreme divine-sight to locate the Buddha's whereabouts. How was the Buddha able to travel to the Trayastrimsas Heaven? This was "deva-foot ubiquity," an ability to appear at will at any place. It was not a case of out-of-body travel, as the Buddha had brought his physical body with him to the Trayastrimsas Heaven.

I have noticed a strange movement during my recent Chi Kung practices. My two arms become fully extended, then start flapping, as if I were a bird in flight. I think this might mean that one day both my body and spirit also will soar up to the heavens to speak on the Dharma. [audience applause]

(6) Knowledge of All Stages of Samadhi

The sixth power of the Buddha is knowledge of the various stages of spiritual levels or realms reached in Samadhi. As a Buddhist practitioner, do you know which level or realm you have reached? How much realization have you attained? How much energy or power do you have? How mature are you spiritually? All these factors determine your spiritual level. Are you at the level of the arhat, or prateykabuddha, or bodhisattva, or Buddha, or Buddha-in-waiting? One of the ten powers of the Tathagata is this ability to observe and determine the spiritual level of an individual.

Buddha Shakyamuni, besides teaching at the Trayastrimsas Heaven, has also taught at the Dragon Palace. If one day I pulled a disappearing act, where would I go? I would go and play chess with Mahakashyapa. [laughter and audience applause] Of course this would have to be done very secretly, so no one would ever become suspicious of my disappearance. Chi practitioners who want to attain the "deva-foot ubiquity" have to scale high on spirit and low on flesh. When the balance is tipped heavily on the side of spirit, and the desires of the flesh are minimal, one's chi will merge into the Universe, enabling one to travel anywhere above or below. With this mighty power, one can even visit the hells. In the Ksitigarbha Original Vow Sutra, when the Kuang Mu Maiden [a former incarnation of Ksitigarbha] asked the Poisonless Ghost King what kind of people could visit the hells, she received this answer, "Only two kinds of people: those who are led there by their own negative karma and those with the mighty power."

A Buddha can visit the hells through his mighty power. I also have traveled to hell to see a student of mine who was having a hard time there. Instead of practicing the True Buddha Tantric Dharma, he had spent his days drinking and offering the excuse, "I can't help it since I have to socialize with my business associates." Socializing? With two mistresses on the outside and a mind that was filled with filthy thoughts and desires, his main preoccupation was to make more money. For whom was he making all this money? For himself? I don't think he got to spend it. For his children and grandchildren? One's descendents have their own fate, so why work so hard for them? Bear in mind that spiritual cultivation is more important. If you don't start now, it might be too late. Some students say, "I will start my practice next year." How many "next years" are there? Maybe you have only half a year left in your life, and by then it will be too late. The one trouble shared by many students is that they keep postponing their practice. They rationalize to themselves, "I have at least taken refuge and been chanting mantras, I will save the precious practice for later when I can spare more time for it."

Therefore, the simple truth is, when the ratio of chi [spirit] to flesh is high, the realm of "deva-foot ubiquity" will manifest and one will ascend to the heavens; when the ratio is low, one will descend to the hells.

(7) Knowledge of the Law of Karma

The seventh power is "knowledge of the law of karma." One reaps whatever one sows. Master Lian-zhi told me this one sign she had seen inside a hospital, "You are what you eat." This sign is stating simply the law of karma. "What you eat" is the cause and "what you will become" is the consequence. As the Chinese saying goes, "One harvests peas by planting peas and melons by planting melons," "Good and bad actions give rise to good and bad results respectively." This is the law of karma. A Buddha is well aware of the direction and consequences of all laws, and knows what one can do to extricate oneself from or avoid the karmic consequences.

(8) Divine-Sight

Among the chief disciples, Aniruddha was known for his supreme "divine-sight" which enabled him to locate the Buddha when the latter went to teach at the Trayastrimsas Heaven. How did this divine-sight power of his come into being? Actually, prior to the development of this power, Aniruddha was most fond of taking naps, just like many of our students here. Whenever the Buddha lectured, Aniruddha would start nodding his head. This was how he would look while chanting and counting the mantra rosary. [Grand Master demonstrates.] "Om, Ah-mi-deh-wah, Seh; Om, Ah-mi-deh-wah, Seh; Om...." [laughter and audience laughter]

When the Buddha saw this he was alarmed, since he was well aware of the direction and consequences of karma. So he spoke to Aniruddha, "If you go on like this, you are going to end up in the Dragon King's Palace." "Dragon King's Palace? It is not bad to be a follower of the Dragon King, is it?" [audience laughter] "Not if you become the palatial clam! Being a deep sea clam lying on the ocean floor is not all that fun. Always covered up by the shell and without any exposure to sunlight, one could easily sleep for several thousand years."

I have mentioned this before: if you tend to fall asleep

during Samadhi practice, keep your eyes open, as closed eyes induce sluggishness. If this fails, try pushing your hands against each other in a hand-shake position. The force generated this way will give you a little energy boost. Also try keeping the spine straight, the chin tucked in, and the eyes focused ahead, just like a soldier. [laughter and audience laughter] If all else fail, get up and walk around while chanting mantra at the same time. Of course, one may be excused if one is not feeling well or has the flu. Also, if one has travelled from afar, such as from Taiwan or Southeast Asia, one may suffer from jet-lag during the first several days, so dozing off is then excusable. However, during ordinary times, one should not doze off every time one does the daily Samadhi practice. As the Buddha has put it, "One might as well go to the Dragon King Palace and learn from the Dragon King. I can't teach you anymore."

Back to Aniruddha. After the Buddha spoke with Aniruddha, Aniruddha vowed never to close his eyes again. He started meditating very diligently while keeping his eyes open. In the end, due to a prolonged period without sleep, he lost his eyesight. At that point, the Buddha taught Aniruddha to develop the divine-sight. One must have determination and an indomitable will if one wants to make progress and attain great accomplishment on the path. [audience applause]

Included in the Fifty Stanzas of Guru Devotion is the recommendation that one should refrain from rocking from side to side when the guru is teaching. When one does that, it is as if one is saying "no" to my teaching and trying to make trouble for me, isn't it? [audience laughter] You are shaking your head to everything that I say. This is showing disrespect for one's guru, [laughter] and it is unacceptable.

The image of our school is also very important. Sometimes during Dharma ceremonies, the Five Buddha Crown headpieces of the masters look like they are about to fall off. [audience laughter] If I appear to be dozing off, I could at least offer the explanation that I am nodding to the Buddhas, [audience laughter] "OK, I know!" [Grand Master nods his head to audience laughter and applause] Although I can justify that I am communicating with the Buddhas, it becomes a problem when those of you sitting around me also start nodding, with your headpieces almost falling off. Therefore, I wish those of you who doze off, or get tired easily, would improve your chi. When your chi is full, your energy will be vigorous. This chi then becomes the "truck" on the "freeway," as I have mentioned, and you can set out like the "dare-to-die corps." A spiritual cultivator should have exuberant energy. Someone who is listless and dispirited does not look at all like an esoteric practitioner.

(9) Access to the Memory Vault

The ninth power is having an access to one's previous memories. Some people say that in the heaven is a memory vault storing the records of the past lives of all humans. If one day one travels to that vault and wants to review the past lives, the official in charge will show one the video tapes, then one will understand the karmic causes and consequences throughout all these lifetimes.

Actually all these review tapes are in our own memories; we do not need to travel to the memory vault in heaven. As long as one opens up the "thousand-petalled chakra" and attains the realization of the Dharma Body Buddha, one will have access to the memory vault. In fact, this power which developed from the thousand-petalled chakra enables a Buddha to find out both his past and future five hundred lifetimes. With this power, a Buddha not only can find out his own history, but also the causes of other people's fate. I have tapped into the memory vault to find out why some of the spiritual teachers are able to build huge temples, attract great following of students, and propagate the teaching so successfully. It turned out that the Brahmadeva is behind some of them. From an analysis of their teaching, we can find out which deva is supporting them.

Many prominent monks and nuns have a long history behind them. When one develops this power to tap into the memory vault, one may perceive clearly which deva is behind and supporting each of them. One day when you attain Enlightenment, you will have this ability to gain access to not just your own past history, but that of others as well.

(10) Eternal State of Non-Birth

The tenth power is entering into the "eternal state of non-birth." The level reached by the Arhats is that of an eternal state of non-birth. This state of eternal non-birth may also be termed the "tranquil state of nirvana." When one attains the ten divine powers of the Tathagata, one knows that all of one's births, present, past, or future, are all fundamentally non-births. When one unifies with the Universal Consciousness, one abides in the condition of nirvana. When one emerges, one is in the state of the Bliss Body and Emanation Body. When one enters into the Universal Consciousness, one abides in the condition of the Dharma Body, or the condition of "non-birth." When you attain this realization, you will transcend all fears and delusions.

If word reached you today that the largest newspaper of a certain country ran a front page article denouncing you, you would have no fear. If little booklets denouncing you were being distributed around the world, you would have no fear. If someone filed a legal suit against you, you would have no fear. If someone warned you to be careful because there were nine people plotting to harm you, you would have no fear. Why would you be able to transcend all fears? Because you have realized that all existences, whether past, present, or future, are fundamentally "non-existences." You are a holy being abiding in the condition of Nirvana and Tranquility — you are totally immovable and beyond any perturbation. This is known as "transcending all fears and delusions." [audience applause]

Therefore, a spiritual adept with clear prescience that someone is laying in wait at a certain place to murder him would still go forward willingly and calmly to meet his own death. What does this prove? It proves that he has already "transcended all fears and delusions"! Take MahaMaudgalyayana, for example. He was well aware that he would be murdered in that lifetime, and he willingly accepted this fate as it was a result of a previous karmic action. When a karmic consequence caught up with him, he knew it was time to face up to it and have it neutralized. After all, what difference did it make? He had already attained the state of mind that transcended all relative existences, past, present, or future, and become totally immersed in the Universal Consciousness. This is abiding in the "eternal state of non-birth" — the tenth power of a Buddha.

To reiterate the ten powers of a Buddha, they are: (1) omniscience,(2) knowledge of the karma of every being, (3) knowledge to end all illusions of every kind, (4) knowledge of the desires and moral direction of every being, (5) knowledge of how to liberate every being, (6) knowledge of all stages of samadhi, (7) knowledge of the law of karma, (8) divine-sight, (9) access to the memory vault, and (10) abiding in the eternal state of non-birth.

"Omniscience," the first of the ten Buddha powers, can also be understood in the following way. Every human being is made up of the elements of "earth, water, fire, and wind" just as the Universe is. The elements in our bodies are interlinked with the corresponding elements of the Universe. If a person understands this truth and is able to respectively unify the elements of "earth, water, fire, and wind" in his body with the "earth, water, fire, and wind" of the universe, then (through the elements of "earth, water, fire, and wind" of the universe) he will be able to identify and corroborate with all phenomena in the world and will gain a clear knowledge about all things. This is a very important point. The chi and meridians [channels through which the chi travels] of the human body and those of the universe are all interlinked. A vajra indestructible body that is immune to all illnesses can only be attained by merging the microcosmic "earth, water, fire, and wind" of one's body with the macrocosmic "earth, water, fire, and wind" of the Universe.

The Ten Epithets of a Buddha

What is a Buddha? There are ten epithets used to describe a Buddha.

The first epithet is "Tathagata," literally the thus-gone one. What is a thus-gone one? A thus-gone one is also a thus-come, thus-perfected one. Paradoxically, the thus-gone or thus-come one has actually never come or gone anywhere. This is one of the ten chief titles of a Buddha.

The second epithet is "worthy of offerings." When you meet with a truly Enlightened person, a Buddha, you should make offerings to him because he is worthy of it. Although you have not meditated on it, you will find yourself voluntarily making offerings to him. Why? Because he is the embodiment of the Universal Consciousness, and a magnetizing power from him will cause veneration to spontaneously sprout in your heart.

The third epithet is "fully Enlightened one." This refers to the power of omniscience that I have just discussed. The pervasive radiance of a Tathagata also shines in the world of darkness, that is why he possesses a true knowledge of every event and phenomenon.

The fourth epithet is "gifted in knowledge and conduct." A Buddha knows what spiritual pathways to take and how many practice stages one must go through to reach liberation.

The fifth epithet is "well-gone one." A Tathagata goes and comes as he wishes. He is completely in control of his own births and deaths. A "well-gone one" can disappear or appear in any wonderful way he chooses. These transformations are just a form of transcendental play the Buddha or Tathagata engages in. When he wants to leave, he will leave. When he wants to come, he will come. He is completely free.

Lately I have been contemplating the place of my next birth. The idea of being born a Westerner does not appeal too much to me. I have been thinking about whether to be born in mainland China or not. We know that, in the past, people from Hong Kong treated people from Taiwan quite highhandedly [audience laughter] and used to take advantage of them because the Taiwanese were much more uncouth. That was why the Taiwanese were nicknamed "the sweet potatoes." [audience laughter] But I have discovered that people in Hong Kong now are being taken advantage of by people from mainland China. The Chinese from mainland China are smarter, so we call them "taros." "Taros" seem to be more valuable than "sweet potatoes." The role of feng shui does make a difference. You know, the facial features of girls from Taiwan do somewhat resemble sweet potatoes. [audience laughter] Girls from mainland China, due to the influence of different feng shui, are "taros" and have different dispositions and temperaments. Different geographical environments nurture and produce different types of people. For example, the Kaoshan and Yamei tribesmen of Taiwan, the Tibetans, and the American Indians all have distinct temperaments and dispositions of their own.

So, which country should I pick as the place of my next birth? Although Thailand is a Buddhist country, the Hinayana Buddhism prevalent there does not offer a very broad vision. Ceylon was one of the countries which was directly introduced to the original Buddhism from India, and many of its Buddhist canons still exist in the form of Pali, but their culture is too sheltered from the rest of the world. In India, one would have to contend with Hinduism and Sikhism, and the country is impoverished and underdeveloped, so I am not counting on it. The idea of being born in mainland China is frightening [laughter and audience laughter]. To be born in Taiwan is to be the "sweet potatoes" again. Hong Kong — truthfully, I have an aversion to the Cantonese dialect. [audience laughter] Really, Cantonese is so stiff sounding that it is harsh on one's ears. My "corresponding office" has become "a little Hong Kong" now since most of the volunteers working there are students from Hong Kong. When they talk, harsh sounding Cantonese flies around as if they are quarrelling with each other.

So, if neither a Western nor Eastern birth appeals to me, where will my next birth be? I have not come to a decision yet.

A "well-gone one" comes and goes in wonderful ways.

A Tathagata is a "well-gone one" because he engages in the creative transformation of himself in wonderful and subtle ways. He is completely free and has mastery over his own births and deaths. The spiritual practice I teach you today can liberate you from births and deaths and allow you to experience what it is like to be a "well-gone one." [audience applause]

The next epithet is "knower of the worlds." What is a "knower of the worlds"? A Tathagata understands all world knowledge. The "five sciences or studies" in Buddhism refer to world knowledge such as the art of healing and the art of crafts. The art of crafts can run the gamut from video-taping to sculpture, painting, and poetry writing.

Another epithet is "unsurpassable teacher" or "supreme master." This means that no one else in the world is higher than the supreme master, a Tathagata is always the highest teacher. One might wonder, among the Five Directions Buddhas, who is ranked the first? If Mahavairocana is the first, then is Amitabha the second, Amoghasiddhi the third, Akshobhaya the fourth, and Ratnasambhava the fifth? No, they are all ranked the first! One way of describing them is to consider Mahavairocana as number one, Amitabha as the first of number one [audience laughter], Amoghasiddhi as the second of number one, so on and so forth — they are all number ones. When you become a Tathagata, you reach the highest rank, surpassing everything else.

Another epithet is "taming master." In Chinese this term is rendered as "taming husband." A "husband" is a giant, do not take it literally as in "husbands and wives." Who had Buddha Shakyamuni as a husband? Yashodhara? [laughter] Here husband means a giant or great person. To tame is to adjust, a little higher here or a little lower there, to strike a balance. The task of a living Tathagata in the world is to help human beings adjust their psyche. If there is misalignment, he aligns it. If it is too tight, he loosens it. If it is too loose, he tightens it. A taming master is thus a great engineer of the psyche.

"Buddha" is also one of the ten epithets, and it means an

"awakened one." The remaining epithet is "world honored one."

I shall repeat the list once more, the ten epithets are: "Tathagata," "worthy of offering," "fully enlightened one," "gifted in knowledge and conduct," "well-gone one," "knower of the worlds," "unsurpassable teacher," "taming master," "awakened one," and "world honored one." Sometimes in the place of the "awakened one," "teacher of gods and men" is used. A Buddha is a teacher of humans, as well as heavenly beings.

Today I have discussed the "ten powers" and "ten epithets" of a Buddha" in addition to analyzing the three types of Enlightenment. Although this discourse is entitled "An Overview of the Buddhadharṁa," it is actually more accurate to call it "A Discourse on the Focal Points in Buddhism." One cannot really do justice to a subject as broad as an overview without devoting a significant amount of time to it. Buddha Shakyamuni spent forty-nine years expounding on the Dharma; how can we expect to cover all of his teachings in a mere seven or eight days? It is impossible. So what I have done is to extract the essential points and lay them down as groundwork for you.

This, then, is the summary of this discourse outlined in a numerical system:

"One" refers to the "initial" step consisting of the graduated stages of "Faith, Comprehension, Practice, and Realization."

"Two" refers to the two doorways of "theoretical" versus "practical" approaches, and how to make a selection between the two.

"Three" refers to the Three Non-outflow Studies of Discipline, Stability, and Wisdom.

"Four" refers to the Four Noble Truths, a very important as well as one of the earliest teachings of Buddha Shakyamuni. "Accumulation" causes "suffering" while "paths" results in "extinction of sufferings." An understanding of the Four Noble Truths is one good way to enter into the door of the Buddhadharma.

"Five" refers to the Five Roots and the Five Positive Agents. By engaging in the Five Positive Agents [faith, energy, thought, stability, and wisdom], one can uproot the various negative tendencies of the Five Roots [five sensory organs].

"Six" refers to the Six Perfections. A great bodhisattva practices the Six Perfections in myriad ways to help sentient beings to reach liberation. Bodhicitta, the limitless compassion to attain liberation for the sake of the welfare of all beings, is a very great aspiration. Although a bodhisattva may have not yet attained Enlightenment, he or she is able to learn and teach at the same time. Thus the monks and nuns command our respect even though they have not yet reached realization.

"Seven" refers to the Seven Bodhyanga, or the Seven Factors of Enlightenment.

"Eight" refers to the Eightfold Noble Path.

"Ten" refers to the Ten Powers of the Buddha.

With the founding of our school, the traditional "ten" schools in [Chinese] Buddhism now becomes the "eleven" schools. [audience applause]

How about "Twelve"? It refers to the twelve links that constitute the chain of conditioned arising. Although I have not touched on this topic, I have written a great deal about this subject in my books. This time I also did not explain in great length the Eightfold Noble Path because a thorough discussion of the subject was given during my discourse on the Prajnaparamita Heart Sutra.

As a matter of fact, an understanding of the doctrines referred to in the above system is tantamount to an understanding of "the Focal Points in Buddhadharma." If you want to expand your knowledge to include all the various doctrines advocated by the ten other schools, such as "the three aspects of the one mind," "calming the mind and developing the special insight," "teachings of Monk Tu Shun, the founder of the Hua Yan School," "the doctrine that nothing exists from mind," and "the three treatise" etc., you may do so. However, if you are already a master of our school, you should study and obtain a very clear understanding of the doctrines of the ten other schools. In the future, when people from the other schools come to ask you questions, you will not be entirely ignorant and will be able to answer them. You have to have a fundamental knowledge of all the doctrines of every school and be able to explain and penetrate deeply into them. By studying and practicing the True Buddha Tantric Dharma, you should be able to understand all Buddhist doctrines. In that sense, this discourse of the "focal points" also would become "an overview" of the Buddhdharma. [audience applause]

This concludes the discussion of "An Overview of the Buddhadharma." Tomorrow will be a "question and answer session." Write down your questions on a piece of paper. They will be collected and I will answer them. Do not ask any personal questions. It is important that only questions pertaining to this discourse on the Buddhadharma be submitted.

The day after tomorrow has been scheduled for "empowerments." You should discuss among yourselves which particular empowerments you would like to receive.

This then brings this discourse of An Overview of the Buddhadharma to an auspicious completion. Thank you for your attendance.

Om Mani Padmi Hum.

Eighth Day:
May 3, 1993

Question and Answer Session

Masters, fellow cultivators, good afternoon. [audience applause] On this eighth day of the discourse on An Overview of the Buddhadharma, we are going to have a Question and Answer session. I have here a pile of papers with questions submitted by many of you. On going over them briefly, I noted that many people listed several questions on one sheet. I hope I have enough time to answer all of them. Thank you. [audience applause]

[The Grand Master then proceeded to answer the questions, after first reading the questions aloud.]

[Q-1] Grand Master Lu, although the other day you explained how "all phenomena arise and disintegrate due to causes and conditions," I am so thick that I still have trouble understanding it. May I ask, from where do causes and conditions arise? [laughter and audience laughter] What determines the duration of the various phases of transmigration? Why do some ghosts stay around in the world for a couple of decades? Don't they have to be reborn to another realm? What is a human? Why do humans act in a certain way? Why do humans have thoughts? What gives rise to thoughts?

[A] It was signed "a student" and no name was given. Very well. [laughter and audience laughter] If I find out who he is, he is going to get three big strikes from me, [audience uproar and applause] because these are very rigorous questions put up to test the speaker.

When the Buddha discussed that "all phenomena arise and disintegrate due to causes and conditions," he was referring to the "doctrine of interdependence," although he did not elaborate on the specific "causes and conditions." However, he taught that the first of the "twelve links of existence" is "ignorance." "Ignorance" gives rise to "separate existence." In the absence of "ignorance," there is no "separate existence." In the Buddhist doctrine of "twelve links of existence," "ignorance" is the earliest cause. I can only offer you this explanation.

Why are you born? Dark clouds precede rain. Without dark clouds, there would not be any rain. What precedes dark clouds? Water vapors. What precedes water vapors? Water. What precedes water? Rain. [audience laughter] The "causes and conditions" are undergoing transmigration.

Then you ask, "Where do causes and conditions come from?" The Buddha said that "ignorance" is the first cause. Thus, to undo "ignorance" is to understand that there is "no separate existence of the self." This is the answer to the first question.

What determines the duration of the various phases of transmigration? Why do some ghosts stay around in the world for a couple of decades without having to undergo transmigration? The spirits are not the only ones who stay around here for twenty plus years; many more men stay around in this world for even longer. So what is there to wonder about? People nowadays may expect to live seventy or even eighty years. If we can stay around here for this long, why can't those spirits? [audience laughter]

"What is a human?" This is very serious [in Taiwanese]. [audience laughter] I can tell you what is a Buddha, but I can't tell you what constitutes a human being. [laughter] [audience laughter and applause]

These questions of yours, "Why do humans act in a certain way? Why do humans have thoughts? What gives rise to thoughts?" are what I referred to during these last seven days as the "conceptual issues." These are what you have to study if you adopt the "theory or conceptual approach." Fortunately for us, today's True Buddha School has adopted the "practice or experiential approach." We will temporarily lay aside these "theories" and concentrate first on the "actual practice." [laughter] [audience laughter and applause] The complete discussion of these questions of yours could take up a whole day.

[Q-2] During meditation practice, should one visualize the enshrined bronze statue of Padmakumara, or should one transform it into the face of the Grand Master?

[A] Visualize the bronze statue because my face changes

with time. As I have explained before, if you see a picture taken of me right after I was born, wearing only my birthday suit, my face was that of a baby. Now I have a middle-aged look, and soon I shall look elderly and completely different. Therefore, base your visualization on the bronze statue.

[Q-3] The Grand Master mentioned previously that there is the presence of Buddhas and Bodhisattvas in every shrine. Is the employment of the Vajra Hook during the step of invocation necessary to ensure that the Deities will descend? When one combines several practices together in one meditation session, may one visualize multiple Vajra Hooks ascending at once to invoke the Deities?

[A] Wow, you know how to make use of variation! [audience laughter] You are right. Normally when we sit at the shrine, we visualize the Wisdom Deity to be in the Empty Space, so we send the Vajra Hook up to the Empty Space. While the Dharma Body of the Buddha resides permanently in the Empty Space, the Bliss Body emerges from the Empty Space, and it is the Emanation Body who reaches our shrine. Bearing this concept in mind, you will be able to do your invocation well.

[Q-4] After employing the Vajra Hook to invoke the Deities to descend, and after the appearance of the Personal Deity from the revolving seed syllable, should one then integrate these two with the Deities in the shrine, and then visualize the empowerment of the three lights coming from this integrated Deity? Or should one just visualize the empowerment of the three lights from the Personal Deity after he has emerged from the seed syllable?

[A] This question is worded in a very complicated way, and it has made my thoughts complicated. [audience laughter] I guess the question is, "Is it permissible to visualize the Personal Deity in the Empty Space to unify with the Personal Deity at the shrine before one performs the visualization of the empowerment of the three lights?" Yes, you may visualize the Personal Deity at the shrine to ascend to dissolve into the Personal Deity at the Empty Space before the empowerment of the three lights. You may do so.

[Q-5] After a student receives the fire puja empowerment, can he go home and start doing fire pujas to help others? Can a student conduct a Fire Puja Dharma Ceremony?

[A] Well, to conduct a Dharma ceremony — this is going to pose some business competition for us! [audience laughter] According to one Tantrayana rule, as the fire puja is an important "generation stage practice," a student has to do 200 sessions of it to become skillful in the unifying of fire, Personal Deity, and self. When one is able to perform a fire puja from beginning to end without any error, then one may perform them to help others.

Regarding public fire pujas, it is best to leave them to be conducted by the acharyas. If heads of local chapters want to conduct them, they may do so, but only if they are already very proficient in the practice and do not make any mistakes. One first should help oneself and one's family members remove karmic obstacles, deferring for a later time the conducting of public fire pujas. One should only perform a public fire puja on behalf of others when one can carry it out without any error.

[Q-6] After a director of a local chapter receives the fire puja empowerment, may he or she go back to the local chapter and hold Fire Puja Dharma Ceremonies open to public registration?

[A] I have already answered this question.

[Q-7] Can a student practice fire pujas without receiving the fire puja empowerment from the root guru?

[A] No, this is not permitted because Tantrayana takes the matter of lineage transmission very seriously. During these past seven or eight days, I have discussed the necessity to receive the empowerment prior to the practice. Without the fire puja empowerment, one should not do any fire pujas.

[Q-8] Can fire pujas be used as a deliverance ritual?

[A] Yes, one may use the fire pujas for deliverance purposes.

[Q-9] May one ask for a remote empowerment for fire

pujas?

[A] It is better to receive it directly from the root guru.

[Q-10] Buddhas are awakened beings who have transcended all mental activities, and the Buddha Nature is present in everyone. Thus there is no discrimination among all beings and all beings are equal. The crux of meditation is to visualize the merging of the Offspring Light with the Mother Light, i.e., the union of the microcosm with the macrocosm. As a whole, the practice of Buddhadharma returns one to the "original nature." Herein also lies my problem. If everything originates from the same source then, at the very beginning, was the first karmic cause originated by the Buddhas? How could that be if the Buddhas abide in the state of "non-thought"? Ultimately one is saving oneself. For example, the Great White Padmakumara's revolving heart gave rise to the Padmakumaras of other colors, and the latter gave rise to us. So the originator of the act ends up having to save himself. If that is the case, why take the trouble to act in the first place? [audience laughter]

[A] OK, very well, this is a "test" question. All these "creative plays" of the Thus Come One happen because he is too bored. [audience laughter and applause] The Thus Come one is so bored with himself that he wants to have some fun. So he creates a game of chess by manifesting all these people or chess pieces and sending them down. Eventually he recalls all of them. [laughter and audience laughter] I can only offer you this simplest of all answers. I don't know how to explain it in a more profound way. [laughter and audience laughter]

[Q-11] How many lotuses from the Great Twin Lotus Ponds have come down to the human realm? If the Padmakumaras create karmic hindrances, how are they resolved? [audience laughter] In the future, when Grand Master Lu enters into Nirvana, who has the authority to certify future acharyas for the True Buddha School? What kinds of moral guidelines should the future True Buddha School students follow? Whom should they rely on in the future? When the Grand Master comes back to the world in the next life,

will he choose the same method of incarnation as adopted by the Dalai Lamas, so as to provide the students with some sense of continuous spiritual leadership?

[A] All these are very good questions. In the past when the Buddha was entering into Nirvana, Anada also asked these same questions. But I am not yet entering into Nirvana! [laughter and audience laughter] When the Padmakumaras commit transgressions, how are the karmic consequences resolved? They themselves have to bring their businesses to an end. [laughter and audience laughter] After I enter into Nirvana, students can use their own judgment to decide on future True Buddha acharyas. What moral guidelines should future students follow? My books, our monastic precepts, the Fourteen Tantrayana Root Precepts, and the Fifty Stanzas of Guru Devotions can all serve as moral guidelines. Whom should they rely on in the future? The same precepts I have just mentioned. Regarding my future incarnations, will I adopt the way of the tulkus? I have not decided yet. [audience laughter and applause]

[Q-12] In Issue 32 of the True Buddha News, the Grand Master made an announcement that no local temple or branch within the school would be singled out as the headquarters. Who then provides the central guidance for all these future students?

[A] As I have just explained, everyone should look to the Dharma, the True Buddha Tantric Dharma, for central guidance. Do not deviate from the Dharma teachings. Take the tree as an example, the tree trunk gives rise to many branches and much foliage as it grows and expands. To deviate from the Dharma is to break away from the main trunk and to lose the lineage transmission. So, one must regard the main trunk, the True Buddha Tantric Dharma, as one's main guidance. [audience applause]

[Q-13] What criteria and conditions does the Grand Master use in the selection of acharyas? Are acharyas in the True Buddha School ranked? Since Tibetan lamas are ranked, does our school announce the rankings of our acharyas? By making this information public, students will be able to select

and learn from the correct acharyas.

[A] My criteria for the selection of an on the teachings of the Buddha. First of all, h have a strong and determined aspiration to se Second, he or she supports the True Buddha Sch root guru. Third, he or she is committed to the bodhi The other two requirements are compassion and equa These five qualities are the only requisites for an achary

Has every acharya met these five requirements? W honestly, the answer is no. [laughter] It is very difficult to mee all these five criteria. So, what should they do if they have not met the requisites? They should work very hard to fulfill the requirements.

Are there different ranks of acharyas? Of course. They are: 1) acharyas, 2) great acharyas, 3) vajra acharyas, and 4) Enlightened acharyas. I have previously covered this subject in my books. To find a qualified acharya from whom to learn, students should employ their wisdom, making discriminations and observations accordingly. [audience applause]

[Q-14] Does the ritual of bestowing food on the Garuda and Ghost require an empowerment? Ever since a fellow student started making these food offerings, his family has experienced unrest, health problems, and misfortunes. Are these related to inadequate skill, using the wrong methodology, or performing poor visualizations while doing the practice?

[A] First, let me say this. As long as one is a student, one may perform this type of offering. If one understands the liturgy clearly and follows it accordingly, one will not make any errors. If one's family fortunes plummeted following this practice, then this was because one's fortunes were supposed to be down during that period of time. It has nothing to do with the practice. [audience applause]

[Q-15] During the ritual of empowerment, a seed is instilled deeply in the eighth level of consciousness. What kind of visualizations during empowerment should I perform in order to facilitate that instillation?

[A] The eighth level consciousness is a very subtle realm

f consciousness, and it is truly the "seed" consciousness. Nonetheless, during an empowerment, you only need to concentrate on the clear visualization of the particular Deity above your head, and the instilling of the Universal energy into your body, filling it up completely.

[Q-16] Is the realm described in the True Buddha Sutra the Realm Where Ordinary and Holy Beings Dwell? Why did the Grand Master say it is the Realm of Eternal Rest and Light?

[A] There is no contradiction here. If the Realm of Eternal Rest and Light is described in the True Buddha Sutra, you will not find a single word in the entire book. There are no words that can be used to describe the Realm of Eternal Rest and Light. I don't know if you understand this or not. You will not find any words at all when you open the true book of the True Buddha Sutra.

[Q-17] Grand Master, please compassionately teach us. Is Enlightenment divided into "conceptualized" and "experiential" types? Or, is an Enlightened person someone who has achieved both conceptually and experientially and, thus, someone who is an accomplished adept in both external and internal practice?

[A] I have discussed this already. Conceptual realization is different from experiential realization. When an Enlightened person achieves experiential realization, he will develop power in the inner world of subtle energy as well as in the exoteric level of practices.

[Q-18] I suddenly feel that we are now in the middle of the Maha Twin Lotus Ponds. The Maha Twin Lotus Ponds actually exist here in the world. It is all a matter of one's mind. This is why Instantaneous Enlightenment is possible and why all forms such as devas, humans, hells, and pure lands are manifestations of the mind. Put another way, the pure lands have never come or gone, neither have the hells and heavens. There is no above nor below. All phenomena are just transformations manifested by the mind. Spiritual practices can transform and purify the mind of illusion and enable one to experience directly — right here in this world — the existence

of the Maha Twin Lotus Ponds. How can the Maha Twin Lotus Ponds not exist in the human world when the Ksitigarbha Hospital of hell realm does exist here? This has made me more appreciative of the remarkableness of the True Buddha Tantric Dharma, and has made me cherish its practices more. This is a practice that can transform our egotistical heart into the heart of the Maha Twin Lotus Ponds' Pure Land. Will the Grand Master please give us further teachings on the manifestation of hells and pure lands right here in the human world?

[A] There is no need to answer your question because you have already given us the teachings. [laughter] [audience laughter] You have done a very good job, and your view is correct. The One Mind indeed undergoes transformations.

[Q-19] Grand Master, please give us the teaching on "the returning of zero to emptiness."

[A] "Zero returning to emptiness"? Well, I have taught "one returning to zero." How did this turn into "zero returning to emptiness"? [laughter and audience laughter] Zero is already emptiness. [audience laughter and applause] Zero is just a mathematical symbol used to represent emptiness. Since "zero" represents a unit, and emptiness is without any unit, I can only tell you that "the returning of zero to emptiness" is the returning of "unit" to "non-unit."

[Q-20] The process of transmigration cannot extinguish the "Innate Self," is this true? May one apply the same description to alaya, the eighth consciousness?

[A] The answer to both of your questions is "yes."

[Q-21] I have noticed that some masters of our school teach practices not taught by the Grand Master. Does this contradict the rules of Tantrayana and how should students react to this? Apart from the root guru, may other masters of the True Buddha School give remote empowerments of the True Buddha Tantric Dharma to students?

[A] Regarding the first question, I have explained earlier that there can be offshoots branching from the main trunk of the True Buddha Tantric Dharma. As long as they are Buddhist practices transmitted by the Buddha himself and are found in the Buddhist scriptures, then the masters may teach them even though I have not taught them. This poses no contradiction. However, the True Buddha Tantric Dharma must serve as the principal basis of their teachings.

Regarding the second question, remote empowerment is an expedient means. If a master of the True Buddha School feels that he or she can perform remote empowerment for others, he or she may do so if the following two conditions are met. First, the master has developed the siddhi of "deva-foot ubiquity" and can travel in spirit body to give the student the empowerment. Second, the master is able to call upon dakinis to come and carry the "water used for empowerment" to where the student is to perform the ritual on behalf of the master. When one has acquired these abilities, then one may perform remote empowerment for others.

[Q-22] I am curious and would like to find out why the Grand Master looked twice toward the door to his left during yesterday's discourse. [audience laughter] It is my observation that the Grand Master is usually very concentrated during his talks and not affected by external influences. [audience laughter]

[A] This is a very sharp and attentive student, and he is also the reason why I could not cough during the discourse. [audience laughter] Many of you have come down with colds, and I had to fight the urge to cough. Actually I don't have a cold, but I sometimes do have to pay attention to details. For example, when one of my buttons becomes undone, the attentive student thinks, "I wonder what happened that caused him to forget to button up." [laughter and audience laughter] He was even aware that I had taken a look in that direction. [audience laughter]

What happened was, during that moment in our teaching, a group of people were walking around outside. They came up to the door suddenly and then walked away. Perhaps no one was watching the gate at that moment. Was the gate open or closed [to the security staff]? [A security staff member answered, "The door was half closed."] Oh, that explains why there were outsiders. Since they were not our students, I paid a little attention to see if they were fire fighters or some other officials. I wanted to make sure that no accident had happened.

[Q-23] The True Buddha News is like the Buddhist scriptures and books to us. Therefore, how should we handle the newspapers after we finish reading them? Should we recycle them, burn them, or just dispose of them in the garbage can? Are there any rituals we should perform?

[A] Well, you are very concerned about their disposal. But actually, after you finish reading the newspapers, you can pass them along to other people until they become worn out. When they are worn out, you do not have to do anything about them anymore. [laughter] Since there are many meaningful articles in the newspapers, pass them along to other people when you are done with them.

[Q-24] Grand Master Lu, please explain the significance of the ring of light that appeared around the sun above the Rainbow Villa last Sunday?

[A] The Buddhas and Bodhisattvas often manifest their commendation of successful events through unusual astronomical and physical signs. A solar aureole or the sudden blooming of flowers is their way of singing praises. It can be regarded as an encouragement for all of us. [audience applause]

[Q-25] The Grand Master has taught us that vibrations from mantra sounds can open up the throat and heart chakras. What kind of sensations accompany such a phenomenon? Several months ago, while chanting the Padmakumara Heart Mantra, I experienced chest pains that were caused by the sound of the mantras. After praying intensively to the Buddhas for blessings and removal of my obscurations, the throat and heart areas stopped hurting. Now my chanting of the Padmakumara Heart Mantra using the vibrating sound method goes very smoothly. Does this mean that I am getting efficacious results from the chanting?

[A] Yes, that is a positive experience that happens during cultivation. In the Treasure Vase Breathing and Inner Heat Practice, one will experience the upsurging of a brisk heat which may cause aches in the head, eyes, or gum tissues. When this happens, one should stop for a while and visualize an icy cold lake appearing on one's head, the water from the lake filling one's body like the Universal energy to extinguish the fire. When the aches subside and the inflamed tissues are healed, one may resume the practice as before.

[Q-26] Does the thought "All beings are the seed syllable Hum" mean that one can visualize all Buddhas, deities, oneself, the six realms of beings, and all phenomenal manifestations as the seed syllable Hum? Does this mean treating every being equally without grasping onto and judging their forms and actions?

[A] In accordance with the meaning of Om Ah Hum, wherein "Om" is the Universal consciousness, "Ah" is Buddha, and "Hum" is all beings, one may visualize all phenomenal manifestations as the Hum syllable. Does this mean treating every being equally without grasping onto and judging their forms and actions? Yes, this is how Buddhas and Bodhisattvas act.

[Q-27] "All Dharmas arise and extinguish dependent on causes and conditions." Are these Dharmas the Buddhadharma or non-Buddhadharma? Or do they include all phenomena?

[A] The term "all Dharmas" does not refer just to the Buddhadharma. It refers to a condition or an environment and every element in that condition. The word "Dharmas" that appear often in Buddhist sutras do not mean only the Buddhadharma or practices such as the Four Preliminary Practices or Guru Yoga. The term "all Dharmas" refer to all phenomenal manifestations in the realm of form.

[Q-28] To benefit all beings, will the Grand Master again compassionately demonstrate to us the employment of the vajra and bell and their secrets. This tape will be produced with special slow motion as a teaching aid to spread the Dharma and help all beings.

[A] [Grand Master demonstrates.] This is to set the Dharma boundary or create a sacred space. This is for purification. This is for magnetization. This is for enhancement. This is for subjugation. While carrying out the various yogic intents, you can maneuver the vajra and bell in graceful ways and visualize lights radiating from these various mudras or movements. The secret lies in the integration of your mental energy with the light and the vajra and bell. [Grand Master repeats demonstrations.] [audience applause]

[Q-29] What is the "Dharma realm"?

[A] In general, the "Dharma realm" refers to the "four holy realms" and "six ordinary realms," ten different Dharma realms in total. The "four holy realms" are the Buddhas, Bodhisattvas, solitary-Buddhas, and arhats. The "six ordinary realms" are devas, humans, asuras, hell beings, hungry ghosts, and animals.

The "Dharma realm" may also be divided into many other systems and dimensions. As a whole, "Dharma realm" refers to the various kinds of levels of existence in the entire Universe.

[Q-30] Since Buddhas have the siddhi of omniscience, why doesn't the Buddha know how to speak English? [audience laughter]

[A] Lianhua Ling-sheng, let me ask you, since you raised this question, how do you know the Buddha does not know how to speak English? Just because he does not speak it does not mean he does not knows it. Let me say something to you in English! [audiencc laughter and applause]

I can speak English. This morning I washed my car. [audience laughter and applause] Some people have asked me, Why have you changed cars? Before you drove a Rolls Royce; now you drive a Mercedes. Why? Because the Rolls Royce is no good. In Washington State, just one person services Rolls Royces, and the service no good. [audience laughter and applause] There were constant troubles. Sometimes, no not sometimes — always, always the car leaked oil. Seriously, the Roll always leaked oil. [audience laughter and applause] Now, have a Mercedes and I like my car. I like its white color. Yes, it is white, the same as my lotus color. [audience laughter and applause] Anyway, yes I can speak English. But I speak English so slowly. My first language is Chinese. English is a second language. [audience applause]

If the Buddha had been born in the Western world, his English would have been top-notch. Now you have forced me to speak in English. [audience laughter and applause]

[Q-31] What is achieved in having sariras in the whole body? How does this achievement differ from the rainbow body transformation?

[A] Sariras are produced when essences in the physical body become condensed. When condensation of the secretions of these life essences occurs in the whole body, it produces sariras all over the body. To transform into the rainbow body is to further transform these condensed essences into light. Therefore the rainbow body transformation is the highest achievement. [audience applause]

[Q-32] Why do sariras generate smaller sariras on their own?

[A] This happens because Buddhas and Bodhisattvas in the spirit dimension have empowered and energized the sariras. When there is generation of new sariras in the spirit realm, new ones are also generated in the physical world. This involves the process of miraculous appearance.

[Q-33] What does this sentence mean, "Perception is forgotten through heightened awareness"?

[A] This is a very good question. I will explain with an analogy: although the intense [camera] lighting is very hot, I have forgotten that it is shining on me because my mind is so focused in answering these questions.

[Q-34] Which one of the following three seed syllables is used in the Ksitigarbha Practice? Ching "ཀྵིཾ," Ha "ཧ," or Seh [hri] "ཧྲཱི"?

[A] You may use Ha "ཧ."

[Q-35] If Amitabha is the Principal Deity, then who is

his Dharma Protector, Wisdom Dharma Protector, and Consort? Which eight offering mudras does the True Buddha School use?

[A] Yamantaka is the Dharma Protector of Amitabha, and Wisdom Dakini is his Wisdom Dharma Protector. I will tell you who his Consort is in the future when I discuss the Consort Practice.

The True Buddha School also has a set of eight offering mudras. I have previously taught the five offering mudras, which are flowers, incense, lamp, tea, and fruit. When you add the mudras for bath water, wish-fulfilling conch, and incense for anointment, then you will have the eight offering mudras.

[Q-36] Can the video tapes of the discourses here at the Rainbow Villa be shown on cable television?

[A] Yes, the more people who view them the better. This will draw more people to come and learn about the Dharma, and to take refuge.

[Q-37] Can internal injuries sustained in the body be healed by special methods associated with the practice of chi?

[A] Yes, there are internal level practices aimed especially at healing internal injuries. Vajra Fist Exercise is one such practice. One method used in guiding the travel of chi inside the body is to visualize the chi and your finger moving together at the same time through the same path. For example, visualize the chi and move your finger from your feet all the way up — this is an integration of touch with chi. In the future, I will elaborate on this method of guiding the chi. When I teach the internal level practice, I will instruct you on how to do "lowering," "elevating," "sustaining," and "releasing." Of these steps, the "elevating" is of greatest importance. I have said before that "with elevation one can leap over Mount Meru." So what is the key to this step? Which part of your physical body is involved? Many people probably think that I am referring to the anus, but this is not so. However, at this point I still cannot divulge it. [laughter and audience laughter] I have to safeguard a few little secrets; otherwise, what is there for me to do when you learn everything from me. [laughter and audience laughter]

[Q-38] How many kinds of chi are there?

[A] Five kinds: shang-hsing chi [which covers an area from tip of the nose to the throat and on to heart]; hsia-hsing chi [which covers an area from the navel to the toes]; p'ien-hsing chi [which covers the four limbs]; ming chi [which covers the genitalia, lower tan-tien, and urinary tract]; and p'ing-hsing chi or teng chi [which covers an area between the heart and the navel].

[Q-39] What is the difference between chi and power or strength?

[A] This pertains to teachings in the internal level practices, just like the shang-hsing chi, hsia-hsing chi, p'ien-hsing chi, ming chi, and p'ing-hsing chi. I will address these topics in the future.

[Q-40] What offerings should one use when a fire puja is offered to the Four Deva Kings? Can the Grand Master give us the Fire Puja Empowerment tomorrow? What visualization accompanies the empowerment?

[A] Tomorrow I plan to discuss how to visualize during this empowerment. Generally, however, during the Fire Puja Empowerment, one raises the inner fire and visualizes this fire entering into the brow-point chakra, then it moves down to the heart chakra. After the fire covers up the upper half of the body, it spreads to the lower half, and one then becomes united with the fire. Tomorrow, during the empowerment, you may also do it this way: when I touch your crown, visualize a swirl of fire entering into your body, igniting your whole body, and transforming it into a fireball. The secret lies in the "integration of fire, Personal Deity, and yourself."

What kind of offerings should one use for the Four Deva Kings? Since one prays to the Four Deva Kings for prosperity and enhancement, offer fruits and wines which are yellow in color. One may offer anything that is inflammable and yellow in color.

[Q-41] If one's ancestor has passed away in Nanking or Shanghai or gone up to heaven, can one dedicate a "spirit

plaque" in his name at the Ling Shen Ching Tze Temple, and would it be of any help to the ancestor's spirit?

[A] Dedicating a "spirit plaque" at the Ling Shen Ching Tze Temple for one's ancestor would help him regardless of where he passed away and whether or not he has gone up to heaven.

[Q-42] As a vajrayana practitioner, what should one's mind be thinking of as one carries out the normal activities of a day? What should one do if the mind gets too busy?

[A] As a vajrayana practitioner going about his or her daily life, nothing should be occupying his or her mind at all. What should one do if the mind gets too busy? When there is nothing in one's mind, it does not get busy. If one is not yet able to empty one's mind, one should rest the mind on "One."

[Q-43] To what does the "nine phoenixes" refer in the "nine phoenixes purifying water method that removes filth"? [taught in one of Grand Master Lu's Taoist books] How does one visualize them?

[A] The phoenix is a spiritual bird of ancient times. According to ancient legends, the nine phoenixes can neutralize many kinds of poisons and are feared by all poisons and filth. Do you know what a phoenix looks like? Just visualize nine of them, and that will do.

[Q-44] According to Tantric rules, one must receive empowerment before learning each mantra, mudra, and liturgy. Does this apply to the Manjusri Rebirth Mantra that is practiced before meals? Is it bad if one does the practice without receiving an empowerment?

[A] It is true that Tantric rules require one to receive an empowerment before practicing each mantra, mudra, and liturgy. Regarding mudras such as the one used in the Manjusri Rebirth Mantra, one may ask for an empowerment if one wants to. If, however, one already knows the meaning of the practice and uses the mantra very devoutly then, even though one has not received any empowerment or blessing, one's sincerity will one day move Manjusri in the spiritual realm to give a blessing which is equivalent to an empowerment.

Therefore, it is best if one can receive an empowerment. If not, use one's sincerity to move Manjusri into giving one an empowerment. This will allow the Manjusri Rebirth Mantra and Mudra that one employs to be efficacious.

[Q-45] What are the differences between the hells in the Vajra Hells and those described in the book Yu Li Bao Chao [the Jade Almanac]? Is "visualization" the same as the term "thinking with closed eyes"?

[A] "Visualization" and "thinking with closed eyes" are just different terms describing the same process.

Yu Li Bao Chao describes the ten hells of the Yama King or the eighteen hells, whereas Vajra Hells are hells for vajrayana practitioners who have made transgressions in vajrayana precepts, samaya precepts, or other precepts.

[Q-46] Grand Master, why are plants not included in the six realms of transmigration? What is the Universal Consciousness? Is "samadhi" the only way to attain the Universal Consciousness? When the Grand Master mentioned "lotuses as big as cart wheels," were you referring to them as symbols for the different local chapters of the True Buddha School (seating many people) and the personal shrine (seating one person)?

[A] Plants also go through transmigration.

Can Universal Consciousness be attained only through "samadhi"? Actually, the Universal Consciousness is what is known as the "Dharma realm," "the Divine Energy." It is not attained only through "samadhi." As long as one can open up and become one with the Universal Consciousness, one attains "It." There are many ways to attain It. Any method can lead one to It. The eighty four thousand doorways mentioned by the Buddha are all equal because they can all lead one to the Universal Consciousness.

"Lotuses as big as cart wheels" does not mean lotuses for local chapters are bigger while lotuses for individual practitioners are smaller. This is not what it means. [laughter]

[Q-47] In the Zen riddles, some masters ask their students if they are "full." What should the reply be? What do

the answers of "yes" and "no" mean?

[A] If the answer is "yes," it means he is full and can leave! [audience laughter] If the answer is "no," then he can go on and eat some more! [laughter and audience laughter and applause] Actually, the meaning behind it is this: When a master asks if one is "full," the answer that "one is full" confirms one's realization. By answering "not full," one has to work harder to make more progress on the path. This is a very simplistic answer. I won't go into other explanations that are deeper.

[Q-48] Monks or cultivators can become enlightened suddenly when they drop and break a cup, see a falling leaf, or hurt their big toe by stumbling on a brick. What is the lesson of Zen in these incidences?

[A] If one kicks one's big toe into a piece of brick, the Zen lesson here is that "the toe will become swollen." [laughter and audience laughter] Do not think so much! [audience laughter] Be simple. Go at once to buy some medicine ointment to put on it. [laughter and audience laughter]

Breaking a cup and getting the hand scalded was what happened to the Venerable Master Hsu Yun. The breaking of the cup had enabled him to suddenly intuit the Truth. This intuition of Truth is considered an "initial rupture on the egoic hold." The breaking of the cup represents the breaking of the boundary between "outside" and "inside." In other words, one is just like a cup when one contracts and recoils into the limited "self." Why doesn't one just smash the body and expand one's consciousness to that of the Universal Consciousness? Isn't that much better? This is Abolition of Duality.

With fallen leaves, go and sweep them up. [laughter and audience laughter] Indeed, if there are fallen leaves, and one's master hands one a broom, one goes and sweeps them. Well, leaves fall every day. One day, one tells one's master, "Master, there is no need to sweep." "Why not?" "Because after today's sweeping, they will fall still tomorrow. After tomorrow's sweeping, they will fall again the day after tomorrow. So, why bother?" As soon as the master hears that, he knows the student has achieved Enlightenment. [laughter and audience laughter and applause] Sweeping leaves also can lead to Enlightenment! The leaves represent "problems perceived by one." There will be "problems perceived by one" every day, so why sweep or tackle them, just let them be blown away by the wind. Here at the Rainbow Villa, it is very windy. When the wind comes, it will blow all of the leaves to someone else' property. [audience laughter] Sometimes one has to sweep, sometimes one does not have to sweep — it depends on how one's interpretation is.

[Q-49] Humans and animals are living creatures. Why is it that after an earth worm is cut into two halves, both halves can still move? In this case, how does one determine which half has the Buddha Nature? [laughter and audience laughter]

[A] You do know how to ask a question. This has been asked by someone before. Since an earth worm has Buddha Nature, and when it is cut into two moving halves, which half has the Buddha Nature? In general people will say the Buddha Nature is in both halves. The true answer is that "Buddha Nature is inherent in everything," not just in the two halves, but also in the spiritual realm and in the empty space. The existence of Buddha Nature is not confined to only living and moving creatures! No, being alive is not equated to Buddha Nature; these are two completely different things. So, it is baffling to ask this question. [laughter and audience laughter] Do not equate moving creatures with Buddha Nature.

[Q-50] Why are mudras released at the brow point? Is there any subtle reason for doing this?

[A] Mudras are released at the brow point because that is the most beautiful gesture. [laughter and audience laughter] One may release mudras at the throat or other areas, but it is most reverent to release it at the brow point or at the crown. Among the descriptions of the Dharma Body of all Buddhas is the "Supreme Crown" or "the Most Honorable and Victorious Buddha Crown," thus the crown of the Buddha is the most victorious area. The releasing of mudras at the crown area constitutes something that is most honorable, victorious, and remarkable.

[Q-51] What kind of preparation should a vajrayana practitioner make before attending oral teachings given by the Root Guru? Should he do visualization and chant mantras? How can one obtain the benefits of "mouth-to-ear transmission"?

[A] In general, the term "mouth-to-ear transmission" refers to teachings on a "one-to-one basis." For example, I talk and you listen. In the past, "mouth[whisper]-to-ear transmission" was on a one-to-one basis and more secretive. What we have here today at this public teaching is different, but it also may be termed "mouth-to-ear transmission." I also talk and you listen.

What kind of preparation should one make before attending the Root Guru's teachings? Go and use the toilet first! [laughter and audience uproar] There is no need to use visualization or mantra when you use the toilet. [audience laughter] That should be sufficient preparation.

[Q-52] The Guru Yoga and Personal Deity Yoga are two separate practices. But if there is a constraint of time, may one integrate the two practices?

[A] You may do so. In Tantrayana, many practices may be combined. The Four Preliminary Practices may be combined with the Guru Yoga. One may also combine the Four Preliminaries with Guru Yoga and Personal Deity Yoga.

[Q-53] In one of the tape recordings made in 1991 at the True Buddha Tantric Quarter, the Grand Master said the following, while explaining the Hundred Syllable Mantra: "je-you-mi-ba-wa, je-zuo-mi-ba-wa." Since the original Hundred Syllable Mantra does not contain the phrase "je-you-mi-ba-wa," should we insert this one particular phrase into the mantra when we chant it now?

[A] What you are doing is looking for my shortcomings! [laughter and audience laughter] There is only "je-zuo-mi-ba-wa" and not "je-you-mi-ba-wa." "Je-you-mi-ba-wa" came out because I was not able to tell right from left at that time. [laughter and audience laughter] ["Zuo" and "you" sound the same as "left" and "right" in Chinese respectively.] Actually many close students know that I sometimes have trouble telling right from left. Finally someone showed me a way to remember it. Since we always answer roll call by answering "you [equivalent to "here" in English]! I will just raise my right hand whenever I say "you." This has helped me to distinguish left from right. "You!" [Grand Master raises his right hand to audience laughter] When I was in the army, and the captain called out "turn to the right" [audience laughter], I always turned to the left. [laughter and audience uproar] You know I was the shortest and stood at the end. When everyone was turning right and marching away, I was the only one ... [laughter and audience laughter and applause] This was true. I had no problem with "turn to the back," but I sometimes had trouble with left and right. When I couldn't figure it out right away, I would turn arbitrarily to one side, and each time it would turn out to be the opposite direction from that the whole troop had turned. After I started off, I would turn to take a look [laughter] and everybody else was very far away. [audience laughter] So this business of "left versus right" has been troubling me for many years. After I started driving and came to America, it took me a while to straighten out the traffic signs of "Turn Right" and "Turn Left." [audience laughter] This inability to figure out right from left is my shortcoming. Very good! Now the questioner has brought it all out in public. [laughter and audience laughter]

[Q-54] Beings who are reborn in Sukhavati will have limitless lifespans. How about beings reborn in other Buddha Pure Lands, do they also enjoy such infinite longevity?

[A] Yes, lifespans in many Buddha Pure Lands are very long, so long that they are beyond counting. That is why they are called "infinite lifespans."

[Q-55] Is the visualization of the transformation of the seed syllable into the Personal Deity very important? If one mixes the seed syllables up, does this mean one cannot attain yogic response?

[A] The transformation of the seed syllable into the Personal Deity is one among a series of steps in visualization. First a moon disc appears, followed by the appearance of the seed syllable on the moon disc. The seed syllable then rotates to transform into the Personal Deity, who then bestows the three lights of blessing on one. Furthermore, the Personal Deity moves to the top of one's crown, contracts to a very miniature size, and enters into one's central channel. After stopping at the heart chakra, it enlarges to become one with one. This is the visualization of the "merging of one with the Personal Deity."

This kind of visualization entails many steps, and requires an intensity of involvement. The transformation of the seed syllable into the Personal Deity is, of course, a very important step. If the wrong seed syllable is visualized, one cannot attain yogic response. If one does not know that one has made a mistake, there is nothing one can do about it. It is considered an error. But when one finds out about it, one can correct it. This is very important.

That is why there is the "Remedy Mantra," which is used when one notices that errors have been made during the practice. One chants the Remedy Mantra to mend those mistakes. The chanting of the Hundred Syllable Mantra also serves this same purpose. During the practice, if any mistakes happen, such as unclear visualization, bad thoughts, wrong mudra, or even yawning or coughing, one may chant the Hundred Syllable Mantra to make amends for them.

Among all the seed syllables is one which is universal to all Buddhas and Bodhisattvas. This is the seed syllable "Ah (ཨཱཿ)." One may visualize this seed syllable to appear on the moon disc regardless of which Personal Deity Yoga one practices. There is no error when one visualizes "Ah" transforming into the Personal Deity, since it is the universal syllable shared by all Buddhas and Bodhisattvas.

[Q-56] Does the seed syllable on the moon disc turn clockwise or does it vacillate vertically from left to right?

[A] Oh, this is a question about left and right. In my visualization, the seed syllable turns in a clockwise fashion, whether it is horizontal or vertical. Generally speaking, in Tibetan Buddhism, the seed syllable is vertically placed, though it may sometimes be horizontal. Regarding my own habit, the seed syllable is vertical when it is on top of a moon disc and horizontal when it is on my navel or heart chakra.

[Q-57] How did the Five Great Buddhas evolve?

[A] The Five Great Buddhas all emerged from the Great Sun Buddha. What were the steps of evolution? We can use a Chinese means of interpreting it. I have been asked this question before, but I have not come across any explanation of this in the Buddhist sutras. Let us look at the five elements of metal, wood, water, fire, and earth, of which the central element, earth, is the beginning. Earth gives rise to metal, which is associated with the west, and thus Amitabha. Metal gives rise to water, which is associated with the north, and thus Amoghasiddhi Buddha. From water is wood generated which is the east, and thus Akshobaya Buddha. Isn't this right? Wood gives rise to fire, which is associated with south, and thus Ratnasambhava Buddha. These are the steps of evolution of the Five Great Buddhas or Buddha Wisdoms. Others might offer a different interpretation.

[Q-58] How does one close the lower gap in the central channel during the practice of Inner Heat?

[A] I will teach you in the future, as it has to do with the "internal practice" of Inner Heat. How does one close the upper and lower gaps in the central channel? How can the inner fire be kindled? Since there is a distance between the starter and the kindling, one cannot start the fire. How can one bring the starter and the kindling together so that one may ignite the kindling and produce the inner fire? This is a secret. If I taught you today, then I would have no classes to offer in the future. So, let us postpone it for a future teaching.

[Q-59] If the right and left sides of a piece of property are unbalanced in terms of feng shui, besides using the method of invoking "devas" to suppress the noxious energy, can one

invoke the Buddhas to use their Ten Transcendental Powers to help one?

[A] Actually it is much more difficult to invoke the Buddhas than to invoke the devas. Your land is unbalanced in energy, so you want to invoke the Buddhas. How can the Buddhas be bothered with your business all the time? You may invoke them, but it is quite difficult to get a response from them unless one has already cultivated to a level almost the same as that of the Buddhas. Otherwise, just arbitrarily assign a child to call aloud, "The Thus Come One, please come!" Will they come? [audience laughter] The Thus-Come One will not thus come. [audience laughter] It is not easy to invoke the Buddhas unless one is almost at the same level as they. But then, if one has reached the same level as the Buddhas, why would one want to ask help from the devas, one could just ask oneself. [audience laughter and applause]

[Q-60] Yesterday when the Grand Master told us that he would give us some empowerments tomorrow, my heart was filled with joy. I sincerely ask the Grand Master to give us the White Tara Purification Empowerment. Since the Twenty One Taras include outstanding practices such as the Kuan Yin, White Tara, and Green Tara, if the Grand Master will compassionately disseminate this teaching to us, it will make the lineage of the True Buddha School more magnificent.

[A] Who has access to the mantras of the Twenty One Taras? [Several masters raise up their hands.] I have given away my copies of the text with the Twenty One Taras' mantras to some of the masters in our school, and they have them now. You may ask the masters for the mantras of the Twenty One Taras. We will have the empowerment tomorrow. [audience applause]

[Q-61] I have read an article called "The Dharani of All Tathagata Heart Secret Body Relic Treasure Case." It is accompanied by an illustration of a Five Wheels Stupa which resembles the shape of a human body. There is this passage in the article, "At the time the Buddha saw the rotting stupa, he took off his top dress to drape over it, and started to cry. When

he finished crying, he smiled. At this time, all Buddhas in the ten directions witnessed this, and they also started crying and shining light on the stupa." Was this the origin of the later enshrining of relics in stupas? The illustrated stupa consisted of five shapes: square, circle, triangle, semi-circle, and heart. Can we also set up a shrine using this same model? The more I read this sutra, the more I feel that it is a description of the past, present, and future of Grand Master Lu. Is my intuition correct? If it is correct, can the empowerment of "All Tathagata Heart Secret Body Relic" be added to tomorrow's program? Are there any special prerequisites prior to receiving this empowerment? What are the visualizations? Is this practice the "Padmakumara Practice"?

[A] This is a scripture from the Buddha Tantra. The Five Wheels Stupa of "earth, water, fire, wind, and space" symbolizes the Great Sun Buddha in the Garbhadhatu. Therefore, these five elements make up the heart mantra of the Garbhadhatu Great Sun Buddha. On the other hand, the mantra for the Vajradhatu is "Om, Be-ja-dha-du, Xun." As mentioned in my True Buddha Tantric Quarter teachings, I have done drawings of the Five Wheel Stupas. Your intuition is not bad. We can have this empowerment tomorrow if other people are also interested in it; otherwise, I will just give it to you yourself.

[Q-62] How long does the effect of an empowerment last? Will it last till the next life?

[A] It is generally fine if one receives many empowerments. One may also ask for a certain empowerment to be bestowed when one decides to pursue that particular practice. What it means is that, after receiving many different empowerments, the power of lineage transmission will manifest when one starts to do the practice. The power from the empowerment, like a seed planted in soil, remains dormant. When one starts doing the practice, which is equivalent to the giving of water, sunlight, and air, the seed will germinate. Otherwise, if one does not do the practice, it will remain forever as a seed.

[Q-63] Does "Namo Western Paradise Thirty Six Tril-

lion One Nineteen Thousand Five Hundred Amitabhas" represent all Buddhas and all beings? Or does it refer only to the Buddhas and beings in the Pure Lands of the east, south, west, and north directions?

[A] When we chant "Namo Western Paradise Thirty Six Trillion One Nineteen Thousand Five Hundred Amitabhas," we refer to the Amitabhas in the Western Paradise. It does not represent all Buddhas and all beings. In the east, south, and north Pure Lands, the number of beings is also very great. In the eyes of the Buddhas, the number of realms of beings is unaccountable and indescribable. The same can be said about the Buddha realms.

[Q-64] Grand Master Lu, are the signs of yogic responses classified into different levels? If so, how may one distinguish the different levels?

[A] Regarding the signs of yogic response, I already discussed this last Saturday evening. I can expand on it using the example of Inner Fire Practice. Of course, the Inner Fire Practice has its own signs: the first sign is the appearance of smoke, the second sign is the appearance of a small fire, the third sign is a huge and powerful fire and, finally, the appearance of light. The emergence of the stage of light is tantamount to arriving at a very high level of response. Just as the Inner Fire Practice has four different levels of response, other practices are characterized by their own different levels of response.

[Q-65] My first question pertains to attaining the state of "non-leakage." How can the "stopping of menstrual flow" be achieved? How does one achieve the state described by the Taoist term of "conquering the dragon and tiger"? Where are the "three hun and seven pa" [a term that describes the different constituents of a person's soul] located? What are the Four Deva Kings' mantra seed syllables and their colors?

[A] Writings on the "three hun and seven pa" may be found on page 83 of my 98th book, *Transpersonal Experiences in the Ocean of Beings*. The mantras of the Four Deva Kings may be found in my 49th book, *The Method of Vajrayana*.

I shall address now the questions pertaining to "non-leakage" and "stopping of menstrual flow." It is known in Taoism or Tantric Buddhism that when one exhausts the vital essences in one's body, one dies. It is therefore best if one can achieve a state wherein there is no leakage of any of the vital essences of one's body. Simply put, males have to be able to keep light drops from leaking. Light drops include both the non-physical "wisdom light drops" and the physical "semen." For females, it would be non-physical "wisdom light drops" and the physical "menstrual blood." How does one stop these light drops from leaking? These are "internal level" practices. First, one must learn to do the Treasure Vase Breathing to fill the whole body with a vigorous chi. Sometimes the hand can be used as a tactile guide for the movement of chi. When the finger moves upward, visualize chi also moving upward along with the finger. Eventually, the chi will move upward without any tactile guidance. By practicing the Treasure Vase Breathing, one's whole body becomes like a treasure vase filled with vigorous chi that filters down to the capillary level.

Next, chi is gathered and transformed into an inner fire that is used to burn up all those physical light drops [which would normally lead to a cascade of events resulting in end products] that are discharged from the body. The physical light drops, which are fluids, will turn into vapors when this inner combustion takes place. As vapors, they arise. When they ascend to the five chakras, they condense and turn into sariras. Internal Practices are thus methods employing chi in one's body to transport these fluids — which emerge as a result of the "inner fire" combustion process — to the five chakras.

Light drops that are about to leak can be elevated by assuming a certain body position or posture. In the tempering process, the inner fire is used to burn these light drops and transform them into vapor. The vapor will rise inside the central channel and, upon reaching the five chakras, transform into sariras.

In Taoism, this process is known as "conquering the dragon and subjugating the tiger," "non-leakage of light drops," and "cessation of the menstrual flow." It is easy to speak about this process but, in reality, in order to achieve the "non-leakage of light drops," one has to lower one's desires. The six senses of sight, hearing, smell, taste, touch, and thought have to be shut off. When one is desire-free, an inner peace is sustained. Then one may practice the four steps of "lowering, elevating, sustaining, and dispersing," and use the "elevating" method to raise light drops, temper them with the inner fire, and transform them into vapor. This is also what is termed in Taoism the practice of "ching, chi, and shen." Ching transforms into chi, which transforms into shen, which then returns to the void. This is the Taoist method of cultivation to return to the Original Source.

In Tantric Buddhism, "non-leakage of light drops" is also the goal. In Vajrayana Buddhism, engaging in consort practice, while one still has leakage of light drops, constitutes a breaking of the vajrayana precepts and can cause one to descend to the vajra hell. Consort practice is engaged in vajrayana because it is an effective way to induce the lowering of the fluid known as "white bindu." While still engaging in consort practice, chi is transferred and instilled into the other party's central channel to open it up. In this process, chi is transformed through skillful means into "wisdom chi," which is used to open up the central channel. This is tantamount to helping the other party to experience the state of liberation. The circulation of chi enables the other party to enter into the same realm as one is in oneself. This is the reason why this very secret yoga is practiced in Tantric schools. However, if the female party is not able to consciously achieve cessation of menstrual flow and the male party is not able to prevent the lightdrops from leaking, then engaging in such practices can cause one to descend to the vajra hell. The successful practice of "non-leakage of lightdrops" is a minimum prerequisite before one should attempt the consort practice. Padmasambhava had five female consorts with whom he entered into sexual union practice for the above reasons.

[Q-66] As I am now just starting to do the daily practice following the guidelines in the practice text, I am not clear on

many things. When should I attempt the meditation [samadhi] step?

[A] Actually, students in general have to practice entering samadhi every time they do the practice. They may do "breath counting," and try to first quiet their mind down a little bit. Start out slowly and, over time, you will be able to enter into a deeper and subtler state of consciousness. You must include this exercise in every single one of your practices.

However, if you are a new refuge student and are starting out with the Four Preliminary Practices, then you do not have to do the samadhi step yet. Just work with one preliminary practice at a time or combine all four practices together.

[Q-67] Is there any connection between the "nine levels of existence" in the Western Pure Land of Ultimate Paradise [Sukhavati] and the Grand Master's Siddhi, the Maha Twin Lotus Ponds?

[A] Yes, there is.

[Q-68] Many students are muddled and do not have a clear understanding of Grand Master and the True Buddha School when they take refuge. If, later on, they decide to leave the school due to personal problems with fellow students or masters in the school, would they be considered to have broken the Samaya Pledge?

[A] Yes, that would constitute a breaking of the Samaya Pledge. I would like to point out to everyone that "taking refuge" and the "Samaya Pledge" are very serious matters. If you have, in the beginning, taken refuge in a muddled state, then you have to learn to do the practice carefully and to hear clearly the teachings and precepts I transmit to you. When you do this, you will not remain in a muddled state and leave. [audience applause]

[Q-69] Going too far is as bad as not going far enough. Are there examples of "excessiveness" in the practice and propagation of the Buddhadharma that can serve to alert us that we should do everything just right? When we witness fellow students or directors of local chapters acting inappropri-

ately, may we give them advice?

[A] Both going too far and not going far enough are undesirable. The Buddha has made an analogy of this issue using the strings of a zither. When the strings are too tight, they break. When the strings are too loose, the music does not sound good. When one plays a guitar, the tension of the strings have to be set just right in order to produce the most beautiful sound quality. It is the same with learning to meditate. The most beautiful moment occurs when we are neither too tight nor too loose.

Regarding whether one should give advice, one must use one's wisdom. Personal affairs are among the most difficult problems. If you know how to use your wisdom to do tasks of mediation, you could become a "taming husband" [an epithet of the Buddha]. [laughter]

[Q-70] How may one differentiate the light circle at the third eye chakra from the white bindu? Is it white in color? If not, what practice should one do to change it to white? Does the light circle at the third eye chakra move? How should one practice to assure that one is on the right path and has not turned into a lunatic? When karmic hindrances emerge in thoughts, what is the proper treatment?

[A] Regarding the light circle at the third eye chakra and the white bindu, we usually refer to them as white. White is used as an representation of their color. Is the light circle moving? If you observe that it is moving, then you are right.

How does one know if one is on the right path or has become a lunatic? It again comes down to wisdom. One must ask oneself if all the things that one is doing are reasonable. Do they make sense? Are they in accordance with the teachings of the Buddhadharma? One must constantly ask oneself these questions.

What is the proper treatment for karmic hindrances emerging in thoughts? Visualization is the proper treatment. If ill thoughts pop up in one's mind, one must constantly visualize the compassionate faces of Buddhas and Bodhisattvas to displace those undesirable thoughts. Visualization is the technique used in esoteric Buddhism to replace one thought with another thought.

[Q-71] Grand Master, please explain the application of the view of "sui san" [literally: to let it disperse] and the areas that one must pay attention to in this practice.

[A] What is the view of "sui san"? It is a view wherein one's consciousness rests in the immense and expansive nature of the mind. For example, one always holds the thought that one abides in Emptiness, a condition wherein one is not abiding anywhere at all. One's mind is not focused here, there, or at any particular point; neither does it spread anywhere. Just let it be dispersed by the wind. This is the view of "sui san." It is a condition wherein the mind becomes equated with Emptiness and is not attached to any place.

[Q-72] I have been practicing Food Bestowing to Spirits for some time now. Grand Master Lu has said that the front door is used to welcome the spirits and the back door is used to see them off. But, is it all right if I carry out the ritual in my backyard, and do my invocation of the Grand Master and the seven Buddhas to bless my practice there?

[A] Yes, you can do that, because you regard your back door as your front door and vice versa.

[Q-73] Should I chant the Food Transformation Mantra and the Nectar Mantra at my shrine or in my backyard?

[A] You can do either one.

[Q-74] Must I sprinkle the water energized with the mantras outside the house? May I sprinkle it on the wall enclosing my backyard?

[A] You may do either.

[Q-75] What is the best time for doing Food Bestowing?

[A] You can do it anytime. [laughter] [audience laughter and applause]

[Q-76] Is it right or wrong if one's desires gradually decrease and disappear over time with the practice of the True Buddha Tantric Dharma?

[A] It is of course right!

[Q-77] My family members do not believe or practice the True Buddha Tantric Dharma; they believe in a different

religion. What should I do with these feelings of loathing that have sprung up in me?

[A] Do not detest them, because other religions also have their own strong points.

[Q-78] If we do not yield to each other, am I causing my family to break one of the Five Precepts?

[A] It is you, not they, who is breaking the Five Precepts. [audience laughter] Therefore it is all right to yield to them.

[Q-79] In trying to introduce and explain the True Buddha School to others, I have met rejection and sometimes heard slandering of the school. How should I ask the Buddhas to forgive their ignorance?

[A] You can chant mantra and do practices for them.

[Q-80] At places where there are no earth energy and no Buddhas and Bodhisattvas, how can I invoke the Buddhas to empower my practice so it will be efficacious?

[A] What makes you think a place does not have earth energy or Buddhas and Bodhisattvas? [audience laughter] Buddhas and Bodhisattvas exist everywhere. Earth energy is found everywhere on earth.

[Q-81] After using the method of patting one's left and right thighs to invoke the Dharma Protectors during emergencies, how should one thank them?

[A] Just make offerings to them.

[Q-82] If there is something weighing on one's mind, and one cannot concentrate on doing the practice, may one chant the Guru's Heart Mantra instead? Or, what else should one do?

[A] If one is unable to do the practice, chanting the mantra is fine. Mantra chanting is also a kind of practice.

[Q-83] According to Rule 37 of the Fifty Stanzas of Guru Devotion, when women attend Dharma teachings, they have to sit in a dignified way, join palms and pay attention. Should female students sit properly with palms joined while attending this series of lectures, as well as during group practices and other Dharma ceremonies?

[A] Just joining palms for a moment will do. One can't

just let one's arms get sore.

[Q-84] I have always doubted if the Buddha was able to convince Yashodhara [Buddha's wife] to turn to the path of liberation. Why?

[A] It did happen according to the Buddhist scriptures. Yashodhara was at first quite upset. She lost her loved ones — even her son had become a renunciant. But, at the end, she also realized the emptiness and impermanence in everything, including suffering.

How does one integrate this realization of the inherent emptiness of the self, others, and all phenomenal existence into one's everyday activities, thereby turning it into a living truth? Make time and take time to experience this.

[Q-85] What does the Grand Master like most? What is the Grand Master most afraid of?

[A] There is nothing I am particularly fond of or afraid of. [audience applause] Of course, the Buddha is also like that. The Buddha has no particular likings and fears. The truth is that the self, others, and all conditions in the phenomenal worlds do not inherently exist. [audience applause]

[Q-86] What has caused us to come here to hear the teaching on An Overview of the Buddhadharma? How should each of us repay the Grand Master? I wish Grand Master Lu would stay in the world forever to turn the Dharma Wheel. Many students need to learn from you and would like to get close to you. Yet we are worried that you will soon retire. What can we do to keep you?

[A] "Entreat the Buddha to always stay in the world" — this is the same vow made by Samantabhadra Bodhisattva. Now, why have you come here to hear this teaching on An Overview of the Buddhadharma? Because you wanted to. [audience laughter] As for repaying me, it is not necessary.

[Q-87] To enter into samadhi, one must first enter into the state of "no thought." But the Grand Master has often referred to the accomplishment of many extraordinary tasks during samadhi. For these feats to happen, does the consciousness need to revert to the state of "thoughts"? Is this what is

meant by the phrase "cheng k'ung miao yu" [contained in the true void are all phenomenal existences]?

[A] Yes, "thought" generated from the state of "no thought," or "thought sprung from the ground of mental cessation," is what is spiritual power. After entering into the state of mental cessation, the first thought that is engendered (when you want to accomplish some task) is called "thought sprung from the ground of mental cessation." It is spiritual power. It is "cheng k'ung miao yu."

[Q-88] Can the Grand Master give the following empowerments to those students who missed them when the Grand Master gave them here at the Rainbow Villa last November? They are: the Vajra Empowerment, the Skeleton View, the Body Offering, Vajra Heart Bodhisattva, Guru Yoga, and the Deva of Auspiciousness?

[A] I hope there will be enough time. [audience applause]

[Q-89] I used to practice the "Dan Tao," a type of exercise that promotes health. Now that I have taken refuge in the Grand Master and am learning the True Buddha Tantric Dharma, are there any other things that I should pay attention to?

[A] Although Dan Tao is a Taoist practice, it is also a kind of internal energy practice. In Taoism there is the so-called "nine swirls mystical pill-cauldrons [dan-ding] practice." The nine pill-cauldrons refer to nine locations in the intestine. In this practice, light drops are manoeuvered into the pill-cauldrons where they are further tempered with inner fire. The "pill-cauldron practice" in Taoism and the Tantric internal practice are just two different approaches that produce the same results. For example, the visualization involving the central channel and the right and left channels are different in the two schools.

[Q-90] Please briefly explain the "twelve links of existence."

[A] The so-called "twelve links of existence" refers to the twelve links that constitute the chain of conditioned arising. The first link is "ignorance" and the last link is "old age and death." The chain consists of ignorance—>impulses—>consciousness—>the mental and the physical—>the six sense-object realms—>contact—> sensation—>craving—>grasping—>becoming—> birth—>old age and death. While sitting under the bodhi tree, the Buddha contemplated these twelve terms. These describe the twelve phenomena that constitute the conditioned arising of men from ignorance through old age and death. Meditating on these phenomena finally led him to Enlightenment.

[Q-91] How can one's will power and determination be strengthened so that one will practice energetically and make progress on the path?

[A] By keeping in mind the original aspiration that motivated you to seek Liberation.

[Q-92] As a Buddhist practitioner, what should I do when facing oppression from authorities in the world? Should I use my utmost effort to make known my stand and viewpoint?

[A] Faith cannot be subdued by force. When circumstances permit you to express yourself, do so. When they do not, then do not talk about it.

[Q-93] Since I have not yet achieved enough spiritual power, what can I do to help other people solve their difficulties and problems?

[A] Pray to the Buddhas and Bodhisattvas to intercede for you. There are eight ways to solve emotional afflictions. One of them is through the chanting of sutras.

[Q-94] When I am about to light the incense to start my practice, the hair on my left leg stands up, but just momentarily. During the practice, when I start to chant the High King Avalokitesvara Sutra and the Great Compassionate Dharani, my back feels like there are bugs crawling around. What should I do about this? Also, why do cultivators who meditate several times a day and who know many of Buddhist theories act in contradictory ways and still harbor lust and greed for prestige in their mind? Although in moments of clarity, they do know that those desires are bad for them.

[A] If the hair on your left leg stands up [audience laugh-

[Q-103] What is meant by the Clear Light? How does it differ from ordinary light? Why is the light of the Great Sun Buddha able to pervade every dark corner? Is it a special kind of light that can bend? How may one judge if the different kinds of light that one sees along the path of cultivation are normal or abnormal? It takes three years of full-time devotion to do all Four Preliminary Practices 100,000 times. Does this mean that one needs to become a renunciant in order to practice them adequately?

[A] Regarding the Clear Light, the light of the Great Sun Buddha is a kind of Dharma realm light that is beyond our ordinary imagination. It is different from ordinary light experienced by our sciences and our sensory organs. The kinds of light now seen by us are actually a mental construct of ours and not the same as the Great Sun Buddha's Clear Light.

Does it take three years to complete the Four Preliminary Practices 100,000 times? Go and try it out for yourself. Some people are able to do them in a shorter period.

[Q-104] Is the seventh consciousness the dream subconsciousness?

[A] The seventh consciousness is "manas," which may also be called the subconsciousness. The subconsciousness also manifests through dream states.

[Q-105] How does one have control in dreams?

[A] Pray to the Personal Deity and Root Guru for blessings, so that your mind will remain lucid and have control in your dreams. There is the Dream Yoga that one may practice.

[Q-106] I will soon be returning to Beijing. After I return, I plan to set up a Tantric shrine at home. Due to all kinds of constraints, the shrine will be a very simple one. What should I be aware of during the setup? How should the shrine be consecrated when it is finished? What are the Five Roots and Five Powers?

[A] There is a very detailed description on the setup of a Tantric shrine in my 81st book, Liturgy in the True Buddha School. Just follow the guidelines there.

The Five Roots are "sight, hearing, smell, taste, and

touch." The Five Powers are "faith, vigor, thought, stability, and wisdom."

[Q-107] What is the best and simplest method to bring Buddhists of scriptural schools and non-Buddhists to practice the True Buddha Tantric Dharma? Does the True Buddha School have any material [in English] to help Caucasians and those children of Chinese descent born in America?

[A] You may share with them the various points of remarkableness of the True Buddha School, which we went over the other day. The practice text is now available in English. Also, many groups, such as the Purple Lotus Society, are now translating my work into English.

[Q-108] To seek a Pure Land Rebirth at the time of dying, one has to chant the name of Amitabha, as well as visualize the image of Amitabha. I believe it would be more direct for students of the True Buddha School to visualize the Grand Master. Would it be better for us to chant the Guru's Heart Mantra instead of Amitabha for a Guided Buddhahood?

[A] You may do so. Chanting the Guru's Heart Mantra or visualizing the Grand Master can lead you to rebirth. You may also chant Amitabha or visualize Amitabha, since both are within the realm of Sukhavati. There is an intimate and inseparable relationship between Amitabha and Padmakumara. So, you may do either one of the practices. [audience applause]

Grand Master: We have at long last come to the final question. [audience laughter and applause] Om Mani Padme Hum.

Ninth Day:
May 13, 1993

Instruction before the Empowerments

Today is the day for empowerments. In a while, when you come up, the important thing to bear in mind is to chant the appropriate mantra and visualize the Deity corresponding to each empowerment.

Just now, I have made a "collective invocation" to invoke all Buddhas and Bodhisattvas, as well as all devas from all times and spaces to emerge from the spiritual realm. Thus, during the empowerment, when you visualize a particular Deity to reside above your head, the Deity will appear. I, myself, at the same time will transform into that particular Deity during the empowerment. This is tantamount to having the Personal Deity perform the empowerment for you — a direct transmission from the Divine Realm of Consciousness. [audience applause] Let us begin.

Instruction before Empowerment for Fire Puja

When you come up to receive the empowerment and when I place the empowerment vase upon your head, you should visualize fire descending upon you to burn up your whole body. The mantra to be chanted is: "Om, Be-ja, Da, Du, Fan."

Instruction before Empowerment for Employment of Vajra and Bell

This empowerment enables you to use both the vajra and bell compassionately and wisely, in ways that are specific to each yogic intent you make: purification, enhancement, magnetization, and subjugation. During the empowerment, visualize Vajrasattva appearing above your head. Vajrasattva holds the vajra and the bell in his hands, and he may be considered to be the root transmitter of all Tantric practices. Apart from visualizing Vajrasattva, also chant the Vajrasattva Mantra: "Om, Be-ja, Sat-Do-Ah, Hum-pei."

Instruction before Empowerment for Manjushri

In the past, Manjushri Bodhisattva was the teacher of many Buddhas. He is a Bodhisattva of great wisdom and power. Generally, practitioners of Manjushri Yoga can achieve great intelligence and wisdom. Manjushri is also the Personal Deity of many lineage gurus, including Tsongkhapa. At the same time, many lineage gurus are human incarnations of Manjushri. During the empowerment, visualize Manjushri and chant his mantra: "Om, Ah-la-ba, Zha-na, Di."

Instruction before Empowerment for Twenty-One Taras

The Twenty-One Taras are different manifestations of Tara who is, in effect, equivalent to Kuan Yin. Besides the White and Green Taras, who personify compassion, each of the Twenty-One Taras is in charge of a specific karma yoga. Thus the scope of the Twenty-One Taras covers a wide array of human affairs. If you know the collective mantra as well as each individual mantra of the Taras, you may do their practices to bring certain yogic intents into materialization in the physical realm. In the past, many Tibetan Buddhists engaging in the Twenty-One Tara Practices achieved great accomplishments. So, by learning to visualize the Twenty-One Taras and chant their mantras, you may, in the future, practice the Tara Yogas and enter into communion with Tara or Kuan Yin. The mantra is: "Om, Dah-le, Du-dah-le, Du-le, So-ha."

Conclusion

There are requests for demonstrations of mudras used in

deliverance rituals. Also, I need to give empowerments to several of the masters. Since remote empowerments may be given for the Treasure Boat Practice, Morici Deva Practice, Wealth Gods of Five Directions, Dream Guidance Practice of Deva of Auspiciousness, the Skeleton Visualization, and Body Offering, you may write to me later to request their specific remote empowerments. Or, perhaps in the future, when another occasion arises, you may receive the empowerments directly. Thank you for coming. [audience applause]

Om Mani Padme Hum.

How to Take Refuge in Grand Master Lu

There are three ways of taking refuge in Master Lu and becoming a disciple of the True Buddha Lineage:

1. By appointment

Make an appointment ahead of time to visit the "True Buddha Tantric Quarter" in Redmond, Washington, USA to receive direct initiation empowerment from Master Lu.

2. By writing

It is often not possible for someone who lives far away to come in person to take refuge. Those students who desire to take refuge can, on the first or fifteenth of any lunar month, at 7:00 a.m., while facing the direction of the rising sun, recite three times the Fourfold Refuge Mantra: "Namo guru bei, namo buddha ye, namo dharma ye, namo sangha ye" and prostrate three times.

On the first or fifteenth of every lunar month, at True Buddha Tantric Quarter, Master Lu performs a ceremony of "remote initiation empowerment" --- to give empowerment to all the students who could not journey in person.

A student who takes refuge from a distance, after performing the rites at home, only needs to send a letter to the True Buddha Tantric Quarter stating that he/she is seeking refuge, together with his/her name, address, age, and an offerings to the Buddhas. Upon receiving the letter, Master Lu will send a certificate, a picture of the master, and a note stating the level of practice he/she should start with. The address of the True Buddha Tantric Quarter is:

Sheng-yen Lu
17102 NE 40th Ct.
Redmond, WA 98052, USA Tel:(206)882-0916

3. Through local chapters of the True Buddha School

Contact nearby local chapters of the True Buddha School.

North American Chapters of the True Buddha School

Ling Shen Ching Tze Temple
17012 NE 40th Court
Redmond, WA 98052, USA
Tel:(206)882-0916

Ling Shen Ching Tze Temple
Chicago Chapter
1035 W. 31st Street
Chicago, IL 60608, USA
T:312-927-8807, F:708-392-7591

Kwan Chao True Buddhist Temple
1612 Frontage Road
Cherry Hill, NJ 08034, USA
T:609-795-3055, F:609-795-2157

Waken Ray Tseng Temple
11657 Lower Azusa Road
El Monte, CA 91732, USA
T:(818)455-0077, F:(818)455-0556

True Buddha Diamond Temple
105-107 Washington Street
New York, NY 10006, USA
T:212-732-5264, F:212-732-8478

Chin Yin Buddhist Society
10853-98 Street
Edmonton Alberta, Canada T5H 2P6
T:403-423-0447, F:403-426-3230

PTT Buddhist Society
514 Keefer Street
Vancouver B.C. Canada V6A 1Y3
T:604-255-3811, F:604-255-8894

Pai Yuin Tang Buddhist Congregation
1809 Center Street N.
Calgary Alberta, Canada T2E 2S5
Tel:(403)230-7427, F:(403)230-2558

Lotus Light Lei Zang Si Temple
347 E. Hastings Street
Vancouver, B.C. Canada V6A 1P3
T:604-685-5548, F:604-685-5598

Chan Hai Lei Zang
125 Rue Charlotte
Montreal P.Q.
Canada H2X 1M2
Tel/Fax:514-875-9578

The Universal Enlightenment Society
259 E. Hastings Street
Vancouver, B.C. Canada V6A 3Y3
T:604-683-6802, F:604-683-6873

Rainbow Villa
14302 476th Ave S.E.
Northbend, WA 98045, USA
Tel:(206)888-3677

Purple Lotus Society
636 San Mateo Avenue
San Bruno, CA 94066, USA
T:415-952-9513, F:415-952-9567

Ming Chih Tang
1758 Orchard Hill Lane
Hacienda Heights, CA 91745, USA
Tel:(818)912-9107

Bao Yin Tang
13020 Ramona Blvd.
Baldwin Park, CA 91706
(818) 856-1988

Mui Yin Tong
131 Ladera Street
Monterey Park, CA 91754, USA
T:818-289-4732, F:818-281-5032

True Buddha Temple
7734 Mary Bates Boulevard
Houston, TX 77036, USA
T:(713)988-8822, F:(713)988-8488

Charlotte The True Buddhist Society
1601 E. 4th Street
Charlotte, NC 28204, USA
Tel/Fax:704-370-0440

Hwei Yuan Town
12810 Mission Circle
Anchorage, AK 99516, USA
T:907-345-4401, F:907-345-4334

Guam True Buddha Chapter
P.O.Box 3146
Agana, Guam 96910, USA
T:671-789-1079, F:671-477-9374

Mee Yuan Buddhist Association
360 Ward Street
Newton, MA 02159, USA
Tel/Fax:617-964-5990

Capital Treasure Buddhist Society
13820 Tabiona Drive
Silver Spring, MD 20906, USA
Tel/Fax:301-598-5896

St. Louis Meditation Center
3718 S. Spring
St. Louis, MO 63116, USA
Tel:314-771-1914

True Buddha Vijaya Temple
3526 Gray Street
Oakland, CA 94601, USA
T:510-532-9888, F:510-261-3318

Ling Shen Ching Tze Temple
Jing Sim Branch
21 Milliken BL #C3
Scarb, Ontario, Canada M1V 1V3
Tel/Fax:416-298-1069

Pure Moon Buddhist Association
2517 Danforth Ave
Toronto, Ont., Canada M4C 1L2
T:416-690-7803, F:416-733-7780

Tantric Buddhist Society
#100-11800 Voyageur Way
Richmond, B.C. Canada V6A 1P3
T:604-279-0048, F:604-279-0046

Books available from Purple Lotus Society:

The Inner World of the Lake

by Master Sheng-yen Lu

In this book, Master Lu weaves the insights he has at the edge of Lake Sammamish (in Washington State) with his episodes of seeing Dakinis above the lake, saving water spirits, and reading messages on the mirror of the lake. The lake is no longer an ordinary body of water in Master Lu's sight but is transformed into the Lake of Self Nature (Buddha Nature). Sharing his thoughts, feelings, and happenings at the edge of the lake, in simple but graceful language, the reader can easily glimpse into the mind of this enlightened sage, and comprehend the esoteric wisdom of Tantric Buddhism. The appendices provide valuable teachings on some of the basics of Tantric Buddhist Practices.

$13.95 retail

Mystical Experiences of the True Buddha Disciples

by Master Sheng-yen Lu

Through the practice of Tantric Buddhism, an individual can develop his/her spiritual energy to a degree that many wondrous events will occur around him or her. Such happenings are not just reserved for the advanced practitioner but also occur to the initiate through the power of one's teacher. This book chronicles the many remarkable things that have happened to students of Master Lu such as clairaudience, mystical phenomena in meditation, a Buddha appearing in the sky, foretelling dreams, remission of serious illnesses and much more.

$10.00 retail

Four Essays on Karma

by Yüen Liao Fan

Written back in the Ming Dynasty, this book contains many gems on how to transform one's karma. The workings of the laws of cause and effect come to life in the many examples outlined in the book. The book follows the lives of various individuals faced with difficult circumstances and how they were able to avert them and live successful lives by understanding the concept of karma. What is more is that the techniques mentioned in the book for transmuting karma are simple and easy to apply by anyone at anytime to achieve a better life.

$5.00 retail

Encounters with the World of Spirits

by Grand Master Sheng-yen Lu

Grand Master Lu's unique spiritual odyssey began one day in 1969. While disinterestedly watching a Buddhist Festival, Grand Master Lu was called out from the crowd by a trance medium and told the Buddhas wanted him to spread the Dharma. That night, Grand Master Lu was magically transported to the magnificent Buddha realm known as the Maha Twin Lotus Ponds and greeted by many Bodhisattvas. During the next several years many remarkable and mysterious happenings transformed Grand Master Lu's life. An invisible teacher from the spiritual realm came to teach Grand Master Lu various esoteric arts and an old Taoist teacher in the Taiwan Mountains taught Grand Master Lu ancient Taoist techniques. In the meantime, Grand Master Lu exorcised spirits from the spiritually possessed, assisted various departed spirits, and spoke with various heavenly beings. This book will inspire anyone oriented towards the esoteric arts.

$10.00 retail

Dharma Talks by a Living Buddha

by Grand Master Sheng-yen Lu

From Dragon Kings to Buddhahood, Grand Master Sheng-yen Lu covers the gamut of esoteric subjects in his many dharma talks. Recognized as a Living Buddha by many Tibetan Tulkus including Kalu Rinpoche, Grand Master Lu brings a unique perspective to the Buddhadharma. Making arcane subjects easily accessible, Grand Master Lu opens the Inner Way to all people. This book is tremendously rich in teachings, including the invocation of the Six Wealth Deities, the method of inner cultivation, purification of meat, and guidance for entering the Buddha Pure Lands. By opening one's heart to these teachings, one will find the darkness of one's being suddenly flooded, illuminated by the Light of Truth.

$10.00 retail

A Complete and Detailed Exposition on the True Buddha Tantric Dharma

by Grand Master Sheng-yen Lu

The nuances and subtleties required for successful Tantric Buddhist Practice were meticulously laid out by Grand Master Lu in a series of discourses at the Rainbow Villa in western Washington in 1992. Grand

Master Lu, in these talks, shares the wealth of information he has obtained from his twenty spiritual masters so that practitioners can quickly attain spiritual response from their Personal Deity. Showing the various visualizations, mantras, hand gestures, and breathing techniques for a highly successful practice, Grand Master Lu enables the practitioner to quickly progress towards Buddhahood. The reader can learn the methods for invoking deities, paying homage to the deities, guarding against negative forces, merging consciousness with one's Personal Deity, and entering into samadhi.

$10.00 retail

Order Form

	Qty.	Price	Cost
The Inner World of the Lake	____	13.95	____
Four Essays on Karma	____	5.00	____
Mystical Experiences of the True Buddha Disciples	____	10.00	____
A Complete and Detailed Exposition on the True Buddha Tantric Dharma	____	10.00	____
Encounters with the World of Spirits	____	10.00	____
Dharma Talks by a Living Buddha	____	10.00	____

Tax CA residents add 8.25% sales tax. ____

Shipping ____

$2.00 shipping for the first book and $1.00 for each additional book. Outside the United States, please include $3.00 for the first book and $1.50 for each additional book.

Total ____

To order, please send order and payment to:
Purple Lotus Society, Publishing
627 San Mateo Ave.
San Bruno, CA 94066
T: (415) 589-9559 F: (415) 588-1785

Offerings from Purple Lotus Society

A Local Chapter of the True Buddha School in San Francisco

Free Subscription
Purple Lotus Journal

The Purple Lotus Society has a free bilingual Journal for anyone with an interest in Buddhism. Articles and speeches by Grand Master Lu concerning Vajrayana, Chan (Zen) Buddhism, Pure Land Buddhism, and Taoism are featured in the Journal.

Group Meditation

The Purple Lotus Society holds meditation every Saturday evening at 8:00 pm. On Tuesday nights when Master Samantha Chou is in town, a Bardo Ceremony is held.

Spiritual Assistance

Master Samantha Chou, a manifestation of the Purple Lotus Bodhisattva, uses her spiritual power to help individuals every Tuesday and Saturday afternoons. Please call for an appointment.

Purple Lotus Society

636 San Mateo Ave.
San Bruno, CA 94066
T: (415) 952-9513 F: (415) 952-9567